Discover
New York City

Experience the best
of New York City

This edition written and researched by

**Michael Grosberg,
Cristian Bonetto, Carolina A Miranda,
Brandon Presser**

Discover
New York City

Lower Manhattan & the Financial District (p47)

Iconic monuments, riverfront access and Wall St mingle at the island's southern end.

Don't Miss Statue of Liberty, Ellis Island

SoHo & Chinatown (p73)

Soup dumpling parlors and hawkers selling bric-a-brac next door to cobblestone streets and big-name stores.

Don't Miss Chinatown

East Village & Lower East Side (p97)

Two of the city's hottest 'hoods that lure students, bankers and scruffier types alike.

Don't Miss St Marks Place

Greenwich Village, Chelsea & the Meatpacking District (p121)

Quaint, intimate streets plus trendy nightlife, shopping and art galleries galore.

Don't Miss The High Line

Union Square, Flatiron District & Gramercy (p149)

A bustling, vibrant park binds surrounding areas filled with good eats.

Don't Miss Union Square

Upper
West Side &
Central Park
(p219)

Upper
East Side
(p199)

Midtown
(p165)

Greenwich Village,
Chelsea & the
Meatpacking
District (p121)

Union Square,
Flatiron District &
Gramercy (p149)

SoHo &
Chinatown
(p73)

East Village
& Lower
East Side
(p97)

Lower Manhattan &
the Financial
District (p47)

Midtown (p165)

Times Square, Broadway theaters, canyons of skyscrapers, and bustling crowds that rarely thin.

Don't Miss Times Square, Museum of Modern Art

Upper East Side (p199)

High-end boutiques, sophisticated mansions and Museum Mile – one of the most cultured strips in the world.

Don't Miss Metropolitan Museum of Art, Guggenheim Museum

Upper West Side & Central Park (p219)

Home to the premier performing arts center and the park that helps define the city.

Don't Miss Central Park

Contents

Plan Your Trip | Discover New York City

In Focus

Survival Guide

Welcome to New York City

Loud, fast and pulsing with energy, New York City (population 8.3 million) is symphonic, exhausting and always evolving. Maybe only a Walt Whitman poem cataloging typical city scenes – from the humblest hole-in-the wall to grand buildings – could begin to do the city justice.

It remains one of the world's creative and business centers. Fashion, theater, food, music, publishing, advertising and, of course, finance, all thrive here. As Groucho Marx once said, 'When it's 9:30 in New York, it's 1937 in Los Angeles.' Coming to NYC from anywhere else for the first time is like stepping into a movie; one you've probably been unknowingly writing; one that contains all imagined possibilities.

Almost every country in the world has a presence here. From Brooklyn's Russian enclave in Brighton Beach to the mini South America in Queens, and from the middle of Times Square to the most obscure corner of the Bronx, you'll find extremes.

You can experience a little bit of everything. You can decide if you'd like your day to be filled with high culture in an uptown museum and trendy eating in the Village, or – if you like your city to be tougher – you can choose to spend an afternoon wandering through the twisting streets and art galleries of downtown. Just don't be too shocked if your day of high culture turns gritty when you come across a gifted jazz singer on the subway platform, or if your bohemian day gets fancy when a trendy boutique seduces you and you're shelling out for the perfect pair of shoes before you know it.

New York City is constantly in the process of reinventing itself. And so too are the successive waves of immigrants who have populated the city and the striving artists who have pinned their hopes and dreams on making it here.

> You can experience a little bit of everything in NYC

New York City

ASTORIA

SUNNYSIDE

Calvary Cemetery

EAST WILLIAMSBURG

39th St

Queens Blvd

Greenpoint Ave

Northern Blvd

Thomson Ave

LONG ISLAND CITY

Long Island Expwy

Newtown Creek

McGuinness Blvd

Humboldt St

Manhattan Ave

McCarren Park

East River Park

21st St

21st St

Vernon Blvd

East River

Hallets Cove

Rainey Park

Queensbridge Park

Roosevelt Island

Queensboro/59th St Bridge

Queens-Midtown Tunnel

STUYVESANT TOWN

East River

Carl Schurz Park

FDR Dr

FDR Dr

John Jay Park

York Ave

FDR Dr

First Ave

FDR Dr

UPPER EAST SIDE

YORKVILLE

E 86th St

E 79th St

E 72nd St

E 65th St

Lexington Ave

E 59th St

E 57th St

Second Ave

Third Ave

E 42nd St

E 40th St

E 34th St

E 23rd St

E 14th St

Madison Ave

Fifth Ave

Park Ave

Park Ave S

Irving Pl

2

22

Jacqueline Kennedy Onassis Reservoir

11

Central Park

6

1

Central Park West

19

The Lake

Central Park South

10

Seventh Ave

Broadway

TIMES SQUARE

7 3

Fifth Ave

FLATIRON DISTRICT

Broadway

MEATPACKING DISTRICT

24

CHELSEA

W 14th St

3.5 mi

20

West End Ave

W 86th St

W 81st St

W 77th St

W 72nd St

UPPER WEST SIDE

W 66th St

17

W 60th St

W 57th St

Tenth Ave

THEATER DISTRICT

HELL'S KITCHEN

Eighth Ave

Ninth Ave

W 34th St

W 23rd St

8

Riverside Dr

Riverside Park

West Side Hwy

Dewitt Clinton Park

W 42nd St

Twelfth Ave (West Side Hwy)

18

Hudson River

UNION CITY

Lincoln Tunnel

John F Kennedy Blvd

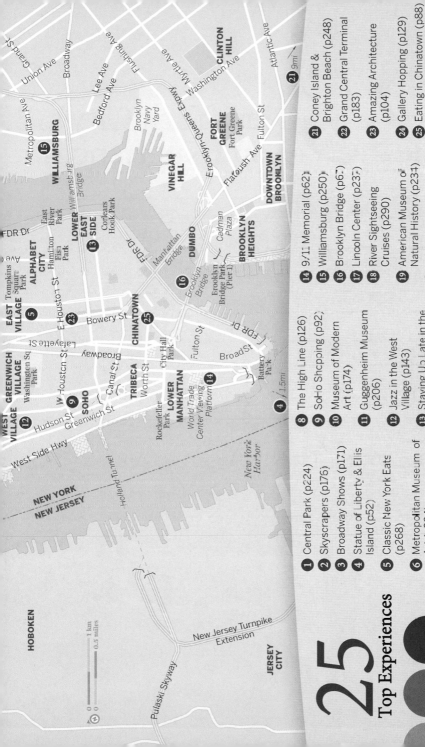

25
Top Experiences

25 New York City's Top Experiences

Central Park (p224)

London has Hyde Park. Paris has the Bois de Boulogne. And New York City has Central Park. One of the world's most renowned green spaces, it checks in with 843 acres of rolling meadows, boulder-studded outcrops, elm-lined walkways, manicured European-style gardens, a lake and a reservoir – not to mention an outdoor theater, a memorial to John Lennon, an idyllic waterside eatery (the Loeb Boathouse) and one very famous statue of Alice in Wonderland. The big challenge? Figuring out where to begin.

2

Skyscrapers

Ah, the skyscraper – mankind's phallic homage to progress. New York City has plenty of 'em, from the imposingly elegant Chrysler Building (p176) to the dainty Flatiron Building (p156) facade. And while staring into the city's infinite abyss of twinkling lights from atop a skyscraper ranks high on everyone's to-do list, we often prefer those quintessential New York moments down on the street when the crown of a soaring spire winks hello amid honking taxis. Empire State Building (p184)

Broadway Shows (p171)

Only London's West End can rival Midtown's Theater District; a sea of premieres, revivals, smash hits and flops. Stretching from 40th St to 54th St, between Sixth and Eight Aves, this is NYC's 'Dream Factory' – a place where romance, betrayal, murder and triumph come with dazzling costumes and stirring scores. Yet, the district is more than just the wicked vaudevillians of *Chicago*, or the in-tune wildlife of *The Lion King*, with enough off-Broadway and off-off-Broadway drama – both new and classic – to please the highest of theater brows.

The Best...
Restaurants

LE BERNARDIN
Triple Michelin-star earner and New York's holy grail of fine dining. (p185)

LOCANDA VERDE
Insanely flavorful Italian grub from one of New York's most beloved chefs. (p64)

REDFARM
Savvy Sino-fusion dishes boast bold flavors, but this place doesn't take itself too seriously. (p134)

DOVETAIL
Vegetarians unite on Mondays for a divine tasting menu at this Upper West Side stunner. (p233)

DANJI
Masterfully prepared and wildly inventive 'Korean tapas.' (p185)

The Best...
Free Activities

STATEN ISLAND FERRY
Hop on the ferry for postcard-perfect views of Manhattan's southern edge. (p71)

CHELSEA GALLERIES
More than 300 galleries open to the public along Manhattan's West 20s. (p129)

NEW MUSEUM OF CONTEMPORARY ART ON THURSDAY NIGHTS
Contemporary art that's free for visitors on Thursday evenings. (p104)

GOVERNORS ISLAND
Take a quick ferry ride to explore this island with priceless views. (p70)

NEW YORK PUBLIC LIBRARY
Experience the stunning Reading Room, as well as diverse exhibits. (p177)

4 Statue of Liberty & Ellis Island (p52)

Since its unveiling in 1886, Lady Liberty has welcomed millions of immigrants sailing into New York Harbor in the hope of a better life. It now welcomes millions of tourists, many of whom head up to her crown for one of New York City's finest views. Close by lies Ellis Island, the American gateway for more than 12 million new arrivals between 1892 and 1954. These days it's home to one of the city's most moving museums, paying tribute to these immigrants and their indelible courage.

HUW JONES/LONELY PLANET IMAGES ©

5 Classic New York Eats (p268)

If you want a real bite of the Apple, chow down a fat, juicy NYC classic. Start with a 'bagel and a schmear' – a boiled-and-baked bagel with cream cheese. Order an all-beef hot dog with the works, and bust your jaw with pastrami on rye and a side of pickles. But you're not done yet! Leave room for a slice of thin, cheesy New York–style pizza (tackled folded in half), and a slab of extra-creamy graham-cracker crust cheesecake.

BEVERLY LOGAN/GETTY IMAGES ©

Metropolitan Museum of Art (Met; p204)

Home to a staggering two million works of art, the Met hosts some of the city's best-known exhibits, and its permanent collection covers every conceivable genre from the last 5000 years – from Egyptian artifacts to contemporary rooftop installations. Without a map, you'll get lost inside this sprawling museum and its priceless collections.

Times Square (p170)

Times Square is more than just where Broadway and Seventh Ave meet, it's America in 'concentrate' – an intense, blinding, electrifying rush of Hollywood billboards; glittering cola signs; and buffed, topless cowboys. True to the American dream, this 'Crossroads of the World' has invented and reinvented itself, from 1920s music-hall mecca to 1970s porn peddler to glossy, nonsmoking 21st-century role model. You might love it, you might loathe it, but do not miss it, especially when the sun goes down and its JumboTron screens turn night back into day.

The High Line (p126)

A resounding triumph of urban renewal, the High Line is New York's proudest testament to the continuous effort to transform scarring vestiges of the city's industrial past into eye-pleasing spaces that foster comfortable city-center living. Once an unsightly elevated train track that snaked between butcheries and low-end domestic dwellings, today the High Line is an unfurled emerald necklace of park space. Unsurprisingly, it has acted as a veritable real estate magnet, luring world-class architects to the neighborhood to create residential eye candy.

The Best...
Religious Architecture

ST PATRICK'S CATHEDRAL
A glorious neo-Gothic masterpiece – the largest cathedral in America. (p180)

TRINITY CHURCH
This gorgeous Anglican church was the tallest building in NYC in the mid-1800s. (p60)

CATHEDRAL CHURCH OF ST JOHN THE DIVINE
The largest place of worship in the US was begun in 1892 – and still isn't finished. (p249)

TEMPLE EMANU-EL
One of New York's most beautiful synagogues. (p212)

ELDRIDGE STREET SYNAGOGUE
After a multimillion-dollar restoration, the hallowed hall is now a museum space. (p105)

SoHo Shopping (p92)

With enough opportunities for retail therapy to cure Woody Allen of his many neuroses, New York is a beacon of the material world, where hundreds of creators – both local and international – descend upon the city with alacrity to display their wares. You'll find dozens of ways to empty your coffers but, at the end of the day, shopping in New York isn't about collecting a closet full of items – it's about accessing the city's myriad subcultures through their art and artifacts. Opening Ceremony (p95

The Best...
Green Spaces

CENTRAL PARK
The city's most famous park has more than 800 acres of rolling meadows and boulder-topped hillocks. (p224)

BROOKLYN BRIDGE PARK
A brand new park lines the waterfront along Dumbo to Atlantic Ave. (p247)

THE HIGH LINE
A thin stripe of green that unfurls up the western slice of downtown. (p126)

RIVERSIDE PARK
A 100-block park alongside the Hudson on Manhattan's west side – ideal spot for a bike ride. (p230)

Museum of Modern Art (MoMA; p174)

Quite possibly the greatest hoarder of modern masterpieces on earth, MoMA is a cultural promised land. It's here that you'll see Van Gogh's *The Starry Night*, Cézanne's *The Bather*, Picasso's *Le Demoiselles d'Avignon*, Pollock's *One: Number 31, 1950* and Warhol's *Campbell's Soup Cans*. Just make sure you leave time for Chagall, Rothko, de Kooning and Haring, a free film screening, a glass of vino in the Sculpture Garden, a little designer retail therapy, and a fine-dining feed at one of its lauded in-house restaurants. MoMA exterior (architects: Yoshio Taniguchi & Kohn Pedersen Fox)

Guggenheim Museum (p206)

This museum's organic shape and sweeping spiral staircase – the work of Frank Lloyd Wright – is a superb sculpture in its own right. Inside in its permanent collection are 20th century paintings by modern heavy hitters such as Picasso, Pollock and Chagall; its temporary exhibits run the gamut from massive retrospectives and large-scale installations to in-depth country surveys. In 1992 the Robert Mapplethorpe Foundation donated 200 photographs, spurring curators to devote the fourth floor to photography exhibitions.

THE SHAPES OF SPACE, SOLOMON R GUGGENHEIM MUSEUM 14–APRIL–5 SEPTEMBER 2007 ©THE SOLOMON R GUGGENHEIM FOUNDATION, NEW YORK. USED WITH THE PERMISSION OF JEAN-PIERRE LESCOURRET/LONELY PLANET IMAGES ©

12

Jazz in the West Village (p143)

The Village Vanguard and Blue Note may not ring a bell to most, but jazz aficionados raise an eyebrow in interest when these names are uttered amid music-savvy circles. Although the plumes of smoke have cleared from the West Village's coterie of clubs, the venues are all still alive and riffin' to a mixed bag of local and international talent. This isn't just another soulful pocket in an anonymous, tower-clad city; this is the heart of one of the most artistic and expression-filled genres of music. Village Vanguard (p143)

13

Staying Up Late in the City That Never Sleeps (p112)

An all-night lounge tucked behind a Chinese restaurant, taco shops that host late-night tranny cabarets, and after-after-after-parties on the roof as the sun rises; the Lower East Side is one of the epi-centers of the city's nightlife universe. An alternate universe lurks between the cracks of everyday life, and it welcomes savvy visitors just as much as locals in the know. Scissor Sisters performing at Bowery Ballroom (p117)

9/11 Memorial (p62)

After years of delays and controversy, the National September 11 Memorial (designed by Michael Arad) finally opened to the public in the fall of 2012. Where the north and south towers of the World Trade Center once stood are two large pools with dramatically symbolic cascading waterfalls that appear to fall into an abyss. Hundreds of swamp white oaks dot the surrounding site, a place of reverie and contemplation as well as a close-up vantage of the $3.1 billion Freedom Tower – since renamed One World Trade Center – that already peeks out over the Lower Manhattan skyline.

The Best...
Vintage Drinking Holes

WHITE HORSE TAVERN
Dylan Thomas and Jack Kerouac drank at the long oak bar here. (p141)

CAMPBELL APARTMENT
A railroad baron's 1920s-era secret hideaway at Grand Central. (p186)

OLD TOWN BAR & RESTAURANT
The classic, preserved decor here offers a turn of the-century vibe. (p161)

MCSORLEY'S OLD ALE HOUSE
A cobwebby, sawdust-floor East Village dive since 1852. (p112)

The Best...
Discount Designer Clothing Stores

CENTURY 21
An enormous vault of super-priced top labels. (p69)

YOUNG DESIGNERS MARKET
Up-and-coming designers sell their wares at this weekend Nolita market. (p95)

BARNEYS CO-OP
Semiannual warehouse sale and relatively affordable year-round. (p145)

TOKIO 7
Consignment store with reasonably priced high-end designer brands for men and women. (p118)

Williamsburg (p250)

Retro cocktail lounges peddling a Depression-era vibe. Artsy eateries dishing out everything from humble pizza slices to Michelin-star gastronomy. And enough music halls and rowdy beer gardens to keep the most dedicated night owls up for weeks. Prefer the daylight hours? Williamsburg is stocked with an array of home design shops, plus fashion outposts of all stripes, from vintage thrift emporiums to design-y boutiques. It's not for nothing that this Brooklyn neighborhood – just one subway stop from downtown Manhattan – is the city's trendiest hangout. Above and left: Bedford Ave, Williamsburg

MIKE HIPPLE/ALAMY ©

Brooklyn Bridge (p67)

Completed in 1873, this Gothic Revival masterpiece – crafted entirely from granite – has inspired poetry (Jack Keroauc's 'Brooklyn Bridge Blues'), music (Frank Sinatra's 'Brooklyn Bridge') and plenty of art (Walker Evans' 1920s photography). A stroll over the graceful bridge, linking lower Manhattan and Brooklyn, is a rite of passage for New Yorkers and visitors alike. Nighttime is especially cinematic, when the city lights reflect off the waters below and the bustling streets seem like a distant memory.

Lincoln Center (p237)

With the billion-dollar-plus redevelopment virtually complete, the world's largest performing arts center is in stunning shape. The dramatic Alice Tully Hall anchors one end of the property, and other venues surround a massive fountain and public space. Every genre has a stage here: you can see the New York Philharmonic, the Chamber Music Society of Lincoln Center, the New York City Ballet, the Metropolitan Opera and more. Metropolitan Opera House (architect: Wallace Harrison) and Avery Fisher Hall (designed by Max Abramovitz)

RICHARD CUMMINS/LONELY PLANET IMAGES ©

River Sightseeing Cruises (p290)

Manhattan is an island and is thus surrounded by water, even if many New Yorkers forget it. The Roosevelt Island tram provides aerial views of the East River, while Riverside Park is the place to go for sunsets over the Hudson River and the Jersey Shore. Brooklyn Bridge Park, that borough's newest, has wide open views of the Brooklyn and Manhattan bridges and East River boat traffic. The best way to take it all in is hopping on one of the various sightseeing cruises that circumnavigate Manhattan.

The Best...
City Stages

BROADWAY
Near Times Square, several dozen theaters host the city's most famous (and priciest) productions. (p171)

JOYCE THEATER
An innovative line-up of contemporary ballet, flamenco, jazz-tinged tap dancing and theatrical modern dance. (p144)

DAVID H KOCH THEATER
Home to the New York City Ballet, all the great works are here, from *Swan Lake* to *The Nutcracker,* with choreographies by ballet legends. (p239)

LA MAMA ETC
East Village icon continues to push boundaries in its genre-defying performances. (p117)

BROOKLYN ACADEMY OF MUSIC
An array of cutting-edge fare in theater, dance and music. (p252)

The Best...
Musical Performance Spaces

METROPOLITAN OPERA HOUSE
Home to one of the world's most venerated opera companies. (p238)

CARNEGIE HALL
The world's greatest musicians have worked this hallowed stage. (p192)

SMALLS JAZZ CLUB
A jazz basement with emerging talents and late-night jam fests. (p143)

PIANOS
A hipster-loving music hall with up-and-coming rock bands. (p117)

LE POISSON ROUGE
A 'multimedia art cabaret' with a staggering variety of music. (p143)

ZEBULON
Funk, Afro-Brazilian and jazz in Williamsburg. (p253)

American Museum of Natural History (p234)

19

Kids of all ages will find something intriguing here, whether it's the stuffed Alaskan brown bear, the Star of India sapphire, or the skullcap of a pachycephalosaurus. Gazing at the Rose Center for Earth & Space – a massive glass box containing a silver globe, home to space-show theaters and the planetarium – is mesmerizing, especially at night, when all of its otherworldly features are aglow. Ecosphere at the Rose Center for Earth & Space, designed by James Stewart Polshek and Todd H Schliemann

⑳ Yankee Stadium (p247)

Though not a thing of beauty (it looks like it was designed by Mussolini), this rebuilt South Bronx arena is home to one of the most storied outfits in American baseball: the Yankees. This was once the home of history-making players like the 'Sultan of Swat' Babe Ruth and 'Joltin' Joe' DiMaggio. These days, it gets packed with baseball fanatics who pour in to root, root, root for the home team, while inhaling pulled-pork sandwiches and cold beer. In other words: an all-American good time.

MICHAEL TAYLOR/LONELY PLANET IMAGES ©

Coney Island & Brighton Beach (p248)

Coney Island achieved worldwide fame as a working-class resort area at the turn of the 20th century. Though no longer the booming attraction it was then, it's blossomed in recent years with new crowds, fresh rides and plentiful places to dine. A five-minute stroll along the boardwalk brings you to Brighton Beach, where Russian old-timers play chess and locals enjoy vodka shots in the sun. Wonder Wheel fairground, Coney Island

Grand Central Terminal (p183)

Even if you're not boarding a train, it's worth exploring the vaulted main concourse at Grand Central Terminal and gazing up at the restored ceiling, decorated with an image of the night sky. The lower floor has a truly excellent array of eateries, bringing the idea of 'food court' to grand new levels. The balconies overlooking the main concourse afford an expansive view; perch yourself here at 5pm on a weekday to see the grace that this terminal commands under pressure.

Amazing Architecture

New York's architectural history is a layer cake of ideas and styles – one that is literally written on the city's streets. Humble colonial farmhouses and graceful Federal-style buildings are found alongside ornate beaux arts palaces. There are the revivals (Greek, Gothic, Romanesque and Renaissance) and the unadorned International Style. And in recent years, daring 'starchitects' and cutting edge firms have designed both torqued forms and boxy buildings – like the New Museum of Contemporary Art (p104) – that artfully integrate neighborhoods' past aesthetic with modern ethereal elements. Chrysler Building (p176)

The Best...
Must-See
Architecture

CHRYSLER BUILDING
Manhattan's most elegant skyscraper. (p176)

EMPIRE STATE BUILDING
This Depression-era skyscraper never ever gets old. (p184)

GRAND CENTRAL TERMINAL
A classic beaux arts stunner, with an astronomical pattern on the ceiling. (p183)

NEW MUSEUM OF CONTEMPORARY ART
A sexy stacked-cube structure with a translucent aluminum exterior. (p104)

WHITNEY MUSEUM OF AMERICAN ART
Modernism doesn't get more brutal than this. (p208)

Gallery Hopping (p129)

Dozens of galleries pack the streets (with many more hidden in upper-level floors) of Chelsea, an industrial 'hood turned art mecca. Opening nights, usually on Thursdays, bring out avant-loving crowds, style hounds and wannabe players in the art arena. And while Chelsea's allure is undeniable, smaller pockets of edgier galleries have popped up in other neighborhoods, mainly the Lower East Side, Williamsburg in Brooklyn and Long Island City in Queens. *The Chelsea* bike rack, designed by former Talking Heads member David Byrne, in the Chelsea gallery district

The Best...
Places to
Relieve Stress

RUSSIAN & TURKISH BATHS
Alternate between steam rooms, sauna, cold baths and borscht. (p119)

CHELSEA PIERS COMPLEX
Hit the driving range, bowling alley, gym or climbing wall at this sports complex. (p147)

BOATING IN CENTRAL PARK
Rent a rowboat from the Loeb Boathouse in Central Park. (p241)

CYCLING IN CENTRAL PARK
Pedal the park for a light aerobic workout and bucolic vistas. (p241)

(25)

Eating in Chinatown (p88)

A feast for the senses, Chinatown is the only place in the city where you can simultaneously see whole roasted pigs hanging in butcher-shop windows, get whiffs of fresh fish, and hear the sounds of Cantonese and Vietnamese rise over the calls of knock-off-Prada-bag hawkers on Canal St. Chinatown has the best dining deals around, and locals love to head downtown to satisfy their hankering for hole-in-the-wall fare and dim sum feasts on weekends.

Chinese New Year, Chinatown

Top Days in
New York City

Midtown & Uptown Icons

Landmarks, highlights, big ticket items: this itinerary will allow you to experience the New York City of everyone's collective imagination, including the city's most famous museum and park. Take in the mythic landscape of Midtown's concrete and skyscrapers, from the street and amidst the clouds.

❶ Metropolitan Museum of Art (p204)

Start uptown at the big daddy of museums. Check out the Egyptian Wing and the European paintings on the second floor.

METROPOLITAN MUSEUM OF ART ◐
CENTRAL PARK
🏃 Walk into Central Park at the 79th St entrance.

❷ Central Park (p224)

Get some fresh air in Central Park, the city's spectacular public backyard. Walk south to the Conservatory Pond where toy boats ply the waters.

CENTRAL PARK ◐ TIMES SQUARE
🚕 Exit the park on Fifth Ave however far south you'd like, and grab a cab for Times Square.

❸ Times Square (p170)

Soak up the Vegas-like atmosphere of Times Square from the TKTS Booth and get discounted tickets for that night. Head to the newly formed pedestrian plaza at the southern end where you can take in the dazzling tableau.

TIMES SQUARE ◐ ROCKEFELLER CENTER
🏃 For more elbow room walk up Sixth Ave to 49th St.

❹ Top of the Rock (p187)

Ride to the open-air observation deck at the Top of the Rock in Rockefeller Center for stunning vistas.

ROCKEFELLER CENTER ◐ MARSEILLE
🏃 It's probably quickest to walk crosstown to Ninth Ave at 44th St (or the weary can grab a taxi).

❺ Dinner at Marseille (p186)

For Broadway-goers, do an early dinner at this theatrically designed and buzzing French brasserie.

MARSEILLE ◐ BROADWAY THEATER
🏃 Walk east to the theater where you've already purchased tickets.

❻ Broadway Theater (p171)

Check out a blockbuster musical for an only-in-New-York spectacle. Afterwards, swig cocktails late into the night at the Edison Hotel's restored piano bar, Rum House (p191).

Central Park (p224)
RICHARD I'ANSON/LONELY PLANET IMAGES ©

Riverine Lower Manhattan

Surprisingly, for this part of downtown dominated by the canyons of Wall St,
this day takes in broad horizons and river views, not to mention an iconic
historic sight. This itinerary requires a little planning – book your tickets
for the Statue of Liberty and Ellis Island as well as the 9/11 Memorial in
advance.

1 Statue of Liberty & Ellis Island (p52)

Time your arrival with your ferry's departure (with advance reservations). Ellis Island will likely occupy the majority of the morning's visit unless you've also arranged a trip to the statue's crown.

ELLIS ISLAND ○ BATTERY PARK CITY
Walk from Castle Clinton north and west to the riverfront promenade.

2 Battery Park City (p61)

This residential area backed by apartment towers offers unobstructed views of the Hudson River and New Jersey. Grab a bench and watch a parade of runners, office workers and other visitors.

BATTERY PARK CITY ○ 9/11 MEMORIAL
Walk north until you reach the World Financial Center. Enter the atrium and cross the West Side Hwy through the covered walkway.

3 9/11 Memorial (p62)

This is the former World Trade Center site. Visit the WTC Tribute Visitor Center for photographs, artifacts and a historical context before lining up (online reservations in advance required).

9/11 MEMORIAL ○ JOE'S SHANGHAI
S Take the N from the Cortlandt St station to Canal St; walk east on Canal and turn south on Mott St. Cross Bayard and turn left on Pell St.

4 Lunch at Joe's Shanghai (p88)

Savor soup dumplings at Joe's Shanghai, a local staple. After lunch, enjoy the bustling streets and Buddhist temples. Pop into a cafe for almond ice cream or bubble tea.

JOE'S SHANGHAI ○ BROOKLYN BRIDGE
Walk south on Bowery and turn west on Worth St and then south again on Centre St; the access road to the bridge is on your left.

5 Brooklyn Bridge (p67)

Join the Brooklynites and hordes of other visitors making this magical pilgrimage on one of the city's most beautiful landmarks.

BROOKLYN BRIDGE ○ BROOKLYN BRIDGE PARK
Walk over the bridge from Manhattan to Brooklyn. Watch out for cyclists!

6 Brooklyn Bridge Park (p247)

The biggest new park to be built in Brooklyn since Prospect Park in the 19th century has staggering views of Manhattan, the Brooklyn Bridge and a fully restored 19th-century carousel.

BROOKLYN BRIDGE PARK ○ GRIMALDI'S
Walk from up Old Fulton St to the corner of Front St.

7 Dinner at Grimaldi's (p251)

Legendary lines and deservedly legendary thin-crust pies in a new location only a few doors up from the old.

GRIMALDI'S ○ VILLAGE VANGUARD
S Walk up Old Fulton St to the High St A train stop. Take the A to W 4th St. Go north on Waverly to 7th Ave.

8 Village Vanguard (p143)

End your day in the West Village taking in some of the world's best jazz beats at this world famous club.

Statue of Liberty (p52)
JEAN-PIERRE LESCOURRET/LONELY PLANET IMAGES ©

West Side Culture

Not everything in this day is lofty-minded. The morning is spent exploring Chelsea, including the High Line – New York's golden child of urban renewal – and the galleries of the West 20s. Cap off the night at Lincoln Center, the stunning campus of some of the country's top performance spaces.

DAY 3

❶ The High Line (p126)

Take a taxi down to the stroll-worthy High Line, an abandoned railway 30ft above the street, now one of New York's favorite downtown destinations. Enter at 20th St and walk the meandering path for views of the Hudson River and city streets below.

THE HIGH LINE ❍ CHELSEA GALLERIES
🏃 Exit at the 26th St stairway and explore the surrounding neighborhood on foot.

❷ Chelsea Galleries (p129)

One of the hubs of the city's art-gallery scene, here you can ogle works by up-and-comers and established artists alike, and maybe even take home an expensive souvenir. Some of the blue-chip galleries to check out are Andrea Rosen, Mary Boone and Matthew Marks.

CHELSEA GALLERIES ❍ CHELSEA MARKET
🏃 Walk to Ninth Ave and south to 15th St.

❸ Lunch at Chelsea Market (p129)

This building, a former cookie factory, has a huge concourse packed with shops selling fresh baked goods, wines, vegetables, imported cheeses and other temptations.

CHELSEA MARKET ❍ AMERICAN MUSEUM OF NATURAL HISTORY
Ⓢ Grab an uptown C train at Eighth Ave and 14th St and take it to 86th and Central Park West.

❹ American Museum of Natural History (p234)

No matter what your age, you'll experience childlike wonder at the exceptional American Museum of Natural History. Be sure to save time for the Rose Center for Earth & Space, a unique architectural gem in its own right.

AMERICAN MUSEUM OF NATURAL HISTORY ❍ BARCIBO ENOTECA
🏃 Walk west to Amsterdam Ave and turn south; veer left on Broadway at 71st St.

❺ Drink at Barcibo Enoteca (p236)

Stop in for a pre-show glass of expertly curated Italian wine, or go for some grub if you're seeing a full-length show.

BARCIBO ENOTECA ❍ LINCOLN CENTER
🏃 Walk south on Broadway to 63rd St.

❻ Lincoln Center (p237)

Head to the Lincoln Center for opera at the Metropolitan Opera House (p238) (the largest in the world), a symphony in Avery Fisher Hall, or a play at one of its two theaters – a promise of a great show in an architecturally mesmerizing setting. Don't miss the choreographed 'water shows' at the plaza fountain.

LINCOLN CENTER ❍ DOVETAIL
🏃 Walk north to 77th St and Columbus Ave.

❼ Dovetail (p233)

Hit up the neighborhood's Michelin-starred new foodie hotspot for a delectable post-performance dinner. Chef John Fraser has attracted a following with fare that focuses on only the freshest produce.

DAY 4

Eastside & Down

Gain insight into immigrant history, grab ethnic eats, check out cutting edge art and theater as well as cheap booze and live music; walk up and down the tiny blocks and peek into stylish boutiques. As a general rule, the further east you go the looser things get.

1 Lower East Side Tenement Museum (p115)

Fantastic insight into the life and shockingly cramped living conditions of immigrants during the 19th and early 20th centuries at this brilliantly curated museum. Sign up for a walking tour for more thorough exploration.

LOWER EAST SIDE TENEMENT MUSEUM ➡ LITTLE ITALY

🚶 Walk west on Delancey St through Sara D Roosevelt Park to Mulberry St.

2 Little Italy (p84)

Although it feels more like a theme park than an authentic Italian strip, Mulberry St is still the heart of the 'hood. Drop into Ferrara Cafe & Bakery (p89) brimming with classic Italian pastries and old-school ambience.

LITTLE ITALY ➡ LA ESQUINA

🚶 Walk two blocks east to Centre St and two blocks north to Kenmare.

3 Lunch at La Esquina (p87)

Grab some lunch at this funky and popular Mexican eatery housed in a former old-school diner. Standouts include chorizo tacos and mango and jicama salads, among other authentic and delicious options.

LA ESQUINA ➡ NEW MUSEUM OF CONTEMPORARY ART

🚶 Walk several blocks east to Bowery and turn north.

4 New Museum of Contemporary Art (p104)

Symbolic of the once gritty Bowery's transformation, this uber contemporary

museum has a steady menu of edgy works in new forms. Stop by the bookstore with an eclectic mix of cutting edge publications.

NEW MUSEUM OF CONTEMPORARY ART ➡ ST MARKS PLACE

🚶 Turn right on Houston and then left up Second Ave until you reach Ninth St.

5 St Marks Place (p102)

Stroll this famous street past the cheesy T-shirt shops, tattoo parlors, punk rock stores like Trash & Vaudeville (p119), and sake bars, then head to the neighboring streets for a quieter round of nibbling and boutique-ing.

ST MARKS PLACE ➡ PS 122

🚶 Head to First Ave and turn north one block to Ninth St.

6 PS 122 (p116)

This black box theater is an experimental performance space for up-and-coming artists as well as established edgy groups and performers.

PS 122 ➡ KATZ'S DELI

🚕 Walk or cab it down First Ave to Houston St and turn left two blocks to Ludlow St.

7 Dinner at Katz's Delicatessen (p110)

The quintessential old-school Jewish Lower East Side eatery serves up smoked meat sandwiches that will please even the biggest kvetchers.

Daniel Guzmán and Steven Shearer's 2008 *Double Album* exhibition at the New Museum of Contemporary Art (p104)

Month by Month

 ## January

 Winter Restaurant Week

You're not allowed to lose that extra holiday weight just yet! Usher in the new year with slash-cut meal deals at some of the city's finest eating establishments during New York's Winter Restaurant Week (www.nycgo.com/restau rantweek).

February

Lunar New Year

One of the biggest Lunar (Chinese) New Year (www. explorechinatown. com) celebrations in the country, this display of fireworks and dancing dragons draws mobs of thrillseekers into the streets of Chinatown.

 ## March

St Patrick's Day Parade

A massive audience, rowdy and wobbly from cups of green beer, lines Fifth Ave on March 17 for this popular parade (www.nyc stpatricksparade.org) of bagpipe blowers, sparkly floats and clusters of Irish-lovin' politicians. The parade, which was first held here in 1762, is the city's oldest and largest.

April

 Tribeca Film Festival

Created after the tragic events of 9/11, Robert De Niro's downtown film festival (www.tribecafi lm.com) has quickly become a star in the indie movie circuit. Gaggles of celebs come to walk the red carpets each spring.

 ## May

Fleet Week

For one week at the end of the month, Manhattan resembles a 1940's movie set as clusters of fresh-faced, uniformed sailors go 'on the town' to look for adventures. The ships they leave behind, docked in the Hudson River, invite the curious to hop aboard for tours.

June

 Puerto Rican Day Parade

The second weekend in June attracts thousands of flag-waving revelers for the annual Puerto Rican Day Parade (www.nationalpuer toricandayparade.org). It runs up Fifth Ave from 44th to 86th Sts.

SummerStage

With over 100 performances – from spoken word

to Top 40 jams – spread across the five boroughs, SummerStage (p239) is NYC's biggest free performing arts festival.

Gay Pride

June is Gay Pride Month, and it culminates in a major march down Fifth Ave on the last Sunday of the month.

HBO Bryant Park Summer Film Festival

Beginning in June and ending in August, there are weekly outdoor screenings of some of the most beloved films in Hollywood history during the Bryant Park Summer Film Festival (www.bryantpark.org).

July

Independence Day

America's Independence Day is celebrated on 4th of July with fireworks and fanfare that can be seen from most NYC apartments with river views.

Shakespeare in the Park

The much-loved Shakespeare in the Park (p239) pays tribute to the Bard, with free performances in Central Park. The catch? You'll have to wait hours in line to score tickets, or win them in the online lottery.

August

Fringe Festival

This mid-August theater festival (www.fringenyc.org) presents two weeks of performances from all over the world. It's the best way to catch the edgiest, wackiest and most creative up-and-comers.

September

BAM! Next Wave Festival

Celebrated for 30 years in 2012, the Brooklyn Academy of Music's Next Wave Festival (www.bam.org) showcases the newest iterations of avant-garde performance, music and dance.

October

Open House New York

The country's largest architecture and design event (www.ohny.org) is held at the start of the month. It features special, architect-led tours, as well as lectures, design workshops, studio visits and city-wide site-specific performances.

Halloween

What once started as simple door-to-door knocking, Halloween in the Village has transformed into an all-out parade (www.halloween-nyc.com) with costume-clad locals and interested onlookers gathering in equal numbers.

November

Macy's Thanksgiving Parade

Huge helium-filled balloons soar overhead, high school marching bands rattle their snares, and millions of onlookers bundle up with scarves and coats to celebrate Thanksgiving with this 2.5-mile-long parade.

NYC Marathon

Held in the first week of November, this annual 26-mile run (www.nycmarathon.org) draws thousands of athletes from around the world, and just as many excited viewers line the streets to cheer the runners on.

Oh Christmas Tree

The flick of a switch ignites the massive Christmas tree in Rockefeller Center.

December

New Year's Eve

Times Square swarms with millions of gatherers who come to stand squashed together like boxed sardines, swig booze, freeze in subarctic temperatures, witness the annual dropping of the ball made entirely of Waterford Crystal and chant the '10...9...8...' in perfect unison.

What's New

For this new edition of Discover New York City, our authors have hunted down the fresh, the transformed, the hot and the happening. These are some of our favourites. For up-to-the-minute recommendations, see lonelyplanet.com/new-york-city.

1 SEEING MORE GREEN

Brooklyn Bridge Park – the biggest new park to be built in Brooklyn since Prospect Park in the 19th century – has staggering views of Manhattan, the Brooklyn Bridge and a fully restored 19th-century carousel. Bring it. (p247)

2 MICHELIN FARE FOR A SONG

Chef John Fraser has attracted a strong foodie following and a Michelin star status for the unpretentious Upper West Side eatery, Dovetail, which focuses on only the freshest produce. It's also a deal: on Mondays, the restaurant offers a three-course vegetarian menu for only $46. (p233)

3 EATALY

Eataly is officially the largest Italian grocer and market space in the entire world, commanding over 50,000 sq ft in the heart of the city's Flatiron District. It is, without a doubt, a major game changer in New York's gourmet market scene. Don't miss the beer garden on the roof. (p163)

4 THE HIGH LINE 2.0

New York City's golden child of urban renewal recently made its first of two planned expansions, effectively doubling the size of the thin haven of green, the High Line. Up next? Redevelopment of the veritable urban dead zone orbiting the Javits Center. (p126)

5 CUTTING-EDGE DESIGN, ENTER STAGE RIGHT

The top-notch Signature Theatre – a well known company that champions contemporary American plays – has moved into its impressive new Frank Gehry–designed premises, the Signature Center on 42nd St. The center includes a bookshop, cafe and various performance spaces. (p192)

6 OLD NEW YORK WITH A TWIST... OF LIME

The guys behind cocktail bar Ward III in Tribeca have restored the Edison Hotel's old piano bar in Midtown and opened it as the Rum House. There's a pianist each night and well-mixed drinks; a 'refreshed' slice of old New York. (p66) (p191)

Get Inspired

Books

- **Go Tell It on the Mountain** (James Baldwin) A lyrical novel of a day in the life of a 14-year-old brings readers into Harlem during the Depression.

- **Bonfire of the Vanities** (Tom Wolfe) A gripping novel of an uptown investment banker's entanglement with the world of the black South Bronx.

- **Fortress of Solitude** (Jonathan Lethem) A ballad to the Brooklyn streets and a lyrical journey into race relations and pop culture from the 1970s to the '90s.

- **Lush Life** (Richard Price) A pitch-perfect exploration of the conflict between project residents and interloping hipsters.

Films

- **Taxi Driver** Martin Scorsese's film is a reminder of how much grittier this place used to be.

- **Saturday Night Fever** John Travolta is the hottest thing in bell-bottoms in this tale of a streetwise Brooklyn kid.

- **Manhattan** A divorced New Yorker falls for his best friend's mistress in what is essentially a Woody Allen love letter to NYC.

- **American Gangster** A Harlem-based drug drama, inspired by a true story.

Music

- **'Autumn in New York'** (Billie Holiday) Why *does* it seem so inviting?

- **'Empire State of Mind'** (Jay Z) An instant classic 'These streets will make you feel...'

- **'Chelsea Hotel No 2'** (Leonard Cohen) Sex, grit and bohemia in a NYC landmark.

- **'Lullaby of Broadway'** (*42nd Street* musical-cast recording) A timeless favorite capturing all the hip-hooray and ballyhoo.

Websites

- **Fandango** (www. fandango.com) Movie and theater tickets at venues throughout the city for a $1 surcharge.

- **Metropolitan Transportation Authority** (www.mta.info) Subway map, service updates and other transportation information.

- **Times Square Visitors Center** (www. timessquarenyc.org) Midtown events, deals, news and advice.

Short on time?

This list will give you an instant insight into the city.

Read Dip into any chapter of *Gotham: A History of New York City to 1898*, a hugely entertaining, Pulitzer prize-winning tome.

Watch Cary Grant and Deborah Kerr make a pact to seal their love atop the Empire State Building in *An Affair to Remember*.

Listen Frank Sinatra's *New York, New York* is the ultimate manifesto of NYC exceptionalism.

Log on For comprehensive tourist information check out *NYC: The Official Guide* (www.nycgo.com).

Chelsea Hotel (p132)

Need to Know

Currency
US dollar (US$)

Language
English

Visas
Twenty-seven countries have a visa-waiver agreement with the US (see www.cbp.gov); citizens of these countries can enter for up to 90 days.

Money
ATMs widely available. Credit cards widely accepted. Some smaller eateries are cash-only.

Cell Phones
Most US cell phones, apart from the iPhone, operate on CDMA, not the European standard GSM; check compatibility with your phone service provider.

Time
Eastern Standard Time (GMT/UTC minus five hours)

Wi-Fi
Many cafes, parks and libraries offer free wi-fi. Some hotels many charge per hour.

Tipping
In restaurants tip at least 15% unless the service is terrible; in taxis around 10%.

For more information, see Survival Guide (p286).

When to Go

New York City

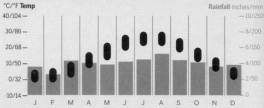

Spring Blossoming trees; rainy days can feel lovely.

Summer Free cultural events everywhere. It can be beastly hot.

Fall Leaves change colors; the air is brisk.

Winter Buildings are festooned with lights; it's the holiday season. Snow, sleet and cold.

Advance Planning

Two months before Book your hotel reservations as soon as possible – prices increase the closer you get to your arrival date. Snag tickets to a Broadway blockbuster.

Three weeks before If you haven't done so already, score a table at your favorite high-end restaurant.

One week before Surf the interwebs for the newest and coolest in the city. Join email news blasts as well.

Your Daily Budget

Budget less than $100
- Dorm bed at Chelsea Hostel $35–$80
- Best pizza slice $2
- Walking the High Line (free)
- Drinks at an East Village dive bar $4
- New York Philharmonic rehearsal performance, Lincoln Center $18

Midrange $100–$300
- Comfortable digs at Country Inn the City $150–$420
- Brunch at Balthazar $40
- Dinner at RedFarm $60
- Discount TKTS tickets to a Broadway show $80

Top End more than $300
- Luxury stay at the Surrey $350–$800
- Snack at the Loeb Boathouse in Central Park $18
- Metropolitan Opera orchestra seats $95–$320

Arriving in New York City

John F Kennedy International Airport (JFK)
The AirTrain ($5) links to the Metropolitan Transport Authority's (MTA) subway ($2.50), which makes the one-hour journey into Manhattan. Shared vans from Grand Central or Port Authority are $15 to $20. Taxis cost a flat rate of $45 excluding tolls and tip.

LaGuardia Airport (LGA)
The closest airport to Manhattan – take the M60 bus from 125th St ($2.50) directly to the airport (30 minutes). Vans and coach buses to Midtown cost $12 to $20. Taxis range from $25 to $45 (excluding tolls and tip) depending on traffic.

Newark Liberty International Airport (EWR)
From Pennsylvania Station, the AirTrain ($12.50) links passengers to the airport with one transfer; shared shuttles from Midtown cost $15 to $20. Taxis range from $60 to $80 (excluding tolls and tip). Allow 45 minutes to one hour of travel time.

Getting Around

Check out the Metropolitan Transportation Authority website (www.mta.info) for public transportation information (buses and subway), including a handy travel planner and regular notifications of delays and alternate travel routes during frequent maintenance.

Walking New York, down deep, can't be seen until you've taken the time to hit the sidewalks. Broadway runs the length of Manhattan, about 13.5 miles. Crossing the East River over the Brooklyn Bridge is a New York classic, and Central Park trails can get you to wooded pockets.

Subway Inexpensive, somewhat efficient and open around the clock, though can be confusing to the uninitiated. A single ride is $2.50 with a MetroCard. A 7-Day Unlimited Pass costs $29.

Taxi Meters start at $2.50 and increase roughly $4 for every 20 blocks. Look for one with a lit light on its roof – this means it's available.

Cycling Always wear a helmet; pedaling on the sidewalk is illegal.

Interborough ferries Hop-on-hop-off service and free rides in the harbor to Staten Island. Check out New York Waterway (www.nywaterway.com) and New York Water Taxi (www.nywatertaxi.com).

Buses Convenient during off hours – especially when transferring between the city's east and west sides. Same price as the subway.

Sleeping

In general, accommodation prices in New York City do not abide by any high season or low season rules; wavering rates usually reflect availability. With more than 50 million tourists visiting in 2011, you can expect that hotel rooms fill up quickly – especially in summer. In addition to the following websites, don't forget about global sites like Hotels.com, Hotwire.com and Orbitz.com.

Useful Websites

○ **newyorkhotels.com** (www.newyorkhotels. com) The self-proclaimed official website for hotels in NYC.

○ **airbnb** (www.airbnb.com) Choose furnished apartments or rooms in a New Yorker's house rather than pricey hotel digs.

○ **Jetsetter** (www.jetsetter.com) Great selection of international sales on luxury hotels; excellent NYC selection.

What to Bring

○ **Walking shoes** Get on your feet and go green. New York City's streets, like Nancy Sinatra's boots, are made for walking.

○ **Extra suitcase** To transport all the goodies you buy here home – from fashion forward clothes to that kitschy Statue of Liberty snow globe.

○ **Swanky clothing** Dress to the nines for a sophisticated night out at the opera, orchestra or meal at one of the city's top restaurants.

○ **Plenty of money** You won't want to skimp on a chance to take in a Broadway show or see world class musicians live.

Be Forewarned

○ **Public restrooms** Few and far between; your best bet is to pop into a Starbucks.

○ **Restaurants** Large parties will have trouble getting seated without reservations.

○ **Subways** Because of constant track work, weekend schedule changes are confusing.

Lower Manhattan & the Financial District

This area packs in a diverse wallop of sights. The borough comes to a pencil point at its southern tip, forming the general swath known as Lower Manhattan. This area is teeming with iconic sights that include the 9/11 Memorial, Wall St, the Brooklyn Bridge and City Hall and, offshore in the near distance, the Statue of Liberty.

It has come back to life slowly and surely, despite seriously delayed redevelopment plans related to the former World Trade Center site. The whole area, in fact, has gone through a recent renaissance, bringing newness in many forms – museums, hotels and trendy restaurants – that has in turn lured more and more visitors. Add those elements to the area's geographic narrowness – waterfront parks and sweeping views are an intimate part of the fabric here – and you've got quite a lively little city corner.

Staten Island Ferry (p71)

Lower Manhattan &
the Financial District Highlights

Walking the Brooklyn Bridge (p67)

The Brooklyn Bridge pedestrian walkway begins just east of City Hall and affords a wonderful view of Lower Manhattan. Observation points offer histories of the waterfront. Take care to stay on the side of the walkway marked for folks on foot – frustrated cyclists, who use it en masse for commuting and pleasure, have been known to get nasty with oblivious tourists.

9/11 Memorial (p62)

Plagued by design controversies, budget blowouts and construction delays, the first part of the World Trade Center redevelopment – known simply as the 9/11 Memorial – opened to the public on September 12, 2011. The wait was worth it. Titled *Reflecting Absence,* its two massive reflecting pools are as much a symbol of hope and renewal as they are a tribute to the thousands who lost their lives to terrorism.

RICHARD LEVINE/ALAMY ©

LEE FOSTER/LONELY PLANET IMAGES ©

3 Battery Park City (p61)

There's a surreal sense to this corner of the city, its clutch of gleaming, modern high-rises and lovely promenades and parks cut off from the rest of the city. Its position at sunset makes it feel like the hovering towers are quietly aglow. By day, you can find peace here, thanks to the 30-acre waterfront stretch of parkland along the Hudson River, making it one of downtown's great opportunities for escape. Fritz Koenig's *Sphere*, Battery Park, previously stood between the World Trade Center towers

GAVIN GOUGH/LONELY PLANET IMAGES ©

4 Ferries (p71)

For a refreshing perspective on the city and its skyline, get yourself out onto the water that surrounds it. Join the commuters on the free Staten Island Ferry and enjoy spectacular views of New York Harbor and the Statue of Liberty, or hop aboard the free Governors Island Ferry for a trip to this small island off the southern tip of Manhattan. Once here, visitors can laze about its massive lawns and enjoy unsurpassed city views. View from Staten Island Ferry

5 Wall Street (p56)

Both an actual street and the metaphorical home of US commerce, Wall St is named for the wooden barrier built by Dutch settlers in 1653 to protect New Amsterdam from Native Americans and the British. Though the New York Stock Exchange has been closed to visitors indefinitely, tourists still gather on the sidewalk to gawk at harried traders who scurry out for cigarettes and food.

Lower Manhattan Walk

Anchored by the mile-long and world-famous Wall St and the reborn World Trade Center Site, this area is steeped in history. Intimate, circuitous and sometimes confusing side streets, Gothic churches and a fine collection of early-20th-century skyscrapers distinguish the concentrated feel of the neighborhood.

❶ La Colombe

Start with coffee at **La Colombe**. In the 19th century, the site was a stop on the antislavery 'underground railway,' a secret network of routes and safe houses allowing African Americans to reach free states and Canada. A plaque on the Lispenard St side of the building commemorates the fact.

❷ 8 Hook & Ladder

Further west, the intersection of Varick and N Moore Sts is where you'll find **8 Hook & Ladder**, better known as ghost-control headquarters in '80s film *Ghostbusters*.

❸ Textile Building

Continue south on Varick St, turn left into Leonard St and stop at the intersection with Church St. On the southeast corner stands the **Textile Building**, built in 1901. Its architect, Henry J Hardenbergh, would go on to design Midtown's monumental Plaza Hotel.

❹ Woolworth Building

Head further south on Church St, turning left into Park Pl and right into Broadway. Before you is the neo-Gothic **Woolworth Building** (p63), the world's tallest skyscraper upon completion in 1913. Security is tight, but you can usually poke your head in to inspect the opulent lobby and blue-and-gold-tiled ceiling.

❺ St Paul's Chapel

Heading south on Broadway, cross Vesey St and you'll see **St Paul's Chapel** (p60) on your right – it's the only pre–Revolutionary War church left intact in the city.

WALK FACTS

- **Start** La Colombe
- **Finish** Wall St
- **Distance** 2.5 miles
- **Duration** 2½ to three hours

6 World Trade Center Site

Continue south on Broadway, turning right into Liberty St, home to the moving **WTC Tribute Visitor Center**. Admission includes access to the neighboring **9/11 Memorial** (p62) – two giant reflecting pools set in the footprints of the destroyed Twin Towers. Soaring above them is the new, 1776ft One World Trade Center, America's tallest skyscraper.

7 Trinity Church

Further south on Broadway, **Trinity Church** (p60) was the city's tallest building upon completion in 1846 and its peaceful cemetery is the final resting place of steamboat inventor Robert Fulton. Designed by English architect Richard Upjohn, the church helped launch the picturesque neo-Gothic movement in America.

8 Wall St

Head east onto Wall St, home of the **New York Stock Exchange** (p61) and the **Federal Hall** (p57). You can visit the latter, in which John Peter Zenger was acquitted of seditious libel in 1735 – the first step, historians say, in establishing a democracy committed to a free press. Just across the street at the southeast corner of Wall and Broad Sts is the former headquarters of the JP Morgan Bank. Examine the pockmarks on its limestone facade on the Wall St side – they're the remnants of the 1920 Morgan Bank bombing.

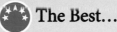

The Best...

PLACES TO EAT

Locanda Verde Simple and relaxed urban Italian. (p64)

Les Halles Meat lovers head downtown to Anthony Bourdain's restaurant. (p64)

Kutsher's Tribeca A hotspot of modern Jewish cuisine with enhanced classic flavors. (p64)

New Amsterdam Market Graze and shop with locavores at this gut-rumbling market. (p65)

PLACES TO DRINK

Macao Downstairs den with eclectic global decor and seriously delicious cocktails. (p66)

Brandy Library Luxury clubbiness and house specialty nibbles. (p66)

Ward III Old-school ambiance and top-notch bar grub. (p66)

Weather Up Effortlessly cool. (p66)

PLACES TO TRACE HISTORY

Federal Hall Site where George Washington took oath of office as first US president. (p57)

Trinity Church Originally founded by King William III. (p60)

St Paul's Chapel George Washington worshipped here. (p60)

Cemetery next to Trinity Church (p60)
MICHELLE BENNETT/LONELY PLANET IMAGES ©

Don't Miss
Statue of Liberty

Lady Liberty has been gazing sternly across the waters to 'unenlightened Europe' since 1886. Dubbed the 'Mother of Exiles,' the statue serves as an admonishment to the rigid social structures of the old world. 'Give me your tired, your poor, Your huddled masses yearning to breathe free, The wretched refuse of your teeming shore. Send these, the homeless, tempest-tost to me, I lift my lamp beside the golden door!' she declares in Emma Lazarus' famous 1883 poem 'The New Colossus.' Ironically, these famous words were added to the statue's base only in 1903, more than 15 years after the poet's death.

📞877-523-9849

www.nps.gov/stli

Liberty Island

🕘9:30am-5pm

Liberty Today

Following the statue's 125th anniversary celebrations on October 28, 2011, the crown, museum and pedestal were closed for a major renovation. Due for completion in late 2012, the improvements will include access to the observation deck for mobility impaired visitors. In the meantime, visitors can still walk around the statue, take an audio tour, and pick up souvenirs in the gift shop. The cafeteria also remains open, though we strongly suggest you miss the sub-par offerings. Bring your own nibbles and (if the weather is behaving), enjoy it by the water, the Manhattan skyline before you.

Once the renovations are complete, folks who reserve in advance (more on that in a minute) will once again be able to climb the (steep) 354 steps to Lady Liberty's crown, where the city and harbor are even more impressive. As for the bad news: crown access is extremely limited, and the only way in is to reserve your spot in advance – and the further in advance you can do it, the better, as up to a full one-year lead time is allowed. Also know that each customer may only reserve a maximum of four crown tickets.

Creating the Lady

One of America's most powerful symbols of kinship and freedom, 'Liberty Enlightening the World' was a joint effort between America and France to commemorate the centennial of the Declaration of Independence. It was created by commissioned sculptor Frédéric-Auguste Bartholdi. The artist spent most of 20 years turning his dream – to create the hollow monument and mount it in the New York Harbor – into reality. Along the way it was hindered by serious financial problems, but was helped in part by the fund-raising efforts of newspaper publisher Joseph Pulitzer. Lending a further hand was poet Emma Lazarus, whose aforementioned ode to Lady Liberty was part of a fund-raising campaign for the statue's pedestal, designed by American architect Richard Morris Hunt. Bartholdi's work on the statue was also delayed by structural challenges – a problem resolved by the metal framework mastery of railway engineer Gustave Eiffel (of, yes, the famous tower). The work of art was finally completed in France in 1884 (a bit off schedule for that centennial). It was shipped to NYC as 350 pieces packed into 214 crates, reassembled over a span of four months and placed on a US-made granite pedestal. Its spectacular October 1886 dedication included New York's first ticker-tape parade, and a flotilla of almost 300 vessels. Put under the administration of the National Park Service in 1933, a restoration of the Lady's oxidized copper began in 1984, the same year the monument made it onto the UN's list of World Heritage Sites.

Need to Know

Although the ferry ride from Battery Park in Lower Manhattan lasts only 15 minutes, a trip to both the Statue of Liberty and Ellis Island is an all-day affair, and only those setting out on the ferry by 1pm will be allowed to visit both sites. Security screening at the ferry terminal can take up to 90 minutes. Reservations to visit the grounds and pedestal (the latter closed until late 2012) are strongly recommended, as they give you a specific visit time and a guarantee you'll get in. Your other option is to buy a Flex Ticket, which lets you enter anytime within a three-day period.

Don't Miss
Ellis Island

Ellis Island is America's most famous and historically important gateway – the very spot where old-world despair met new-world promise. Between 1892 and 1954, more than 12 million immigrants passed through this processing station, their dreams in tow. Among them were Hungarian Erik Weisz (Harry Houdini), Rodolfo Guglielmi (Rudolph Valentino) and British Archibald Alexander Leach (Cary Grant). An estimated 40% of Americans today have at least one ancestor who was processed here, confirming the major role this tiny harbor island has played in the making of modern America.

212-363-3200,
Statue Cruises
877-523-9849

www.statuecruises.
com

ferry departs
Battery Park

admission free,
ferry (incl Statue of
Liberty) adult/child
$13/5

ferries every 15-
30min 9am-2pm

1 to South Ferry;
4/5 to Bowling Green

Main Building Architecture

After a $160 million restoration, the center was reopened to the public in 1990. Now anybody who rides the ferry to the island can experience a cleaned-up, modern version of the historic new-arrival experience at the impressive Immigration Museum, whose interactive exhibits pay homage to the hope, jubilation and sometimes bitter disappointment of the millions who came here in search of a new beginning.

With their Main Building (pictured), architects Edward Lippincott Tilton and William A Boring created a suitably impressive and imposing 'prologue' to America. The designing duo won the contract after the original wooden building burnt down in 1897. The building evokes a grand train station, with majestic triple-arched entrances, decorative Flemish bond brickwork, and granite quoins (cornerstones) and belvederes. Inside, it's the second-floor, 338ft-long Registry Room (also known as the Great Hall) that takes the breath away. It was under this beautiful vaulted ceiling that the newly arrived lined up to have their documents checked, and that the polygamists, paupers, criminals and anarchists were turned back. The original plaster ceiling was severely damaged by an explosion of munition barges at nearby Black Tom Wharf. It was a blessing in disguise: the rebuilt version was adorned with striking, herringbone-patterned tiles by Rafael Guastavino.

Immigration Museum Exhibits

The three-level Immigration Museum is a poignant tribute to the immigrant experience. To get the most out of your visit, opt for the 50-minute self-guided audio tour ($8, available from the museum lobby). Featuring narratives from a number of sources, including historians, architects and the immigrants themselves, the tour brings to life the museum's hefty collection of personal objects, official documents, photographs and film footage. It's an evocative experience to relive personal memories – both good and bad – in the very halls and corridors in which they occurred.

The collection itself is divided into a number of permanent and temporary exhibitions. On the second floor you'll find two of the most fascinating exhibitions. The first, 'Through America's Gate,' examines the step-by-step process faced by the newly arrived, including the chalk-marking of those suspected of illness, a wince-inducing eye examination, and 29 questions in the beautiful, vaulted Registry Room. The second must-see exhibition, 'Peak Immigration Years,' explores the motives behind the immigrants' journeys and the challenges they faced once they were free to begin their new American lives. For a history of the rise, fall and resurrection of the building itself, make time for the 'Restoring a Landmark' exhibition on the third floor; its tableaux of trashed desks, chairs and other abandoned possessions are strangely haunting. Best of all, the audio tour offers optional, in-depth coverage for those wanting to delve deeper into the collections and the island's history. If you don't feel like opting for the audio tour, you can always pick up one of the phones in each display area and listen to the recorded, yet affecting memories of real Ellis Island immigrants, taped in the 1980s. Another option is the free, 45-minute guided tour with a park ranger.

Need to Know

To be sure you get onto a ferry, you should make advance reservations. However, if you're not one for planning in advance, you can take your chances by going for one of a limited number of time passes available to walkups on a first-come-first-served basis. During the especially busy summer months, there is a less crowded approach to Ellis Island, via ferry from New Jersey's Liberty State Park. If you plan on exploring the museum in detail, set aside a good three hours.

Discover Lower Manhattan & the Financial District

🔄 Getting There & Away

○ **Subway** The Financial District is well serviced by subway lines, connecting the area to the rest of Manhattan, Brooklyn, Queens and the Bronx. Fulton St is the main interchange station, servicing the A/C, J/M/Z, 2/3 and 4/5 lines. The 1 train terminates at South Ferry, from where the Staten Island Ferry departs.

○ **Bus** From the Staten Island Ferry terminal, useful routes include the 15 (to East Village, Midtown East and Upper East Side) and the 20 (to Tribeca, West Village, Chelsea and Midtown West).

○ **Boat** The Staten Island Ferry Terminal is at the southern end of Whitehall St. Ferries to Governors Island leave from the adjacent Battery Maritime Building. Services to Liberty and Ellis Islands depart from nearby Battery Park.

George Washington statue, Federal Hall
RICHARD CUMMINS/LONELY PLANET IMAGES ©

◉ Sights

Wall Street & the Financial District

Museum of American Finance   Museum

Map p58 (www.moaf.org; 48 Wall St btwn Pearl & William Sts; adult/child $8/free; ⊙10am-4pm Tue-Sat; S 2/3, 4/5 to Wall St) Money makes this museum go round, its exhibits focusing on historic moments in American financial history. Permanent collections include rare, 18th-century documents, stock and bond certificates from the Gilded Age, the oldest known photograph of Wall St and a stock ticker from c 1875.

The museum also runs themed walking tours of the area, advertised on the museum website.

Once the headquarters for the Bank of New York, the building itself is a lavish spectacle, with 30ft ceilings, high arched windows, a majestic staircase to the mezzanine, glass chandeliers, and murals depicting historic scenes of banking and commerce.

Fraunces Tavern Museum   Museum

Map p58 (www.frauncestavernmuseum.org; 54 Pearl St btwn Broad St & Coenties Slip; adult/child $7/free; ⊙noon-5pm; S J/M/Z to Broad St, 4/5 to Bowling Green) Combining five early–18th-century structures, this unique museum/restaurant combo is an homage to the nation-shaping events of 1783, when the British relinquished control of New York at the end of the Revolutionary War and General George Washington gave a farewell speech to the officers of

Morgan Bank Bombing

If you wander past the former headquarters of JP Morgan Bank on the southeast corner of Wall and Broad Sts, take a minute to examine its limestone facade on the Wall St side. The pockmarks you see are the remnants of the so-called Morgan Bank bombing – America's deadliest terrorist attack until the Oklahoma City bombing of 1995.

The fateful day was Thursday, 16 September 1920, when at exactly 12.01pm, 500 pounds of lead sash weights and 100 pounds of dynamite exploded from a horse-drawn carriage. Thirty-eight people were killed and around 400 injured. Among the latter was John F Kennedy's father, Joseph P Kennedy.

The bomb's detonation outside America's most influential financial institution at the time led many to blame anticapitalist groups, from Italian anarchists to stock-standard Bolsheviks. Yet the crime has yet to be solved, the decision to reopen both the bank and New York Stock Exchange the following day leading to a swift clean up of both debris and vital clues. Almost 100 years on, the shrapnel marks remain, purposely left by banker Jack Morgan as an act of remembrance and defiance.

the Continental Army in the second-floor dining room on December 4.

Today, the museum hosts historical walking tours, lectures, Revolutionary War paintings, and some surprising Washington relics, including false teeth and a lock of hair.

FREE Federal Reserve Bank of New York
Notable Building

Map p58 (212-720-6130; www.newyorkfed.org; 33 Liberty St at Nassau St, entry via 44 Maiden Lane; reservation required; tours 11.15am, noon, 1.15pm, 2.30pm, 3.15pm & 4pm Mon-Fri; S A/C, J/Z, 2/3, 4/5 to Fulton St) The best reason to visit the Federal Reserve Bank is the chance to ogle its high-security vault – more than 10,000 tons of gold reserves reside here, 80ft below ground. You'll only see a small part of that fortune, but signing on to a free tour (the only way down; book around six weeks ahead) is worth the effort.

While you don't need to join a guided tour to browse the bank's museum, which includes an interesting exhibition on the history of money, you will still need to book a time online. Bring your passport or other official ID.

FREE National Museum of the American Indian
Museum

Map p58 (www.nmai.si.edu; 1 Bowling Green; 10am-5pm Fri-Wed, to 8pm Thu; S 4/5 to Bowling Green) An affiliate of the Smithsonian Institution, this elegant museum of Native American culture is set in Cass Gilbert's spectacular 1907 Custom House, one of NYC's finest beaux arts buildings. Beyond a vast elliptical rotunda, sleek galleries play host to changing exhibitions documenting Native American culture, life and beliefs. The museum's permanent collection includes stunning decorative arts, textiles and ceremonial objects.

FREE Federal Hall
Museum

Map p58 (www.nps.gov/feha; 26 Wall St, entrance on Pine St; 9am-5pm Mon-Fri; S J/M/Z to Broad St, 2/3, 4/5 to Wall St) A Greek Revival masterpiece, Federal Hall houses a museum dedicated to postcolonial New York. There's also a visitor information hall which covers downtown cultural happenings.

The building itself, distinguished by a huge statue of George Washington, stands on the site of New York's original City Hall, where the first US Congress

Lower Manhattan & the Financial District

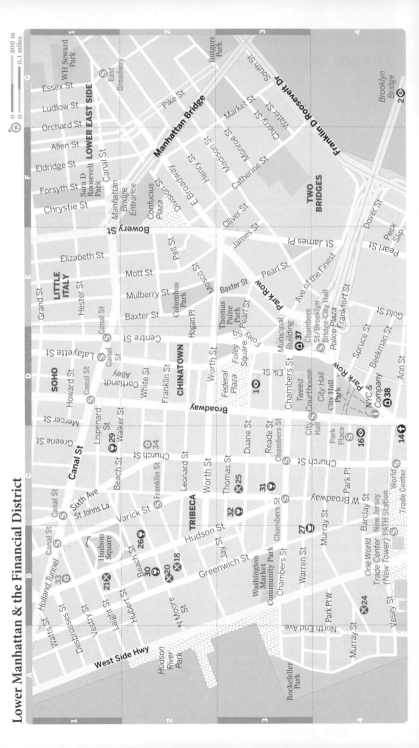

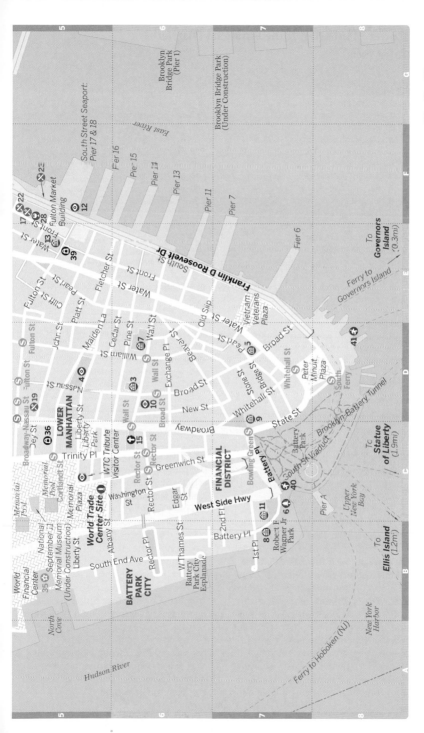

South Street Seaport: Pier 17 & 18

Brooklyn Bridge Park (Pier 1)

Brooklyn Bridge Park (Under Construction)

East River

Fulton Market Building 12

Fer 16

Pier 15

Pier 14

Pier 13

Pier 11

Pier 7

Pier 6

To Governors Island (0.3mi)

Ferry to Governors Island

22

17

28

Front St

13

Water St

39

Front St

South St

Franklin D Roosevelt Dr

Fulton St

Cliff St

Pearl St

Fletcher St

Water St

Front St

Platt St

Jchn St

Maiden La

Cedar St

Pine St

William St

Wall St

Old Slip

Water St

Vietnam Veterans Plaza

Broad St

Pearl St

Fulton St

Fulton St

Nassau St

4

19

John St

Fulton St

3

Wall St

Exchange Pl

Beaver St

South St

Stone St

Whitehall St

Broad St

Peter Minuit Plaza

LOWER MANHATTAN

Dey St

Broadway-Nassau St

Liberty St

Liberty Park

10

Broad St

New St

Whitehall St

41

Broadway

State St

Memorial Pool

Cortlandt St

Memorial Plaza

Trinity Pl

WTC Tribute Visitor Center

36

Rector St

15

Rector St

Greenwich St

9

Bowling Green

Battery Pl

Battery Park

To Governors Island

Memorial Pool

National September 11 Memorial Museum (Under Construction)

Liberty St

World Trade Center Site

Washington St

Rector St

Edgar St

FINANCIAL DISTRICT

40

South St Viaduct

Brooklyn-Battery Tunnel

World Financial Center

35

West Side Hwy

2nd Pl

6

Pier A

Upper New York Bay

To Statue of Liberty (1.9mi)

North Cove

Albany St

Rector Pl

W Thames St

Battery Pl

11

8

1st Pl

Robert F Wagner Jr Park

BATTERY PARK CITY

South End Ave

Battery Park City Esplanade

To Ellis Island (1.2mi)

New York Harbor

Hudson River

Ferry to Hoboken (NJ)

Lower Manhattan & the Financial District

Top Sights
- 9/11 Memorial ... C5

Sights
- **1** African Burial Ground ... D3
- **2** Brooklyn Bridge ... G4
- **3** Federal Hall ... D6
- **4** Federal Reserve Bank of New York ... D5
- **5** Fraunces Tavern Museum ... D7
- **6** Hudson River Park ... C7
- **7** Museum of American Finance ... D6
- **8** Museum of Jewish Heritage ... B7
- **9** National Museum of the American Indian ... D7
- **10** New York Stock Exchange ... D6
- **11** Skyscraper Museum ... C7
- **12** South Street Seaport ... F5
- **13** South Street Seaport Museum ... E5
- **14** St Paul's Chapel ... C4
- **15** Trinity Church ... C6
- **16** Woolworth Building ... C4

Eating
- **17** Barbarini ... F5
- **18** Kutsher's Tribeca ... B2
- **19** Les Halles ... D5
- **20** Locanda Verde ... B2
- **21** Moomah ... B1
- **22** Nelson Blue ... F5
- **23** New Amsterdam Market ... F5
- **24** Shake Shack ... B4
- **25** Tiny's & the Bar Upstairs ... C3

Drinking & Nightlife
- **26** Brandy Library ... B2
- **27** Kaffe 1668 ... B3
- **28** Keg No 229 ... F5
- **29** Macao ... C1
- **30** Smith & Mills ... B2
- **31** Ward III ... C3
- **32** Weather Up ... C3

Entertainment
- **33** 92YTribeca ... B1
- **34** Flea Theater ... C2
- **35** World Financial Center ... B5

Shopping
- **36** Century 21 ... C5
- **37** Citystore ... D3
- **38** J&R Music & Computer World ... D4
- **39** New York Yankees Clubhouse ... E5

Sports & Activities
- **40** Bike & Roll Bike Rentals ... C7
- **41** Staten Island Ferry ... D8

convened and Washington took the oath of office as the first US president on April 30, 1789. After that structure's demolition in the early 19th century, the current building rose in its place between 1834 and 1842, serving as the US Customs House until 1862.

Trinity Church — Church

Map p58 (www.trinitywallstreet.org; Broadway at Wall St; 🕒7am-6pm Mon-Fri, 8am-4pm Sat, 7am-4pm Sun; [S] R to Rector St; 2/3, 4/5 to Wall St) New York City's tallest building upon completion in 1846, Trinity Church features a 280ft-high bell tower, an arresting stained glass window over the altar, and a small museum of historical church artifacts. Famous residents of its serene cemetery include Founding Father Alexander Hamilton, while its excellent music series includes Concerts at One (1pm Thursdays) and magnificent choir concerts, including an annual December rendition of Handel's *Messiah*.

St Paul's Chapel — Church

Map p58 (www.trinitywallstreet.org; Broadway at Fulton St; 🕒10am-6pm Mon-Fri, to 4pm Sat, 7am-4pm Sun; [S] A/C, J/Z, 2/3, 4/5 to Fulton St) Despite George Washington worshipping here after his inauguration in 1789, this classic revival brownstone chapel found new fame in the aftermath of September 11. With the World Trade Center destruction occurring just a block away, the mighty structure became a spiritual support and volunteer center, movingly documented in its exhibition 'Unwavering Spirit: Hope & Healing at Ground Zero.'

The chapel, built in 1766 and considered the oldest building in New York still in continuous use, also hosts workshops, special events and a popular classical-music series.

New York Stock Exchange
Notable Building

Map p58 (www.nyse.com; 11 Wall St; ⊘ closed to the public; **S** J/M/Z to Broad St, 2/3, 4/5 to Wall St) Home to the world's best-known stock exchange (the NYSE), Wall Street is an iconic symbol of US capitalism. About one billion shares, valued at around $73 billion, change hands daily behind the portentous Romanesque facade, a sight no longer accessible to the public due to security concerns. Feel free to gawk outside the building, protected by barricades and the hawk-eyed NYPD.

New York Harbor

Statue of Liberty
Monument

See p52.

Ellis Island
Landmark

See p54.

Battery Park City

Hudson River Park
Park

Map p58 (www.hudsonriverpark.org; Manhattan's west side from Battery Park to 59th St; **S** 1 to Franklin St, 1 to Canal St) Stretching from Battery Park to Hell's Kitchen, the 5-mile, 550-acre Hudson River Park runs along the lower western side of Manhattan. Diversions include a bike/run/skate path snaking along its entire length, community gardens, playgrounds, and renovated piers reinvented as riverfront esplanades, miniature golf courses and alfresco summertime movie theaters and concert venues. Visit website for a detailed map.

Museum of Jewish Heritage
Museum

Map p58 (www.mjhnyc.org; 36 Battery Pl; adult/child $12/free, 4pm-8pm Wed free; ⊘ 10am-5:45pm Sun-Tue & Thu, to 8pm Wed, to 5pm Fri; **S** 4/5 to Bowling Green) This waterfront memorial museum explores all aspects of modern Jewish identity, with often poignant personal artifacts, photographs and documentary films.

Skyscraper Museum
Museum

Map p58 (www.skyscraper.org; 39 Battery Pl; admission $5; ⊘ noon-6pm Wed-Sun; **S** 4/5 to Bowling Green) Fans of phallic architecture will love this compact, high-gloss gallery, examining skyscrapers as objects of design, engineering and urban renewal. Temporary exhibitions dominate the space, with one recent offering

Hudson River Park

ANGELO HORNAK/ALAMY ©

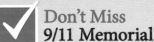 ## Don't Miss
9/11 Memorial

Plagued by design controversies, budget blowouts and construction delays, the first part of the World Trade Center redevelopment – the National September 11 Memorial, or simply the 9/11 Memorial (designer: Michael Arad) – opened on 12 September 2011. The wait was worth it. Titled *Reflecting Absence*, its two massive reflecting pools are as much a symbol of hope and renewal as they are a tribute to the thousands who lost their lives.

Visitor passes for specific times and dates are free and available online. Alternatively, paid admission to the WTC Tribute Visitor Center includes admission to the memorial.

Surrounded by a plaza planted with 400 swamp white oak trees, the 9/11 Memorial's pools occupy the footprints of the ill-fated twin towers. From their rim, a cascade of water pours 30ft down towards a central void. Bronze panels frame the pools, inscribed with the names of those who died in the terrorist attacks of 11 September 2001, and in the World Trade Center car bombing on 26 February 1993. When it opens, the National September 11 Memorial Museum will document the attacks. Until then, the temporary WTC Tribute Visitor Center features a gallery of images and artifacts, and offers tours of the WTC site's perimeter. The temporary 9/11 Memorial Preview Site has models and renderings related to the site and redevelopment.

At the northwest corner is David M Childs' One World Trade Center (1 WTC). Upon completion in late 2012, the skyscraper will be America's tallest, with 105 stories and a total height of 1776ft, a symbolic reference to the year of American independence.

NEED TO KNOW

Map p58; www.911memorial.org; cnr Greenwich & Albany Sts; 9/11 Memorial free; S A/C/E to Chambers St, R to Rector St, 2/3 to Park Pl

showcasing the world's next generation of 'Supertalls.' The permanent collection includes information on the design and construction of the Empire State Building, as well as that of the World Trade Center.

South Street Seaport

South Street Seaport Museum
Museum

Map p58 (212 748 8600; www.seany.org; 12 Fulton St; adult/child/senior & student $10/free/$6; 10am-6pm Wed-Sun; S 2/3, 4/5, A/C, J/M/Z to Fulton St) Recently renovated, this museum offers a glimpse of the seaport's history and a survey of the world's great ocean liners, with permanent exhibits and various other sites dotted around the 11-block area. Spanning three floors, the museum's new galleries include a battalion of model ships, antique shipping tools, as well as left-of-center shows covering anything from New York fashion to contemporary photography. The museum's booty also extends to a group of tall-masted sailing ships just south of Pier 17, including the *Ambrose* and *Pioneer*. Off-limits for restoration during research, access to their windswept decks and intimate interiors are normally included in the admission to the museum. It was hoped that from spring 2012, the gorgeous, iron-hulled *Pioneer*, built in 1885 to carry mined sand, is expected to once again offer two-hour sailing journeys through the warmer months; contact the museum for updates.

City Hall & Civic Center

Woolworth Building
Architecture

Map p58 (233 Broadway at Park Pl; S J/M/Z to Chambers St; 4/5/6 to Brooklyn Bridge-City Hall) The world's tallest building upon completion in 1913, Cass Gilbert's 60-story Woolworth Building is a neo-Gothic marvel, elegantly clad in masonry and terra-cotta. Surpassed in height by the Chrysler Building in 1930, the 792ft-tall tower is off-limits to visitors these days (try to sneak a peak at the beautifully preserved lobby). Alternatively, admire the facade from City Hall Park across the street.

FREE African Burial Ground
Memorial

Map p58 (www.nps.gov/afbg/index.htm; 290 Broadway btwn Duane & Elk Sts; memorial 9am-5pm daily, visitors center 9am-5pm Mon-Fri; S 4/5 to Wall St) In 1991, construction workers here uncovered over 400 stacked wooden caskets, just 16ft to 28ft below street level. The boxes contained the remains of enslaved Africans (nearby Trinity Church graveyard had banned the burial of Africans at the time). Today, a memorial and visitors center honors an estimated 15,000 Africans buried here during the 17th and 18th centuries.

Woolworth Building
COREY WISE/LONELY PLANET IMAGES ©

Tribeca

Taking its moniker from real estate agents who noted the pocket of land sitting in a 'TRIangle BElow CAnal (St),' this intimate neighborhood is composed of landmark 19th-century buildings as well as massive former warehouses that have been pretty thoroughly converted into luxury condos. It's a quiet and unassuming place that hasn't seen a true media frenzy since the decade-old tragic death of John F Kennedy Jr, which still inspires visitors to leave flowers at his former residence on N Moore St. There are plenty of living, breathing stars living here, too – though none so prominent as Robert De Niro, who has put his 'hood on the map as NYC's new center of film with his wildly successful Tribeca Film Festival. Still, local foodies know this as the place to celeb-spot while spending small fortunes on sushi or steak *frites,* and night owls love it for its sultry lounge bars.

First used as farmland for Dutch settlers, the years since have seen it become a center for the textile industry, dairy mercantile exchanges, cheap artists' lofts and, by the 1970s, an urban renewal plan that knocked down many of the old buildings and threw up high-rises, parks and educational facilities, including the Borough of Manhattan Community College. Though Tribeca has not been known as one of the top spots to see art since the '80s (most galleries have fled uptown to Chelsea), there's still plenty to see here.

Tribeca is bordered by Canal St (to the north), West St (west), Chambers St (south) and Broadway (east). For getting around once you're here, walking should suit you fine; otherwise try the M20 or M6 buses or the 1 train to Franklin St or the 1, 2, 3 to Chambers St.

🍴 Eating

Locanda Verde Italian $$$

Map p58 (☎212-925-3797; www.locandaverdenyc.com; 377 Greenwich St at Noore St; pasta $17-19, mains $15-31; [S] A/C/E to Canal St, 1 to Franklin St) Step through the red velvet curtains and into a sexy, buzzing scene of loosened Brown Brothers' shirts, black dresses and slick barmen behind a long, crowded bar. Part of the Greenwich Hotel (p283), this sprawling, brasserie-style hot spot is the domain of celebrity chef Andrew Carmellini, whose contemporary Italian grub is seasonal, honest and insanely flavorful.

Kutsher's Tribeca Jewish $$$

Map p58 (☎212-431-0606; www.kutsherstribeca.com; 186 Franklin St btwn Greenwich & Hudson Sts; mains $19-29; 🕒dinner; [S] A/C/E to Canal St, 1 to Franklin St) Thank Yahweh for new-kid-on-the-block Kutsher's, where Jewish comfort food gets a refreshing makeover. Forget the starch and stodge, here you'll be grazing on crispy artichokes with lemon, garlic and Parmesan; borscht salad with marinated goat cheese; or latkes with local apple compote.

Les Halles French $$

Map p58 (☎212-285-8585; www.leshalles.net; 15 John St btwn Broadway & Nassau St; mains $15-29; 🕒11:30am-midnight; 📶; [S] A/C, J/M/Z, 2/3, 4/5 to Fulton St) Vegetarians need not apply at this packed and serious brasserie, owned by celebrity chef Anthony Bourdain. Among the elegant light-fixture balls, dark wood paneling and stiff white tablecloths you'll find a buttoned-up, meat-lovin' crowd who've come for rich and decadent favorites like *cote de boeuf* and steak au poivre.

Shake Shack
Burgers $

Map p58 (www.shakeshack.com; 215 Murray St btwn West St & North End Ave; burgers $3.50-9; **S** A/C, 1/2/3 to Chambers St) This is fast food at its finest: cotton-soft burgers made with prime, freshly ground mince; Chicago-style hot dogs in poppy-seed potato buns; and seriously good cheesy fries. Leave room for the legendary frozen custard and drink local with a Brooklyn Brewery Shackmeister ale.

New Amsterdam Market
Market $

Map p58 (www.newamsterdammarket.org; South St btwn Peck Slip & Beekman St; ⊙11am-4pm Sun late Apr–mid-Dec; **S** A/C, J/Z, 1/2, 4/5 to Fulton St) Sophisticated locavore or basic glutton, do not miss this Sunday food market outside the old Fulton Fish Market. Usually held from late April to mid-December, its 40-odd stalls showcase some of the region's top food and drink producers. Pick up everything from organic Finnish Ruis bread to handmade sausages and pasta.

Barbarini
Italian $$

Map p58 (www.barbarinimercato.com; 225 Front St btwn Peck Slip & Beekman St; pasta $15, mains $16-20; ⊙10am-10:30pm Mon-Sat, 11am-9:30pm Sun; **S** A/C, J/Z, 2/3, 4/5 to Fulton St) Deli? Cafe? Restaurant? Barbarini is all three, sleekly packaged in a combo of concrete floors, charcoal hues and brickwork. Stock the larder with artisanal pasta, salumi, cheeses and mini pistachio cannoli.... but not before nabbing a table in the light-filled backroom for better-than-mamma offerings like buckwheat pasta with wild boar.

Nelson Blue
Pub $$

Map p58 (☎212-346-9090; www.nelsonblue. com; 233-235 Front St at Peck Slip; mains $15-26; **S** 2/3, 4/5, A/C, J/Z to Fulton St) Good for a drink as well as a lamb curry pie, Nelson Blue is the only Kiwi pub in town. The wine list is heavy on New Zealand drops, a perfect match for standouts like zucchini and corn fritters, and green-lipped mussels in a curry and coconut broth.

Tiny's & the Bar Upstairs
American $$

Map p58 (☎212-374-1135; 135 W Broadway btwn Duane & Thomas Sts; mains $18-29; ⊙11:30am-11pm Mon-Thu, to 1am Fri, 10:30am-1am Sat; **S** A/C, 1/2/3 to Chambers St) Snug and

Locanda Verde

Top Tip

If you're after cut-price tickets to Broadway shows, ditch the main TKTS Booth in Times Square for the TKTS branch at **South Street Seaport** (www.tdf.org/tkts; cnr Front & John Sts; ⌚11am-6pm Mon-Sat, to 4pm Sun; [S] A/C to Broadway-Nassau; 2/3, 4/5, J/Z to Fulton St). Queues usually move a little faster and you can also purchase tickets for next-day matinees (something you can't do at the Times Square outlet). Smartphone users can download the free TKTS app, which offers real-time listings of what's on sale.

adorable (book ahead!), Tiny's comes with a crackling fire in the back room and an intimate bar upstairs – try the signature Hot Buttered Wassail (chamomile, apple cider, allspice, cinnamon and whipped cream). Heading the kitchen is chef John Martinez (formerly of Michelin-starred Jean Georges), whose seasonal, well-balanced dishes are served on vintage porcelain. Expect soulful options like meatballs and garlic toast, beet and crispy goat cheese salad, or a beautifully cooked pan-roasted hake.

Moomah Cafe $

Map p58 (www.moomah.com; 161 Hudson St btwn Laight & Hubert Sts; meals $7-13; ⌚7:30am-6pm Mon-Thu, to 7pm Fri, 8am-7pm Sun, art space 9am-5pm Mon-Thu, to 6pm Fri & Sat ; 📶 👪; [S] A/C/E, 1/2 to Canal St) Bond with your little munchkins at this trendy cafe/creative space hybrid, where you can buy art projects off the shelf and undertake them on-site. Whether you're making jewlery or a superhero costume, you'll be sensibly fueled by wholesome edibles like soups, wraps and salads.

Drinking & Nightlife

Macao Cocktail Bar

Map p58 (☎212-431-8750; www.macaonyc.com; 311 Church St btwn Lispenard & Walker Sts; [S] A/C/E, N/R/Q, 4/6 to Canal St) Skip the lines for Macao restaurant and duck into the dark, red-walled opium den-turned-lounge downstairs. A fusion of Portuguese and Asian grub and liquor, Macao remains a top spot for late-night drinking and snacking, especially if you've a soft spot for creative, sizzle-on-the-tongue cocktails.

Brandy Library Bar

Map p58 (www.brandylibrary.com; 25 N Moore St at Varick St; ⌚5pm-1am Sun-Wed, 4pm-2am Thu, 4pm-4am Fri & Sat; [S] 1 to Franklin St) When sipping means serious business, settle into this uber-luxe library, with soothing reading lamps and club chairs facing backlit, floor-to-ceiling, bottle-filled shelves. Go for top-shelf cognac, malt scotch or 90-year-old brandies (prices range from $9 to $340).

Ward III Cocktail Bar

Map p58 (www.ward3tribeca.com; 111 Reade St btwn Church St & W Broadway; [S] A/C/E, 1/2/3 to Chambers St) Ward III channels old-school jauntiness with its elegant cocktails, vintage vibe (tin ceilings, dark wood and old Singer sewing tables behind the bar), and gentlemanly house rules (No 2: 'Don't be creepy').

Weather Up Cocktail Bar

Map p58 (www.weatherupnyc.com; 159 Duane St btwn Hudson St & W Broadway; [S] 1/2/3 to Chambers St) Softly lit subway tiles, eye candy bar staff and smooth, seductive libations underlie Weather Up's magic. Sweet talk the staff over a None But the Brave (cognac, homemade ginger syrup, fresh lime, Pimeto Dram Allspice and soda). Failing that, comfort yourself with some seriously fine bar grub, including spectacular green chile-spiked oysters.

NATALIE GRONO/LONELY PLANET IMAGES ©

Don't Miss
Brooklyn Bridge

A New York icon, the Brooklyn Bridge (Map p58) was the world's first steel suspension bridge. When it opened in 1883, the 1596ft span between its two support towers was the longest in history. Although its construction was fraught with disaster, the bridge became a magnificent example of urban design, inspiring poets, writers and painters. Today, the Brooklyn Bridge continues to dazzle – many regard it as the most beautiful bridge in the world.

The Prussian-born engineer John Roebling designed the bridge, which spans the East River from Manhattan to Brooklyn; he died of tetanus poisoning before construction of the bridge even began. His son, Washington Roebling, supervised construction of the bridge, which lasted 14 years and managed to survive budget overruns and the deaths of 20 workers. The younger Roebling himself suffered from the bends while helping to excavate the riverbed and remained bedridden for much of the project; his wife Emily oversaw construction in his stead. When the bridge opened to pedestrian traffic in June 1883, someone in the crowd shouted, perhaps as a joke, that the bridge was collapsing into the river, setting off a mad rush in which 12 people were trampled to death.

The pedestrian walkway that begins just east of City Hall affords a wonderful view of lower Manhattan; observation points under the support towers offer brass 'panorama' histories of the waterfront. Just take care to stay on the side of the walkway marked for folks on foot – one half is designated for cyclists, who use it en masse for both commuting and pleasure rides, and frustrated pedalers have been known to get nasty with oblivious tourists who wander, camera pressed to an eye, into the bike lane.

Smith & Mills
Cocktail Bar

Map p58 (www.smithandmills.com; 71 N Moore St btwn Hudson & Greenwich Sts; S 1 to Franklin St) This petite drinking hole marks all the cool boxes: unmarked exterior, kooky industrial interior (think early 20th-century factory) and smooth libations – the 'Carriage House' is a nod to the space's previous incarnation. Space is limited so head in early if you fancy kicking back on a plush banquette. A seasonal menu spans light snacks to more substantial options.

Keg No 229
Beer Hall

Map p58 (www.kegno229.com; 229 Front St btwn Beekman St & Peck Slip; S A/C, J/Z, 1/2, 4/5 to Fulton St) If you know that a Flying Dog Raging Bitch is a craft beer – not a nickname for your ex – this curated beer bar is for you.

On hand to soak it all up is a solid selection of comfort grub, including fried pickles and mini cheeseburgers.

Kaffe 1668
Cafe

Map p58 (www.kaffe1668.com; 275 Greenwich St btwn Warren & Murray Sts; ⊘ 6:30am-10pm Mon-Fri, 7:30am-10pm Sat & Sun; 🛜; S A/C, 1/2/3 to Chambers St) One for the coffee cognoscenti, with clover machines, coffee urns and dual synessos pumping out superlative single-origin magic. Seating includes a large communal table, speckled with a mix of office workers, designer Tribeca parents and laptop-hugging creatives.

⭐ Entertainment

Flea Theater
Theater

Map p58 (www.theflea.org; 41 White St btwn Church St & Broadway; S 1 to Franklin St, A/C/E, N/Q/R, J/M/Z, 6 to Canal St) The Flea is one of New York's top off-off-Broadway companies, performing innovative, timely new works in its two intimate performance spaces. Luminaries including Sigourney Weaver and John Lithgow have trod the boards here, and the year-round program also includes cutting-edge music and dance performances.

Left: World Financial Center; **Below:** Cafe at 92Y Tribeca

World Financial Center
Concert Venue

Map p58 (www.artsworldfinancialcenter. com; 200 Liberty St; **S** E to World Trade Center; R to Cortlandt St) Although the World Financial Center is best known as an office and retail complex, its palm-fringed Winter Garden hosts free concerts, theater and dance performances, as well as art exhibits, throughout the year. Head to the website to see what's on.

92Y Tribeca
Cinema

Map p58 (**J** 212-601-1000; www.92y.org; 200 Hudson St at Vestry St; **S** A/C/E, N/Q/R, J/M/Z, 6 to Canal St) Festival-circuit indies, underground classics, camp tear-jerkers – the film screenings at this Tribeca cultural center are as eclectic as they are brilliant.

92Y Tribeca also hosts regular music, theater and comedy performances, as well as public lectures and themed city tours. Check the website for what's on.

🔒 Shopping

Century 21
Fashion

Map p58 (www.c21stores.com; 22 Cortlandt St btwn Church St & Broadway; ⏱7:45am-9pm Mon-Wed, to 9:30pm Thu & Fri, 10am-9pm Sat, 11am-8pm Sun; **S** A/C, J/Z, 2/3, 4/5 to Fulton St) If you're a fashionista with more style than cents, this cut-price department store is your promised land. Raid the racks for designer duds at up to 70% off. Not everything is a knockout or a bargain, but persistence pays off. It gets crowded and competitive, so if you see something you like, get hold of it fast.

J&R Music & Computer World
Music

Map p58 (www.jr.com; 15-23 Park Row; **S** A/C, J/Z, M, 2/3, 4/5 to Fulton St-Broadway-Nassau St) Located on what was once known as Newspaper Row – the center of NYC's

ISTOCK ©

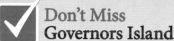

Don't Miss
Governors Island

Off-limits for 200 years, former military outpost Governors Island is now one of New York's most popular playgrounds. Each summer, free ferries make the trip from Lower Manhattan. Among the island's draws is Picnic Point; **Figment** (www.figmentproject. org), a one-weekend-only art festival; and **Water Taxi Beach**, a spit of sand hosting events from dance parties to concerts. There's the 2.2-mile bicycle path around the island, which you can pedal with rental bikes from **Bike & Roll** ($15 per two hours, free on Fridays). Commencing in 2012, a major redevelopment will see the addition of a new park, commercial developments at its eastern and western ends, and a new promenade around its perimeter.

Besides serving as a successful military fort in the Revolutionary War, the Union Army's central recruiting station during the Civil War and the take-off point for Wilbur Wright's famous 1909 flight around the Statue of Liberty, Governors Island is where the 1988 Reagan-Gorbachev summit signaled the beginning of the end of the Cold War. You can visit the spot where that famous summit took place at the Admiral's House, a grand-colonnaded, 1843 military residence that's part of the elegant ghost-town area of Nolan Park. The best way to explore it all is with the **National Park Service** (www. www.nps.gov/gois/index.htm), whose rangers conduct 90-minute guided tours of the historic district, usually on Wednesdays and Thursdays.

NEED TO KNOW

☎ 212-514-8285; www.nps.gov/gois; admission free; ⌚ 10am-5pm Fri, to 7pm Sat & Sun, May 31-Oct 12; ferries leave from Battery Maritime Bldg, Slip 7, hourly 10am-3pm Fri & every 30min 10am-5pm Sat & Sun May-Oct; Ⓢ 4, 5 to Bowling Green, 1 to South Ferry

newspaper publishing biz from the 1840s to the 1920s – this trio of electronics stores sell everything that's related to computers, phones, stereos, iPods, iPads, recording equipment and other electronic gadgetry. It's also packed with CDs, DVDs and video games.

Citystore   Books

Map p58 (www.nyc.gov/citystore; Municipal Bldg, North Plaza, 1 Centre St; ⊘10am-6pm Mon-Fri; S J/M/Z to Chambers St, 4/5/6 to Brooklyn Bridge-City Hall) This small, little-known city-run shop stocks all manner of New York memorabilia, including authentic taxi medallions, manhole coasters, silk ties and baby clothes bearing the official 'City of New York' seal, Brooklyn Bridge posters, NYPD baseball caps, and actual streets signs ('No Parking,' 'Don't Feed the Pigeons'). There's also a great collection of city-themed books.

New York Yankees Clubhouse   Sports

Map p58 (8 Fulton St btwn Front & Water Sts; ⊘10am-9pm Mon-Sat, 11am-8pm Sun; S A/C, J/Z, 2/3, 4/5 to Fulton St) It's on Schermerhorn Row, a block of old warehouses bordered by Fulton, Front and South Sts, that you'll find this commercial shrine to America's mightiest baseball dynasty. Salute the ballpark legends with logo-pimped jerseys, tees, caps... even dog bowls. Hardcore fans will appreciate the booty of signed bats, balls and posters. You can even purchase fee-free game tickets.

🏃 Sports & Activities

FREE **Staten Island Ferry**   Outdoors

Map p58 (www.siferry.com; Whitehall Terminal at Whitehall & South Sts; ⊘24hr; S 1 to South Ferry) Staten Islanders know these hulking, dirty-orange ferryboats as commuter vehicles, while Manhattanites like to think of them as their secret, romantic vessels for a spring-day escape. Yet many a tourist is clued into the charms of the Staten Island Ferry, whose 5.2-mile journey between Lower Manhattan and the Staten Island neighborhood of St George is one of NYC's finest free adventures.

For maximum impact, catch the ferry an hour before sunset – this way your return trip view will be of a glittering, twilight Manhattan skyline.

Bike & Roll
Bike Rentals   Bicycle Rental

Map p58 (www.bikeandroll.com; Pier A, 18 Battery Place; rentals per day $49, tours adult/child $50/35; ⊘9am-7pm Mar-May, 8am-8pm Jun-Aug, 9am-5pm Sep-Nov; S 4/5 to Bowling Green; 1 to South Ferry) Located in Battery Park, this place rents out bikes, as well as leading bike tours along the Hudson River, to Central Park and across the Brooklyn Bridge from April to October.

Battery Park City
Parks Conservancy   Walking Tour

(☎212-267-9700; www.bpcparks.org) The Battery Park City Parks Conservancy offers a range of free or low-fee walking tours, group swims, children's programs and classes. Check the website for upcoming events.

SoHo & Chinatown

Head here to explore ethnic neighborhoods and cool shopping corridors. SoHo (SOuth of HOuston), NoHo (NOrth of HOuston) and Nolita (NOrth of LIttle ITAly) are known for their tangled thickets of hipness in the form of boutiques, bars and eateries. Real estate is through the roof in all three spots, and nights out (or days shopping) can prove to be expensive propositions. But in the end you'll be won over by the unique blend of industrial starkness and cobblestone coziness that lends these areas their character.

There's a palpable anything-goes spirit in Chinatown, where frenzied crowds and hawkers mingle under the winking lights of aging billboards. This, the largest Chinese community outside of Asia (there's a substantial Vietnamese presence as well), is a feast for the senses.

Historic buildings, SoHo

SoHo & Chinatown Highlights

Shopping in SoHo (p92)

Hundreds of stores – big and small – are scattered along SoHo's streets. Broadway is lined with less-expensive chain stores. West along the tree-lined streets are pricier boutiques. Street vendors hawk jewelery, art, T-shirts, hats and other crafts on warm days. On Lafayette shops cater to the DJ and skate crowds with indie labels and vintage shops thrown into the mix. Further east, Nolita is home to tiny jewel-box boutiques.

② Chow Down in Chinatown (p88)

Duck into a produce market to check out oddly shaped fruits and vegetables. Buy three luscious turnip cakes for $1 from a street vendor. Sip bubble teas and slurp noodles. With cuisine from Shanghai, Vietnam and Malaysia, from holes in-the-wall to banquet-sized dining rooms, Chinatown is a true culinary adventure. Experience the area's bustling dining den with friends and eat 'family style.'

Joseph Papp Public Theater (p91)

3

One of the best venues in all NYC for top-quality theater, the Joseph Papp Public Theater has been an important cultural voice for the last half century. Some of the most critically acclaimed off-Broadway productions have been staged here – including many productions that then moved uptown to Broadway – while the attached Joe's Pub draws talented musicians.

JOE'S PUB
PUBLIC

RISTORANTE
UGLIA
STORANTE
Est. 1919

4

Independent Movie Theaters (p91)

Cinephiles can't beat the selection of classic, avant-garde, foreign and themed films on offer at the Film Forum on Houston St. Showings are often combined with director talks. Listen for the roar of the subway under your seat at the Angelika Film Center, where contemporary art-house, independent and the occasional Hollywood movies are screened. Angelika Film Center (p144)

5

Little Italy (p84)

Once known as a truly authentic pocket of Italian people, culture and eateries, Little Italy today is constantly shrinking (a growing Chinatown keeps moving in). Still, the old-world feels like it's hanging on when you take a nighttime stroll down Mulberry St, past turn-of-the-century tenements; loyal Italian Americans still flock here to gather around red-and-white-checkered tablecloths at a handful of long-standing red-sauce restaurants.

SoHo Walk

This walk through the land of acronyms and the concrete catwalks of SoHo takes in some architectural landmarks, but the biggest attraction is the simple beauty of the small tangle of streets that feels like you're walking through an elegant village.

WALK FACTS

- **Start** Cable Building
- **Finish** New York Earth Room
- **Distance** 1.5 miles
- **Duration** One hour

❶ Cable Building

Pop out of the B, D, F, V train and get an immediate sense of old-meets-new with this NoHo beaux arts building built by famed architects McKim, Mead and White in 1894. Originally used as the power plant for the Broadway Cable Car (the nation's first), the **Cable Building** features an oval window and caryatids on its Broadway facade. Today it houses the **Angelika Film Center** (p144).

❷ St Patrick's Old Cathedral

Head east across Houston St and make a right on Lafayette St. Turn left on Prince St and you'll be approaching **St Patrick's Old Cathedral** (p80), which dates from 1809 and is the original location for the famous Fifth Ave cathedral's congregation. Don't miss the ancient, peaceful cemetery.

❸ Elizabeth Street Gallery

Continue along Prince St. If you're hungry, you can stop to fuel up at **Café Gitane** (p87) on Mott St. Otherwise, turn right onto Elizabeth St, where you can pause to admire the fenced-in garden of the curious **Elizabeth Street Gallery** (210 Elizabeth St), part of a fireplace, fountain and garden-ornament shop for the well-off home owner.

4 Singer Building

Turn right on Spring St and walk until you hit Broadway. Just half a block north is the **Singer Building**, one of the post–Civil War buildings that gave this area its 'Cast-Iron District' nickname. This one used to be the main warehouse for the famous sewing-machine company of the same name.

5 Haughwout Building

Head south down Broadway and you'll come to a rather generic Staples store with a surprising history: it's located in the **Haughwout Building**, the first structure to use the exotic steam elevator developed by Elisha Otis. Known as the 'Parthenon of Cast-Iron Architecture,' the Haughwout (pronounced how-out) is considered a rare structure for its two-sided design. Don't miss the iron clock that sits on the Broadway facade.

6 Drawing Center

Continue another block south on Broadway and then turn right onto Grand St and continue three blocks before turning right onto Wooster St. On your right is the **Drawing Center**, the only nonprofit institute in the country to focus solely on drawings, using works by masters as well as unknowns to show the juxtaposition of various styles.

7 New York Earth Room

Continue north on Wooster St and head several blocks up to the **New York Earth Room**, where artist Walter De Maria's gallery filled with cool, moist soil will either thrill you or leave you scratching your head (or maybe a bit of both).

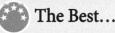

The Best...

PLACES TO EAT

Dutch 'Roots-inspired' locavore American at this award winning restaurant. (p87)

Balthazar Kitchen stays open till 2am from Thursday to Saturday, and weekend brunch is a crowded production. (p86)

Joe's Shanghai A bustling family-style eatery famous for soup dumplings. (p88)

Café Gitane A definite Euro vibe with a stylish downtown clientele and Moroccan cuisine. (p87)

Ferrara Cafe & Bakery Landmark old-school place for pastries and drinks. (p89)

PLACES TO DRINK

Pravda Downtown media types mixing with a slice of Moscow on the Hudson. (p90)

Apotheke Bar Track down this former opium den-turned-apothecary bar. (p90)

Mulberry Street Bar A classic that's hanging on to the past; good for a strong drink. (p90)

FASIONABLE SCENES

Café Gitane Euro, trendy, with good-looking people. (p87)

Pravda Popular hangout for up-and-coming Russians. (p90)

Opening Ceremony Come out looking like a stylish downtowner. (p95)

Balthazar (p86)

Don't Miss
Chinatown

Endless exotic moments await in New York City's most colorfully cramped community, where a walk through the neighborhood is never the same no matter how many times you pass through. Catch the whiff of fresh fish and ripe persimmons, hear the clacking of mah-jongg tiles on makeshift tables, witness dangling duck roasts swinging in store windows and shop for anything imaginable from rice-paper lanterns and 'faux-lex' watches to tire irons and a pound of pressed nutmeg. America's largest congregation of Chinese immigrants is your oyster – dipped in soy sauce, of course.

Map p86

www.explore chinatown.com

south of Canal St & east of Broadway

🚌M1, M6, M9, M15, M22, M103, B39, B51, [S]6, J/M/Z, N/Q/R/W to Canal St Station; B/D to Grand St Station; F to East Broadway Station

Culinary Adventure

The most rewarding experience for Chinatown neophytes is to access this wild and wonderful world through their taste buds. More than any other area of Manhattan, Chinatown's menus sport low prices, uninflated by ambience or reputation. But more than cheap eats, the neighborhood is rife with family recipes passed between generations and continents. Food displays and preparation remain unchanged and untempered by American norms; it's not unusual to walk by stores sporting an array of lacquered animals ready to be chopped up and served at a family banquet. Steaming street stalls clang down the sidewalk serving pork buns and other finger-friendly food. Don't forget to wander down the back alleys for an assortment of spices and herbs to dress up recipes back at home.

Buddhist Temples

Chinatown is home to Buddhist temples large and small, public and obscure. They are easily stumbled upon during a full-on stroll of the neighborhood. The **Eastern States Buddhist Temple** is filled with hundreds of Buddhas, while the **Mahayana Buddhist Temple** holds one golden, 16ft-high Buddha, sitting on a lotus and edged with offerings of fresh oranges, apples and flowers.

Canal Street

Walking down Canal St is like a game of Frogger played on the streets of Shanghai. This is Chinatown's main artery, where you'll dodge oncoming human traffic as you scurry into back alleys to scout treasures from the Far East. You'll pass stinky seafood stalls hawking slippery fish; herb shops displaying a witch's cauldron's worth of roots and potions; storefront bakeries with the tastiest 50-cent pork buns you've ever had; restaurants with whole, roasted ducks hanging by their skinny necks in the windows; produce markets piled high with fresh lychees and Asian pears; and street vendors selling every iteration of knock-off designer goods.

Games in Columbus Park (p85)

Don't Miss List

BY HELEN KOH, EXECUTIVE DIRECTOR OF THE MUSEUM OF CHINESE IN AMERICA

1 CHINESE OPERA

Local opera troupes gather to perform outdoors in the area of Columbus Park closest to Bayard St on any Saturday or Sunday afternoon in good weather. There's also periodic performances on weekends in the basement of the Chinese Consolidated Benevolent Association at 62 Mott St.

2 STREETS TO WANDER

Grand St is a good window on the transformation of the neighborhood: new condo developments and the influx of non-Asians. You walk past little fish and vegetable stores, Vietnamese noodle shops and Italian cafes. The intersection of Doyers and Pell Sts is Chinatown's historical heart; Ting's, at the corner, is a time-capsule curio shop, one of the last to survive. The block of Mott St between Hester and Grand, condensed with groceries, fish shops and meat markets, has lots of energy and is a chance to view a slice of life of local residents.

3 GOOD EATS

Definitely check out renovated Nam Wah, one of the only made-to-order dim sum places and the self-proclaimed first in Chinatown. Besides the food, Red Egg is interesting for the old disco balls in back reminiscent of Hong Kong style from another era. And for late night noodle, congee and rice dishes, one of my favorites is Noodle Town, open to around 4am.

4 GOOD TIME TO VISIT

The neighborhood is especially festive from mid- to late September during the mid-Autumn moon festival; families gather together and bakeries sell delicious mooncakes, pastries with a variety of fillings, from red bean paste to duck egg yolks.

5 BOOKS

The hard-boiled detective novels of Ed Lin and Henry Chang are entertaining fictional tours of the Chinatown streets.

79

Discover SoHo & Chinatown

⊕ Getting There & Away

○ **Subway** The subway lines dump off along various points of Canal St (J, M, Z, N, R, W, Q and 6). Once you arrive it's best to explore on foot. The neighborhood's downtown location makes it easy to access from Midtown and Brooklyn.

○ **Bus & Taxi** Avoid taking cabs or buses – especially in Chinatown, as the traffic is full-on. For SoHo, have your taxi let you off along Broadway if you aren't fussed about your final destination. Don't take cabs south of Canal St if you're simply planning to wander around Chinatown.

◎ Sights

SoHo, NoHo & Nolita

Merchant's House Museum   Museum

Map p82 (☎ 212-777-1089; www.merchantshouse. org; 29 E 4th St btwn Lafayette St & Bowery; adult/senior & student $10/5; ☺ noon-5pm Thu-Mon; Ⓢ 6 to Bleecker St) This elegant, red-brick row house is a family home dating from 1832 – and it's perfectly preserved both inside and out. Home to a prosperous merchant family, the Tred-wells, for nearly a century, the place is in mint condition, allowing you to step back in time through the formal Greek Revival parlors featuring mahogany pocket doors, bronze gasoliers and marble mantelpieces. Bedrooms reveal plenty of other luxuries, from fine antique furniture to a display of dresses, shoes and parasols.

St Patrick's Old Cathedral   Church

Map p82 (www.oldsaintpatricks. com; 263 Mulberry St; ☺ rectory 8am-5pm Mon-Fri; Ⓢ R/W to Prince St) Though St Patrick's Cathe-dral is now famously located on Fifth Ave in Midtown, its first congregation was housed here, in the neighborhood now called Nolita, in this 1809–15 Gothic Revival church designed by Joseph-François Mangin. Its soaring inner vault stands at 85ft, and the or-nate interior features a marble altar and gold-leaf detailing. Back in its heyday, the church was the seat of religious life for the Archdiocese of New York, as well as an important community center for new immigrants, mainly from Ireland. Today it holds regular liturgies in English, Spanish and Chinese. Its ancient cemetery out

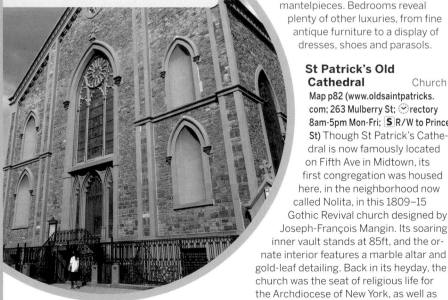

St Patrick's Old Cathedral
DAN HERRICK/LONELY PLANET IMAGES ©

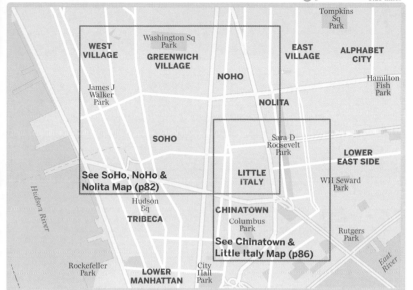

the back is a beautiful respite in the midst of city chaos; if it's not open when you pass by, sneak a peek through the thick, padlocked gate.

Museum of Comic & Cartoon Art
Museum

Map p82 (212-254-3511; www.moccany.org; 594 Broadway; admission $5; noon-5pm Fri-Mon, by appointment Tue-Thu; S R/W to Prince St) Cartoon aficionados can't get enough of this museum and its wealth of graphic novels, comic lore and long-lost posters. Special exhibits include both well-known cartoonists and up-and-coming artists, with frequent opening parties and various festivals. Check the website for online exhibits and upcoming lecture series.

New York City Fire Museum
Museum

Map p82 (212-219-1222; www.nycfiremuseum. org; 278 Spring St btwn Varick & Hudson Sts; suggested donation adult/child $5/1; 10am-5pm Tue-Sat, to 4pm Sun; S C/E to Spring St) Occupying a grand old firehouse dating from 1904, this museum houses a col-

lection of gold, horse-drawn firefighting carriages and modern-day red firetrucks. Exhibits show the development of the NYC firefighting system, which began with the 'bucket brigades.' The museum's friendly staff (and the heavy equipment) make this a great place to bring children. The New York Fire Department (FDNY) lost 343 of its members in the collapse of the World Trade Center, and memorials and exhibits have become a permanent part of the collection.

FREE American Numismatic Society
Museum

Map p82 (212-234-3130; www.numismatics. org; 1 Hudson Sq at Varick & Watts Sts; 9am-5pm Mon-Fri; S 1 to Houston St) The holdings here of more than 800,000 coins, medals and notes are rivaled by only one similar collection in Europe. The items are from all over the map and throughout history, including Greek, Roman, East Asian, medieval and Islamic items. Frequent small special exhibitions and lectures focus on the history of currency, while the society's main exhibition space is at the

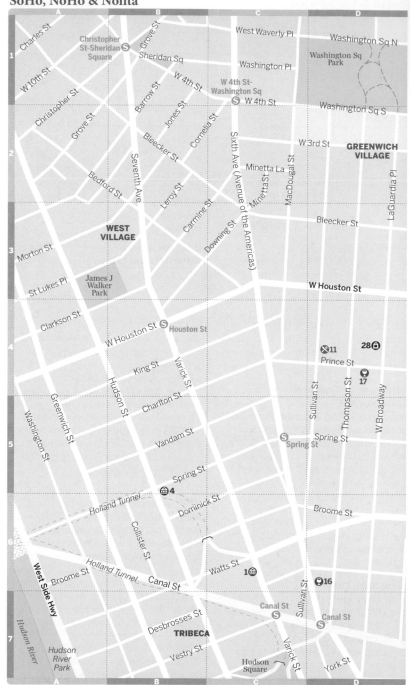

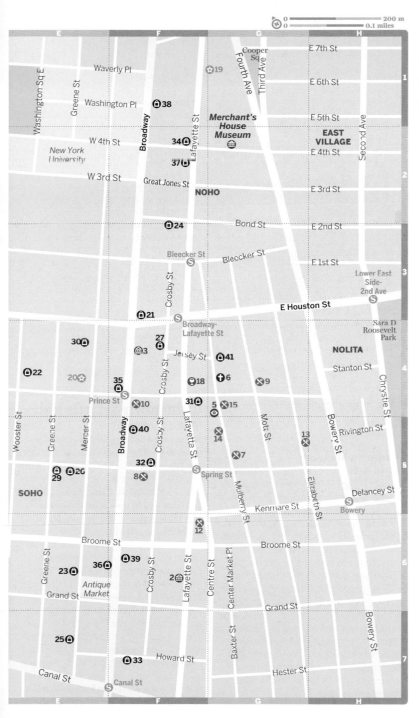

Waverly Pl

Greene St

Washington Pl

⊕19

Cooper Sq

E 7th St

E 6th St

E 5th St

⊕38

Fourth Ave

Third Ave

Merchant's House Museum

EAST VILLAGE

Washington Sq E

Broadway

W 4th St

34⊕

E 4th St

New York University

37⊕

E 3rd St

W 3rd St

Great Jones St

NOHO

Second Ave

⊕24

Bond St

E 2nd St

Bleecker St

Ⓢ

Bleecker St

E 1st St

Lower East Side- 2nd Ave Ⓢ

Crosby St

E Houston St

⊕21

Ⓢ

Sara D Roosevelt Park

30⊕

27⊕

Broadway- Lafayette St

⊕3

Jersey St

⊕41

NOLITA

Stanton St

⊕22

20✪

18

⊕6

✖9

35⊕

Ⓢ

✖10

31⊕

5 ✖15

◎

Chrystie St

Prince St

Wooster St

Greene St

Mercer St

Broadway

⊕40

Crosby St

Lafayette St

✖14

Mott St

13 ✖

Bowery St

Rivington St

32⊕

✖7

8✖

Ⓢ Spring St

⊕ ⊕26
29

SOHO

Kenmare St

Mulberry St

Elizabeth St

Delancey St

Ⓢ Bowery

Broome St

✖12

Broome St

23⊕

36⊕

⊕39

2⊕

Greene St

Antique Market

Crosby St

Lafayette St

Centre St

Center Market Pl

Grand St

Grand St

Grand St

Bowery St

25⊕

⊕33

Baxter St

Howard St

Canal St

Ⓢ Canal St

Hester St

83

SoHo, NoHo & Nolita

Top Sights

	Merchant's House Museum	G2

Sights

1	American Numismatic Society	C6
2	Children's Museum of the Arts	F6
3	Museum of Comic & Cartoon Art	F4
4	New York City Fire Museum	B5
5	Ravenite Social Club	G4
6	St Patrick's Old Cathedral	G4

Eating

7	Balaboosta	G5
8	Balthazar	F5
9	Café Gitane	G4
10	Dean & DeLuca	F4
11	Dutch	D4
12	La Esquina	F6
13	Peasant	G5
14	Rubirosa	G5
15	Torrisi Italian Specialties	G4

Drinking & Nightlife

16	Jimmy	D6
17	MiLady's	D4
18	Pravda	F4

Entertainment

	Joe's Pub	(see 19)
19	Joseph Papp Public Theater	G1
20	Joyce Soho	E4

Shopping

21	Adidas	F3
22	Adidas Originals	E4
23	Babeland	E6
24	Bond 09	F3
25	DDC Lab	E7
26	Evolution	E5
27	Housing Works Book Store	F4
28	Ice Cream & the Billionaire Boys Club	D4
29	John Varvatos	E5
30	Marc Jacobs	E4
31	McNally Jackson	F4
32	MoMA Store	F5
33	Opening Ceremony	F7
34	Other Music	F2
35	Prada	F4
36	Scoop	E6
37	Screaming Mimi's	F2
38	Shakespeare & Co	F1
39	Topshop	F6
40	Uniqlo	F5
41	Young Designers Market	G4

nearby Federal Reserve Bank. It's best to call ahead before setting out to visit the headquarters here.

Children's Museum of the Arts

Museum

Map p82 (☎212-274-0986; www.cmany.org; 182 Lafayette St btwn Broome & Grand Sts; admission $10, suggested donation 4pm-6pm Thu; 🕒noon-5pm Wed & Fri-Sun, to 6pm Thu; [S] N/R to Prince St; 6 to Spring St) A place for kids to unleash their inner artist, this small but worthy stop is home to a permanent collection of paintings, drawings and photographs by local school kids, with adorable exhibit titles like 'Beyond the Refrigerator Door.' For more hands-on activities, check out the museum's vast offering of public programs for kids of all ages, including guided workshops on art forms ranging from sculpture to collaborative mural painting, as well as movie nights and other special treats.

Chinatown & Little Italy

Mulberry Street

Street

Map p86 ([S] 6 to Spring St) Although it feels more like a theme park than an authentic Italian strip, Mulberry St is still the heart of Little Italy. It's the home of landmarks such as **Umberto's Clam House** (**Map p86; ☎212-0431-7545; www.umbertosclamhouse.com; 132 Mulberry St; [S] 6 to Spring St**), where mobster Joey Gallo was shot to death in the '70s, as well as the old-time Mulberry Street Bar (p90), one of the favorite haunts of the late Frank Sinatra. Just a half block off of Mulberry is the legendary Ferrara Cafe & Bakery (p89), brimming with classic Italian pastries and old-school ambiance. You'll see lots of red, white and green Italian flags sold in souvenir shops, and you'll also enjoy the lovely aroma of fresh-baked pastries and pizzas wafting out of doorways. Take a gander at what was once the **Ravenite Social Club** (**Map p82; 247 Mulberry St; [S] 6 to Spring St**) to see how things have really changed around here, as these days it's host to a rotating roster of legit businesses, including clothing and gift shops. It was once an organized-crime hangout (originally known as the Alto Knights Social Club), where big hitters such as Lucky Luciano and John Gotti (as well as the FBI, who kept raiding the place) logged time.

Museum of Chinese In America
Museum

Map p86 (📞 212-619-4785; www.mocanyc.org; 211-215 Centre St near Grand St; admission $7; ⏰ 11am-6pm Tue-Wed & Fri-Sun, to 9pm Thu; S N/Q/R/W, J/M/Z, 6 to Canal St) Housed in a 12,350-sq-ft space designed by architect Maya Lin (who created the famed Vietnam Memorial in Washington DC), the Museum of Chinese in America is a multifaceted space with exhibit galleries, a bookstore and a visitors lounge, which, all together serve as a national center of information about Chinese American life. Browse through interactive multimedia exhibits, maps, timelines, photos, letters, films and artifacts. Its anchor exhibit, 'With a Single Step: Stories in the Making of America,' is an interactive display touching on subjects such as immigration, politics and history.

Columbus Park
Park

Map p86 (Mulberry & Bayard Sts; S J/M/Z, 6 to Canal St) This is where outdoor mah-jongg and domino games take place at bridge tables while tai chi practitioners move through lyrical, slow-motion poses under shady trees. Judo-sparring folks and relaxing families are also common sights in this active communal space originally created in the 1890s and popular with local residents. Visitors are welcome, though (or at least ignored).

FREE Italian American Museum
Museum

Map p86 (www.italianamericanmuseum.org; 155 Mulberry St; ⏰ 11am-6pm Wed, Thu, Sat & Sun, to 8pm Fri; S J/Z, N/Q, 4/6 to Canal St, B/D to Grand St) This small museum sits where one of the most important buildings in Little Italy once stood: the Banca Stabile, which was once the unofficial headquarters of the community, helping immigrants sort their monetary needs and providing a lifeline back to the homeland. Today, the former bank makes up much of the main exhibition space, which tells the New York Italian community's unique story of struggle.

Wing Fat Shopping Mall
Notable Building

Map p86 (8-9 Bowery btwn Pell & Doyers Sts; S J/M/Z, N/Q/R/W, 6 to Canal St) One of the most unique malls you'll ever see, Wing Fat lies underground and has businesses

Columbus Park
IAN DAGNALL/ALAMY ©

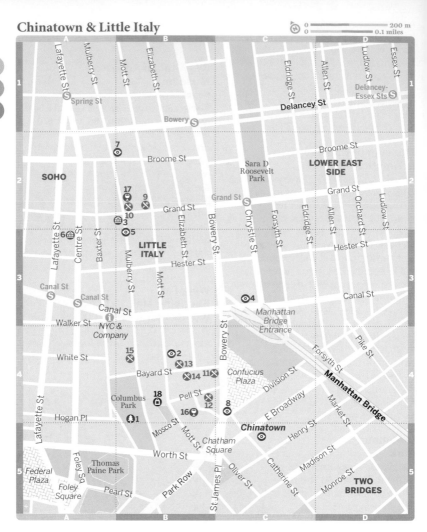

offering reflexology, collectible stamps and feng shui services. The most fascinating aspect is its history, as the tunnel is said to have served as a stop on the Underground Railroad as well as an escape route in the early 1900s for members of rival Tong gangs, who fought up on the street and then disappeared below before police could even begin to search.

 Eating

SoHo, NoHo & Nolita

Balthazar   French $$$

Map p82 (☎ 212-965-1414; www.balthazarny. com; 80 Spring St btwn Broadway & Crosby St; mains $11-34; ☺ breakfast, lunch & dinner daily, brunch Sat & Sun; **S** 6 to Spring St) Retaining its long-held status as a superstar among the city's glut of French bistros, this bustling (OK, *loud*) spot still pulls in the discriminating mobs. That's thanks

Chinatown & Little Italy

to three winning details: the location, which makes it a convenient shopping-spree rest area; the uplifting ambiance, shaped by big, mounted mirrors, cozy high-backed booths, airy high ceilings and wide windows; and, of course, the stellar something-for-everyone menu, which features an outstanding raw bar, steak frites, salad niçoise, roasted beet salad and prawn risotto with sage and butternut squash. The kitchen stays open till 2am Thursday to Saturday, and weekend brunch here is a very crowded (and delicious) production.

Dutch   American $$$

Map p82 (☎212-677-6200; www.thedutchnyc. com; 131 Sullivan St btwn Prince & Houston Sts; mains $16-48; ☺11:30am-3pm Mon-Fri, 5:30pm-midnight Mon-Thu & Sun, 5:30pm-1am Fri & Sat, 10am-3pm Sat & Sun ; Ⓢ A/C/E to Spring St, N/R to Prince St, 1/2 to Houston St) The foodie folks from Locanda Verde have done it again at the Dutch, with simple pleasures on the cobalt-blue chalkboard and a shortlist of supper regulars that draw their inspiration from the new American table. Oysters on ice and freshly baked homemade pies are the notable bookends of the dining experience – in the middle is unfussy cuisine, fresh from the farm, served in casseroles with the perfect amount of ceremony.

Café Gitane   Moroccan $$

Map p82 (☎212-334-9552; www.cafegitanenyc. com; 242 Mott St; mains $12-18; ☺9am-midnight Sun-Thu, to 12:30am Fri & Sat; Ⓢ N/R/W to Prince St) Clear the Gauloise smoke from your eyes and blink twice if you think you're in Paris – Gitane has that louche vibe. Label-conscious shoppers love this authentic bistro, with its dark, aromatic coffee and dishes such as yellowfin tuna seviche, spicy meatballs in tomato turmeric sauce with a boiled egg, Greek salad on focaccia and heart-of-palm salad, with plenty of lusty wines.

La Esquina   Mexican $$

Map p82 (☎646-613-6700; www.esquinanyc. com; 114 Kenmare St; mains $9-20; ☺24hr; Ⓢ 6 to Spring St) This mega-popular and quirky little spot is housed in a former greasy spoon that sits within the neat little triangle formed by Cleveland Pl and Lafayette St. It's three places really: a stand-while-you-eat taco window, a casual Mexican cafe and, downstairs, a cozy, overly hip cave of a dining room that requires reservations.

Balaboosta   Modern American $$$

Map p82 (☎212-966-7366; www.balaboostanyc. com; 214 Mulberry St btwn Spring & Prince Sts; mains $20-29, small plates $5-10; ☺5:30pm-11pm Mon-Thu, noon-3pm Tue-Fri, 5:30pm-10pm Fri & Sat, 11am-4pm Sat & Sun, 5:30pm-10pm Sun;

S J to Bowery, N/R to Prince St, 4/6 to Spring St) 'The Perfect Housewife,' as the Yiddish name suggests, truly does feel like a cram-packed evening at your Bubbie's... if your Bubbie were an amazing cook with an uncanny flair for whipping up delightfully inventive appetizers (crispy cauliflower!) and scrumptious mains (flavor-intensive lamb chops!). Seating is tight, but neighbors become fast friends when united by the collective chorus of 'yums.'

Torrisi Italian Specialties
Italian $$$

Map p82 (☎212-965-0955; www.piginahat. com; 250 Mulberry St btwn Spring & Prince Sts; prix fixe menu $65; S N/R to Prince St; B/D/F, M to Broadway-Lafayette St; 4/6 to Spring St) Torrisi's tasting menu reads like an ode to Italy, with changes each week reflecting the whim of the owners (who also run popular Parm nearby) and the seasonal rotation of fresh ingredients. Expect market produce and less-common items (like rabbit and goat) spun into home-made platters that are both succulent and inspiring.

Peasant
Italian $$$

Map p82 (☎212-965-9511; www.peasantnyc. com; 194 Elizabeth St btwn Spring & Prince Sts; mains $22-39; ☉dinner; S 6 to Spring St) This homey house of gourmet comfort grub has a vibe of old-fashioned simplicity and quality. It has a warm dining area of bare oak tables around a brick hearth and an open kitchen, which lovingly turns out hearty, pan-Italian, mostly meat-based fare. Peasant has made it onto various best-restaurant lists in town, and always seems to be filled with a crowd of sophisticates, who want in on solid stunners like gnocchi with wild mushrooms, grilled hen or octopus and thin-crusted pizzas – not to mention the winning bread and fresh ricotta that start off every meal.

Dean & DeLuca
Deli $$

Map p82 (☎212-226-6800; www.deanandde luca.com; 560 Broadway at Prince St; ☉Mon-Fri 7am-8pm, Sat-Sun 8am-8pm; S R/W to Prince St) New York City loves its luxury grocers

and Dean & DeLuca is one of the biggest names around town; this reputation is well earned, as it boasts a seemingly infinite assortment of edibles from around the globe. Curious palates should make a beeline for the bakery.

Rubirosa
Pizzeria $$

Map p82 (☎212-965-0500; www.rubirosanyc. com; 235 Mulberry St btwn Spring & Prince Sts; mains $12-25; ☉11:30am-11pm Mon-Wed & Sun, to midnight Thu-Sat; S N/R to Prince St, B/D/F, M to Broadway-Lafayette St, 4/6 to Spring St) Rubirosa's infallible family recipe for the perfect, whisper-thin pie crust lures a steady stream of patrons from every corner of the city. Shovel slices from the bar stools or grab a table amid cozy surrounds and make room for savory apps and antipasti.

Chinatown & Little Italy
Joe's Shanghai
Chinese $

Map p86 (☎212-233-8888; www.joeshanghairest aurants.com; 9 Pell St btwn Bowery & Doyers St; mains $5-16; ☉11am-11pm Mon-Sun; S J/Z, N/Q, 4/6 to Canal St, B/D to Grand St) Gather a gaggle of friends and descend upon Joe's en masse to spin the plastic Lazy Susans and savor some of the best dumplings in town. A Flushing transplant, this Chinatown staple also tempts the budget-friendly palate with crispy beef, sticky pork buns and finger-licking shrimp platters.

Nice Green Bo
Chinese $

Map p86 (New Green Bow; ☎212-625-2359; 66 Bayard St btwn Elizabeth & Mott Sts; mains $4-10; ☉11am-11pm; S J/Z, N/Q, 4/6 to Canal St, B/D to Grand St) Not a shred of effort – not even a new sign (you'll see!) – has been made to spruce up Nice Green Bo, and that's the way we like it. It's all about the food here: gorgeous soup dumplings served in steaming drums, heaping portions of noodles, and savory pancakes.

Pho Viet Huong
Vietnamese, Chinese $

Map p86 (☎212-233-8988; www.phoviethuong. com; 73 Mulberry St btwn Bayard & Walker Sts; mains $6-14; ☉11am-10:30pm; S 4/6, J/Z, N/Q/R to Canal St) Shockingly inexpensive

SHERAB/ALAMY ©

dishes is reason enough to visit; the delicious assortment of Vietnamese and Chinese selections will have you coming back for seconds. Slurp-worthy bowls of *pho* and dripping *bahn mi* buns wobble atop the unceremonious scatter of slap-shut tables and chairs.

Bánh Mì Saigon Bakery
Vietnamese $

Map p86 (📞212-941-1514; 198 Grand St btwn Mulberry & Mott Sts; mains $4-6; ⊙10am-7pm Tue-Sun; S J/M/Z, N/Q/R/W, 6 to Canal St) This frequently mobbed, no-frills store-front doles out some of the best *bánh mì* (Vietnamese roast pork sandwiches served on fat baguettes with piles of sliced cucumber, pickled carrots, hot sauce and cilantro) in town. And none will cost you more than $5.

Ferrara Cafe & Bakery
Bakery, Cafe $$

Map p86 (195 Grand St; S B/D to Grand St) Although it feels more like a theme park than an authentic Italian strip, Mulberry St is still the heart of the Little Italy 'hood. Just a half block off Mulberry is the legendary Ferrara Cafe & Bakery, brimming with classic Italian pastries and old-school

ambience. You'll see lots of red, white and green Italian flags sold in souvenir shops around here, and you'll also enjoy the lovely aroma of fresh-baked pastries and pizzas wafting out of doorways.

Original Chinatown Ice Cream Factory
Ice Cream $

Map p86 (📞212-608-4170; www.chinatown icecreamfactory.com; 65 Bayard St; scoop $4; ⊙11am-10pm; 🚻; S J/M, N/Q/R/W, 6 to Canal St) Totally overshadowing the nearby Häagen-Dazs is this busy ice-cream shop, where you can savor scoops of green tea, ginger, passion fruit and lychee sorbet among dozens of flavors.

Great New York Noodle Town
Chinese $

Map p86 (📞212-349-0923; www.greatnynoodle town.com; 28 Bowery St at Bayard St; mains $4-13; ⊙9am-4am; S J/M/Z, N/Q/R/W, 6 to Canal St) The name of this Chinatown stalwart says it all, as the specialties here are endless incarnations of the long and slippery strands, offered up through an easy-to-decipher picture menu. What the no-frills spot lacks in ambience it makes up for in characters – especially once 2am or 3am rolls around.

🍷 Drinking & Nightlife

Pravda   Cocktail Bar

Map p82 (☎212-226-4944; 281 Lafayette St btwn Prince & Houston Sts; Ⓢ B/D/F/V to Broadway-Lafayette St) This subterranean bar and brasserie lays on the Soviet-era nostalgia with heavy brushstrokes, from the Cyrillic lettering on the walls to the extensive vodka menu, including the caviar martini (vodka with dill, cucumber and a spoonful of you-know-what). Red leather banquettes and inviting armchairs provide a fine spot to enjoy blinis, handsomely made cocktails and a bit of eavesdropping on neighboring apparatchiks from the fashion or banking industry.

Apotheke Bar   Bar

Map p86 (☎212-406-0400; www.apothekenyc. com; 9 Doyers St; ⏰6pm-2am Mon-Sat, 8pm-2am Sun; Ⓢ J/M/Z to Canal St) Look for a

Golden Flower sign – that's the clue you've arrived. The sleek red interior, with marble bar and apothecary-type mortars, pestles and cylinders, gives the Apotheke Bar a cool vibe, enhanced when the owner passes around his homemade absinthe.

MiLady's   Bar

Map p82 (☎212-226-9340; 160 Prince St btwn W Broadway & Thompson St; Ⓢ A/C/E to Spring St, N/R to Prince St, 1/2 to Houston St) The last of the dive bars in SoHo where you can still score a brewski for under $5, MiLady's has all the ambiance of the old neighborhood before high-end shops and sleek eats took over. The salads here are surprisingly fresh, and you can't go wrong with the chicken wings and mac 'n' cheese – just avoid everything else.

Mulberry Street Bar   Bar

Map p86 (☎212-226-9345; 176½ Mulberry St btwn Broome & Grand Sts; Ⓢ B/D to Grand St) Frank Sinatra liked this 100-year-old Little Italy hang, which was also used as a backdrop

for scenes in the *Sopranos*, *Godfather III* and *Donnie Brasco*. The gruff, old-school bartenders add to the charm, as does the odd mix of wide-eyed tourists, crusty regulars and the overflow of hipsters.

Jimmy — Bar
Map p82 (📞212-201-9118; www.jimmysoho.com; James Hotel, 15 Thompson St; S A/C/E, 1/2 to Canal St, A/C/E to Spring St) Lofted atop the James New York hotel in SoHo, Jimmy is a sky-high hangout with sweeping views of the city below. The summer months team with tipsy patrons who spill out onto the open deck; in cooler weather drinks are slung indoors from the centrally anchored bar guarded by floor-to-ceiling windows.

 Entertainment

Joseph Papp Public Theater — Theater
Map p82 (📞212-260-2400; www.publictheater. org; 425 Lafayette St btwn Astor Pl & 4th St; ⏱hours vary; S N/R to 8th St-NYU; 6 to Astor Pl) One of the city's most important cultural centers, the Papp was founded by the late, expansive-minded Joseph Papp, who once returned a massive NEA grant rather than sign its conservative anti-obscenity amendment. The theater has had an almost constant roster of can't-miss productions over the years, and staged world premieres of *Hair*, *A Chorus Line*, *Plenty* and *Caroline, or Change*, all of which moved to Broadway. The East Village complex also offers Joe's Pub (below) for top-notch musical and cabaret shows, and every summer it presents its famous productions of Shakespeare in the Park at Delacorte Theater, which Papp began back in 1954, before the lovely, open-air theater was even built.

Joe's Pub — Live Music
Map p82 (📞212-539-8778; www.joespub.com; Public Theater, 425 Lafayette St btwn Astor Pl & 4th St; S R/W to 8th St-NYU; 6 to Astor Pl) Part cabaret theater, part rock and new-indie venue, this intimate supper club stages

the fringe mainstream (eg folks like Aimee Mann). It has a nice, long bar, seats cuddled around a corner stage and a bit of a dress-up atmosphere.

Joyce Soho   Dance
Map p82 (📞212-242-0800; www.joyce.org; 155 Mercer St at Prince St, SoHo; ⓢR/W to Prince St) A more intimate branch of the Joyce Theater in Chelsea, Joyce Soho occupies a former firehouse in SoHo and has dance studios and a performance space that seats just 74.

🛍 Shopping

SoHo

Shakespeare & Co   Books
Map p82 (📞212-529-1330; www.shakeandco. com; 716 Broadway; ⏱10am-11pm Mon-Fri, noon-9pm Sat & Sun; ⓢN/R/W to 8th St; 6 to Astor Pl) This popular New York bookstore is one of the city's great indie options – with other locations, including the **Upper East Side** (Map p210; 📞212-570-0201; www.shakeandco.

com; 939 Lexington Ave at 69th St; ⏱9am-8pm Mon-Fri, 10am-7pm Sat, 11am-6pm Sun; ⓢ6 to 68th St). You'll find a wide array of contemporary fiction and nonfiction, art books and tomes about NYC, plus a small but unique collection of periodicals.

Adidas Originals   Shoes, Clothing
Map p82 (📞212-673-0398; 136 Wooster St; ⏱11am-7pm Mon-Sat, noon-6pm Sun; ⓢR/W to Prince St) This ultrahip Adidas shop stocks a tempting selection of its iconic triple-striped sneakers plus sporty jackets, T-shirts and retro-looking gear. It's a tech-and music-savvy place, with DJs sometimes working the decks, and lawn chairs out front on hot summer days. You can also order custom-made sneakers. For the big-box retail experience, head to the 29,500-sq-ft **Adidas** (Map p82; 📞212-529-0081; 610 Broadway at Houston St; ⏱10am-8pm Mon-Sat, 11am-7pm Sun; ⓢA/C/E to Spring St; N/R to Prince St; B/D/F to Broadway-Lafayette St) sneaker emporium a few blocks back.

Evolution   Gifts
Map p82 (📞212-343-1114; 120 Spring St btwn Mercer & Greene Sts; ⏱11am-7pm; ⓢR/W to Prince St) A great cabinet of curiosities, this old-fashioned storefront sells natural-history collectibles of the sort usually seen in museums. This is the place to buy – or just gawk at – framed beetles and butterflies, bugs frozen in amber-resin cubes, stuffed parrots, zebra hides and shark teeth, as well as stony wonders, including meteorites, fragments from Mars and 100-million-year-old fossils.

**Housing Works
Book Store**   Books
Map p82 (📞212-334-3324; www.housingworks.org/ usedbookcafe; 126 Crosby St; ⏱10am-9pm Mon-Fri, noon-9pm Sat; ⓢB/D/F/V to Broadway-Lafayette St) Relaxed, earthy and fea-

Prada
MARKA/ALAMY ©

turing a great selection of fabulous books you can buy for a good cause (proceeds go to the city's HIV-positive and AIDS homeless communities), this spacious cafe is a great place to while away a few quiet afternoon hours.

McNally Jackson
Books

Map p82 (☏ 212-274-1160; www.mcnallyjackson. com; 52 Prince St btwn Lafayette & Mulberry Sts; ☉ 10am-10pm Mon-Sat, to 9pm Sun; S R/W to Prince St) This inviting indie bookshop stocks an excellent selection of magazines and books covering contemporary fiction, food writing, architecture and design, art and history. The cozy cafe is a fine spot to settle in with some reading material or to catch one of the frequent readings and book signings held here.

Prada
Fashion, Accessories

Map p82 (☏ 212-334-8888; 575 Broadway; ☉ 11am-7pm Mon-Sat, noon-6pm Sun; S N/R/W to Prince St) Don't come just for the shoes: check out the space. Dutch architect Rem Koolhaas has transformed the old Guggenheim into a fantasy land full of elegant hardwood floors and small dressing spaces. Don't be afraid to try something on – those translucent changing-room doors do fog up when you step inside.

John Varvatos
Clothing, Shoes

Map p82 (☏ 212-965-0700; 122 Spring St; ☉ 11am-7pm Mon-Sat, noon-6pm Sun; S R/W to Prince St) One of the city's most coveted menswear designers, John Varvatos creates a classic, timeless look – with a rock-and-roll soul – with his stylish and handsome-fitting sports coats, jeans, footwear and accessories. Head downstairs for JV's younger edgier persona.

MoMA Store
Homewares, Gifts

Map p82 (☏ 646-613-1367; 81 Spring St; ☉ 10am-8pm Mon-Sat, 11am-7pm Sun; S N/Q/R/W to Prince St) This sleek and stylish space carries a huge collection of handsomely designed objects for the home, office and wardrobe. You'll find modernist alarm clocks, wildly shaped vases, designer kitchenware and surreal lamps, plus brainy games, hand puppets,

fanciful scarves, coffee-table books and lots of other great gift ideas.

Bond 09
Beauty

Map p82 (☏ 212-228-1940; www.bondno9.com; 9 Bond St; ☉ 11am-7pm Mon-Sat; S 6 to Bleecker St) 'Making scents of New York' is the motto of this thoroughly unique perfume boutique, where the gimmick is everything NYC. Each bottle of home-brewed potion (prices begin at about $100) not only comes labeled with a trademark round label inspired by an old New York subway token, it gets filled with one of 20 fragrances that are named after and inspired by local nabes. Fragrances include Riverside Drive, Madison Soirée, Central Park, Nuits de Noho and Chinatown, none of which smells like wet pavement, exhaust fumes or simmering hot dogs.

DDC Lab
Clothing

Map p82 (☏ 212-226-8980; 7 Mercer St; ☉ 11am-7pm Mon-Sat, noon-6pm Sun; S N/Q/R/W, 6 to Canal St) A cool boutique for the latest flourishes of urban style, DDC Lab sells a range of nicely designed slim-fitting wares including sleek limited-edition sneakers, superbly comfortable T-shirts, leather jackets and peacoats as well as rubbery Nooka belts and other accessories. DDC Lab also sports a store in the **Meatpacking District** (Map p130; ☏ 212-414-5801; 427 W 14th St).

Uniqlo
Clothing

Map p82 (☏ 917-237-8811; 546 Broadway; ☉ 10am-9pm Mon-Sat, 11am-8pm Sun; S N/R/W to Prince St) The enormous three-story emporium owes its popularity to attractive apparel at discount prices. You'll find Japanese denim, Mongolian cashmere, graphic T-shirts, smart-looking skirts and endless racks of colorful ready-to-wear – with most things at the sub-$100 mark.

Other Music
Music

Map p82 (☏ 212-477-8150; www.othermusic. com; 15 E 4th St; ☉ noon-9pm Mon-Fri, to 8pm Sat, to 7pm Sun; S 6 to Bleecker St) This indie-run CD store has won over a loyal fan base with its informed selection of, well, other types of music: offbeat lounge,

MICHAEL COHEN/GETTY IMAGES ©

psychedelic, electronica, indie rock etc, available new and used. Friendly staffers like what they do, and may be able to help translate your inner musical whims and dreams to actual CD reality. OM also stocks a small but excellent selection of new and used vinyl.

Ice Cream & the Billionaire Boys Club
Clothing, Shoes

Map p82 (☎212-777-2225; 456 W Broadway; ☺noon-7pm; Ⓢ N/R/W to Prince St) Created by pop icon Pharell Williams and Japanese design guru Nigo, this slim little two-floor boutique stocks colorful, one-of-a-kind sneakers and imaginative T-shirts and outerwear. Head up the dark star-lit staircase at the back to check out the BBC part of the brand (more edgy sneakers and T-shirts) while talking a walk in outer space, courtesy of a moon print covering the floor.

Screaming Mimi's
Vintage

Map p82 (☎212-677-6464; 382 Lafayette St; ☺noon-8pm Mon-Sat, 1pm-7pm Sun; Ⓢ 6 to Bleecker St) A warm and colorful storefront that just begs to be entered; you'll find accessories and jewelry up front, and an excellent selection of clothing – organized, ingeniously, by decade – from the '50s to the '90s. It's all in great condition, from the prim, beaded wool cardigans to the suede minidresses and white leather go-go boots.

Topshop
Fashion

Map p82 (☎212-966-9555; www.topshopnyc. com; 478 Broadway at Broome St; ☺10am-9pm Mon-Sat, 11am-8pm Sun; Ⓢ 6 to Spring St) The genius of Topshop is that the clothes always find that sweet spot between trendy and wearable. Everything's up-to-the-minute but still flattering and practical for the average person. Three floors for women, one for men, and all at fairly reasonable prices. Sales can get hectic: be prepared to dig for bargains.

Chinatown

Aji Ichiban
Food & Drink

Map p86 (☎212-233-7650; 37 Mott St btwn Bayard & Mosco Sts; ☺10am-8:30pm; Ⓢ J/M/Z, N/Q/R/W, 6 to Canal St) This Hong Kong–based chain, the name of which means 'awesome' in Japanese, is a ubiquitous sight in Chinatown, as this is just one

DISCOVER SOHO & CHINATOWN SHOPPING

of five locations here. And though it is a candy shop, get ready for something a bit more exciting than malted balls and peppermint sticks. Here's where you'll find sesame-flavored marshmallows, Thai durian milk candy, preserved plums, mandarin peel, blackcurrant gummies and dried guava, as well as savory snacks like crispy spicy cod fish, crab chips, wasabi peas and dried anchovies with peanuts.

Young Designers
Market   Accessories, Clothing
Map p82 (212-580-8995; 268 Mulberry St; ⊙11am-7pm Sat & Sun; S B/D/F/V to Broad-way-Lafayette St) This large colorful market takes over the gym of Old St Patrick's on weekends. As per the name, young and indie designers rule the roost, selling handmade jewelry, unique and witty T-shirts and one-of-a-kind stationery, plus dresses, hoodies and lots of other afford-able items you won't find elsewhere.

Opening Ceremony   Fashion
Map p82 (212-219-2688; 35 Howard St btwn Broadway & Lafayette St; ⊙11am-8pm Mon-Sat, noon-7pm Sun; S N/Q/R/W, 6 to Canal St) Just off the beaten SoHo path, Opening Ceremony is a favorite among fashion insiders for its unique collection of indie labels. Owners Carol Lim and Humberto Leon showcase a changing roster of labels from across the globe – though

the look is always avant-garde, even if the prices are decidedly uptown.

Babeland   Erotica
Map p82 (212-966-2120; www.babeland. com; 43 Mercer St btwn Grand & Broome Sts; ⊙11am-10pm Mon-Sat, to 7pm Sun; S A/C/E to Canal St) This women-owned sex shop is the queen bee of sex toys, aflutter with open and supportive staffers who will gladly talk you through the chore of picking out the very best silicone dildo or butt plug, matching it with an appropri-ate leather harness and inspiring you to toss in a quality vibrator while you're at it. But it's also much more: it's a purveyor of sex-related books, magazines, adult DVDs, flavored lube and Babeland tees, and an educator, with a constant roster of how-to lectures, for all genders, from the knowledgeable staff.

Scoop   Fashion
Map p82 (212-925-3539; 473 Broadway btwn Broome & Grand Sts; ⊙11am-8pm Mon-Sat, to 7pm Sun; S N/Q/R/W to Canal St) Scoop is a great one-stop destination for unearth-ing top contemporary fashion by Theory, Stella McCartney, Marc Jacobs, James Perse and many others. While there's nothing particularly edgy about the selections, there's a lot on offer (over 100 designers covering men's, women's and children's), and you can often score deals at season-end sales.

East Village & Lower East Side

Old meets new on every block of this downtown duo. These are two of the city's hottest 'hoods for nightlife and cheap eats that lure students, bankers and scruffier types alike.

No longer the edgy radical 'hood of decades past, the East Village is still very cool – filled with endless boutiques, bars, restaurants and characters. These days, however, it's developers who are truly shaping the physical landscape. Stick to the area around Tompkins Square Park, and the lettered avenues (known as Alphabet City) to its east, for interesting nooks – as well as a collection of little community gardens that provide leafy respites.

Originally a settlement for Jews and then Latinos, the Lower East Side (LES) has become the place to be seen. It's either about cramming yourself into low-lit lounges and live-music clubs or about snagging a table at a pricey restaurant. A bunch of luxury high-rise condominiums and hip boutique hotels coexist with large public housing projects and blocks of tenement-style buildings.

Mural in Alphabet City, East Village

East Village & Lower East Side Highlights

Bar Scene (p112)

From cocktail bars to dirty dives filled with NYU students or lounges pulling in outsiders wanting to booze in NY punk rock's old HQ, the East Village is the ideal neighborhood for a tippling tour. Meanwhile, the Lower East Side is hipster central. In a relatively concentrated area there are dozens of pick-up spots, low-key hangouts, re-created speakeasies, ironically themed dives, and up-towners wanting 'in' on the cool side of town. McSorley's Old Ale House (p112)

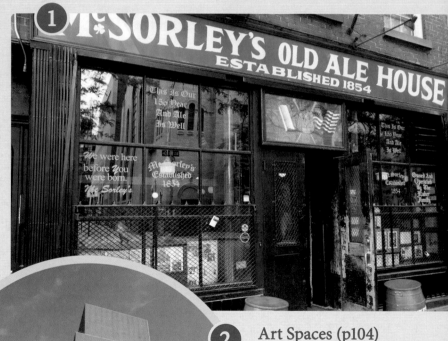

Art Spaces (p104)

A recent anchor in Manhattan's ever-spinning art world, the stacked-box architecture of the New Museum of Contemporary Art offers a transformative take on the typical gallery experience. Exhibitions are mind-bending iterations of art across myriad media. A handful of galleries, including Sperone Westwater (p109), have also thrown open their doors in the Lower East Side, offering cutting-edge fare. New Museum of Contemporary Art (p104) designed by SANAA

RAYMOND PATRICK/CORBIS ©

Tenement Museum (p115)

There's no museum in New York that humanizes the city's colorful past quite like the Lower East Side Tenement Museum, which puts the neighborhood's heartbreaking but inspiring heritage on full display in several recreations of turn-of-the-20th-century tenements. Always evolving and expanding, the museum also has a variety of tours and talks beyond the museum's walls – a must for any curious visitor interested in old New York.

East Village Culinary World Tour (p106)

Mind-blowing variety covering the full spectrum of continents and budgets – in just a single city block. You'll find every type of taste-bud tantalizer under the sun from Ukrainian *pierogi* (dumpling) palaces and sushi joints to pizza parlors and falafel huts galore. There's tons of Indian fare too, especially on the carnival-esque strip of E 6th St between First and Second Aves, otherwise known as Curry Row. Freshly made *pierogies*

Boutique Shopping (p118)

The downtown fashion crowd looking for that edgy, experimental or old-school hip-hop look head to the Lower East Side. Dotted throughout are dozens of stores selling vintage apparel, vegan shoes, one-of-a-kind sneakers, old-fashioned candy, left-wing books and more. In the East Village, you'll still find punk-rock T-shirts, tattoo parlors and dusty stores selling vintage clothing alongside new local designers, sleek shops and even chain stores.

Shop front, East Village

East Village & Lower East Side Walk

If you've been dreaming of quintessential New York – graffiti on crimson brick; punks and grannies walking side by side; religious monuments to an immigrant history down the street from cutting edge art institutions – this walk is for you.

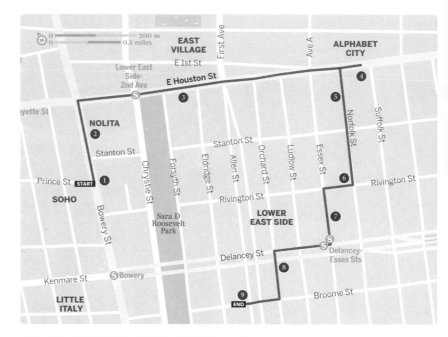

❶ New Museum of Contemporary Art

Kick off by seeing the **New Museum of Contemporary Art** (p104) – one of downtown's most buzzed-about attractions, a stunning work of architecture that towers above the gritty Bowery.

❷ Sperone Westwater

Just up the street on Bowery is **Sperone Westwater** (p109). This prominent gallery is in a startling, eight-story sliver building sheathed in milled glass, with bright-red elevator doors. Entire exhibits are visible from out on the street.

❸ Landmark Sunshine Cinema

Make a right on Houston St and walk east. Just past Forsyth St, on your right, you'll see the **Landmark Sunshine Cinema** (p118) which was shuttered for 70 years before being reopened in its current form as an indie-movie cinema. In its heyday it was a Yiddish theater and a boxing venue, and was originally built as a Dutch church in the 1840s.

4 Participant Inc

Continue east along Houston St until you reach **Participant Inc** (p109); this gallery/performance space was one of the places to jump start the neighborhood's gallery scene.

5 Angel Orensanz Foundation

Turn south down Norfolk St; halfway down the block will be this the neo-Gothic building designed as a synagogue in 1849. Spanish sculptor Angel Orensanz purchased the fading gem in 1986 to use it as his studio; it's now **Angel Orensanz Foundation** (p109) – an arts foundation that hosts performances, exhibits and other cultural happenings.

6 Gallery Onetwentyeight

Continue along Norfolk St, and at the corner of Rivington St you'll get to the always thought-provoking gallery, **Gallery Onetwentyeight** (p109), where installations can range from the playful to the political.

7 Essex Street Market

Turn right on Rivington St and left onto Essex; on your left is the indoor **Essex Street Market** (p119), a great place to browse and indulge in gourmet treats.

8 Lower East Side Tenement Museum

Continue down Essex, turn right onto Delancey and then left onto Orchard. Here you'll find the **Lower East Side Tenement Museum** (p115) visitors center. A tour of former tenements will show you how life was for Jewish and Italian immigrants living in poverty.

9 Kehila Kedosha Janina Synagogue & Musuem

From Orchard St, turn right on Broome St to reach the **Kehila Kedosha Janina Synagogue**, home to the Romaniotes, an obscure branch of Greek Judaism whose ancestors were slaves sent to Rome by ship but rerouted to Greece by a storm. This is their only synagogue in the Western Hemisphere, and includes a small museum, art gallery and costumes from Janina.

 The Best…

PLACES TO EAT

Cafe Orlin Neighborhood hotspot with delicious Middle Eastern fare. (p106)

Westville East New American comfort food; our favorite of the three downtown locations. (p106)

Katz's Delicatessen Perfect for a late night fix of old-school Jewish Lower East Side; sandwiches big enough for two. (p110)

PLACES TO DRINK

McSorley's Old Ale House Rub elbows with long-time regulars at this atmospheric bar – as old-school as it gets. (p112)

Mayahuel About as far from your typical Spring Break tequila bar as you can get – more like the cellar of a monastery. (p114)

Whiskey Ward Enjoy the single mindedness of this brick-walled whiskey bar. (p114)

ALTERNATIVE ARTS SPACES

Performance Space 122 (PS 122) Interdisciplinary pieces from both accomplished award winners and young up-and-comers. (p116)

Amore Opera Humble and committed performances such as *La Bohème* and *The Merry Widow*. (p117)

La MaMa ETC Venerable and renowned, still staging the best thought-provoking experimental theater. (p117)

Pastrami sandwich, Katz's Delicatessen (p110)

Don't Miss
St Marks Place

One of the most magical things about New York is that every street tells a story, from the action unfurling before your eyes to the dense history hidden behind colorful facades. St Marks Place is one of the best strips of pavement in the city for story telling, as almost every building on these hallowed blocks is rife with tales from a time when the East Village embodied a far more lawless spirit.

Map p106

St Marks Pl, Ave A to Third Ave

S N/R/W to 8th St-NYU, 6 to Astor Pl

Third Ave to Ave A

The East Village was once the home base for emerging punk rock acts – many would frequent the clothing shops along St Marks to assemble their trademark looks. Although most joints have gone the way of the dodo in favor of more tourist-friendly wares, there are still a few spots that remain, like Trash & Vaudeville (p119).

Easily one of NYC's most famous streets, St Marks Place is also one of the city's smallest, occupying only three blocks between Astor Pl and Tompkins Sq Park. The road, however, is jam-packed with historical tidbits that would delight any trivia buff. Some of the most important addresses include numbers 2, 4, 96 and 98, and 122 St Marks Place. Number 2 St Marks Place is known as the St Mark's Ale House, but for a time it was the famous Five-Spot, where jazz fiend Thelonious Monk got his start in the 1950s. A cast of colorful characters have left their mark at 4 St Marks Place: Alexander Hamilton's son built the structure, James Fenimore Cooper lived here in the 1830s, and Yoko Ono's Fluxus artists descended upon the building in the 1960s. The buildings at 96 and 98 St Marks Place are immortalized on the cover of Led Zeppelin's Physical Graffiti album. Though it closed in the 1990s, number 122 St Marks Place was the location of a popular cafe called Sin-é, where Jeff Buckley and David Gray often performed.

Tompkins Square Park

St Marks Place terminates at a welcome clearing of green deep in the heart of the East Village. The 10.5-acre Tompkins Sq Park honors Daniel Tompkins, who served as governor of New York from 1807 to 1817 (and as the nation's vice president after that, under James Monroe). It's like a friendly town square for locals, who gather for chess at concrete tables, picnics on the lawn on warm days and spontaneous guitar or drum jams on various grassy knolls. It's also the site of basketball courts, a fun-to-watch dog run, frequent summer concerts and an always-lively kids' playground. The park,

which recently underwent a facelift, wasn't always a place for such clean fun, however. In the '80s, it was a dirty, needle-strewn homeless encampment, unusable for folks wanting a place to stroll or picnic. A contentious turning point came when police razed the band shell and evicted more than 100 squatters living in a tent city in the park in 1988 (and again in 1991). That first eviction turned violent; the Tompkins Sq Riot, as it came to be known, ushered in the first wave of yuppies in the dog run, fashionistas lolling in the grass and undercover narcotics agents trying to pass as druggie punk kids. There's not much drama here these days, unless you count the annual Howl! Festival of East Village Arts, which brings Allen Ginsberg–inspired theater, music, film, dance and spoken-word events to the park each September.

Astor Place

St Marks Place begins on the east side of Astor Place – a crowded crisscrossing of streets anchored by a curious square sculpture that's affectionately (and appropriately) known by locals as *The Cube*. A favorite meeting spot for neighborhood dwellers, this work of art – actually named *Alamo* – weighs more than 1800 pounds and is made entirely of Cor-Tensteel.

Originally Astor Place was the home of the Astor Opera House (now gone), which attracted the city's wealthy elite for regular performances in the mid-1800s. The square was also the site of the notorious Astor Place riots, in which the city's protesting Irish population caused such a stir about their homeland potato famine that the police fired shots into the masses, injuring hundreds and killing at least 18 people.

Today the square is largely known as the home of the Village Voice and the Cooper Union design institute.

103

Discover East Village & Lower East Side

Getting There & Away

- **Subway** Trains don't go far enough east to carry you to most East Village locations, but it's a quick walk (and even quicker cab or bus ride) from the 6 at Astor Pl, the F, V at Lower East Side-2nd Ave or the L at First or Third Aves. The subway's F line (Lower East Side-2nd Ave or Delancey St stops) will let you off in the thick of the Lower East Side.
- **Bus** If you're traveling from the west side, it's better to take the M14 rather than the subway (L), as the bus will take you further into the East Village, making a southern turn along Aves A, B or C (depending on how the bus is marked).

Graffiti, Lower East Side
FREDERIC SOLTAN/CORBIS ©

Sights

East Village

St Marks Place Street
See p102.

St Mark's in the Bowery Church
Map p106 (☎212-674-6377; www.stmarksbowery.org; 131 E 10th St at Second Ave; 🕐10am-6pm Mon-Fri; [S] L to 3rd Ave, 6 to Astor Pl) Though it's most popular with East Village locals for its cultural offerings – such as poetry readings hosted by the Poetry Project or cutting-edge dance performances from Danspace and the Ontological Hysteric Theater – this is also a historic site. This Episcopal church stands on the site of the farm, or bouwerie, owned by Dutch Governor Peter Stuyvesant, whose crypt lies under the grounds.

The 1799 church, damaged by fire in 1978, has been restored, and you can enjoy an interior view of its abstract stained-glass windows during opening hours.

Lower East Side

New Museum of Contemporary Art Gallery
Map p112 (☎212-219-1222; www.newmuseum.org; 235 Bowery btwn Prince & Rivington Sts; adult/child $14/free, 7pm-9pm Thu free; 🕐11am-6pm Wed & Fri-Sun, to 9pm Thu; [S] N/R to Prince St, F to 2nd Ave, J/Z to Bowery, 6 to Spring St) Like any modern-day museum worth its salt, its structure has to be as much of a statement as the artwork inside. The New Museum of Contemporary Art's Lower East Side avatar accomplishes just that and

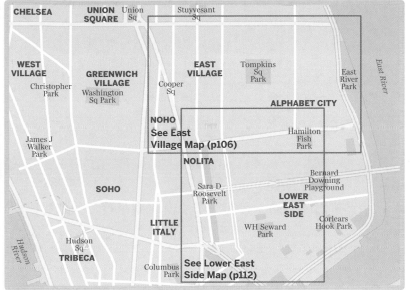

more with its inspired design by noted Japanese architecture firm SANAA. The Lower East Side has seen its fair share of physical changes over the last decade as the sweeping hand of gentrification has cleaned up slummy nooks and replaced them with glittering residential blocks. The New Museum manages to punctuate the neighborhood with something truly unique, and its cache of artistic work will dazzle and confuse just as much as its facade.

Eldridge Street Synagogue   Jewish

Map p112 (☏ 212-219-0888; www.eldridgestreet. org; 12 Eldridge St btwn Canal & Division Sts; donations suggested; ⏱10am-5pm Sun-Thu; S F to East Broadway) This landmarked house of worship, built in 1887, was once the center of Jewish life, before falling into squalor in the 1920s. Left to rot, it's only recently been reclaimed, and now shines with original splendor. Its onsite museum gives tours every half hour ($10; 10am to 5pm), with the last one departing at 4pm.

Orchard Street Bargain District   Neighborhood

Map p112 (Orchard; Ludlow & Essex Sts btwn Houston & Delancey Sts; ⏱Sun-Fri; S F, J/M/Z to Delancey-Essex Sts) Back in the day, this large intersection was a free-for-all, as Eastern European and Jewish merchants sold anything that could command a buck from their pushcarts. The 300-plus shops you see now aren't as picturesque, but it's a good place to pick up some cheap shirts, tees and jeans. If you like to haggle, take a shot at bargaining over the price.

East River Park   Park

Map p106 (FDR & E Houston; S F to Delancey-Essex Sts) In addition to the great ballparks, running and biking paths, 5000-seat amphitheater for concerts and expansive patches of green, this park has got cool, natural breezes and stunning views of the Williamsburg, Manhattan and Brooklyn Bridges. A drawn-out renovation brought great nighttime lighting and surprisingly clean bathrooms to the mix.

 # Eating

East Village

Momofuku Noodle Bar
Noodles $$$

Map p106 (☎212-777-7773; www.momofuku.com/noodle-bar/; 171 First Ave btwn 10th & 11th Sts; ⏰lunch & dinner; ⓢL to 1st Ave, 6 to Astor Pl) Queue up for the namesake special at this outpost of a crazily popular restaurant group (www.momofuku.com): homemade ramen noodles in broth, served with poached eggs, shredded pork, braised oxtail, roasted rice cakes or some interesting combos (the only vegetarian option is a broth-free bowl with ginger and veggies).

Cafe Orlin
Middle Eastern $

Map p106 (☎212-777-1447; www.cafeorlin.com; 41 St Marks Pl btwn First & Second Aves; mains $7-14; ⏰breakfast, lunch, dinner; ⓢL to 3rd Ave, N/R to 8th St-NYU, 4/6 to Astor Pl) Toeing the line between Middle Eastern and home-grown American fare, Cafe Orlin is the star of the brunching and lunching scene along St Marks Pl. The perfect omelets, with fresh fixings folded deep within, lure a colorful assortment of characters from angsty hipster types guzzling red wine while toying with their iPads to hungover SNL cast members recovering from last night's show.

Westville East
Modern American $$

Map p106 (☎212-677-2033; www.westville nyc.com; 173 Ave A; mains $12-20; ⏰Mon-Fri 11:30am-11pm, Sat & Sun 10am-11pm; ⓢL to 1st

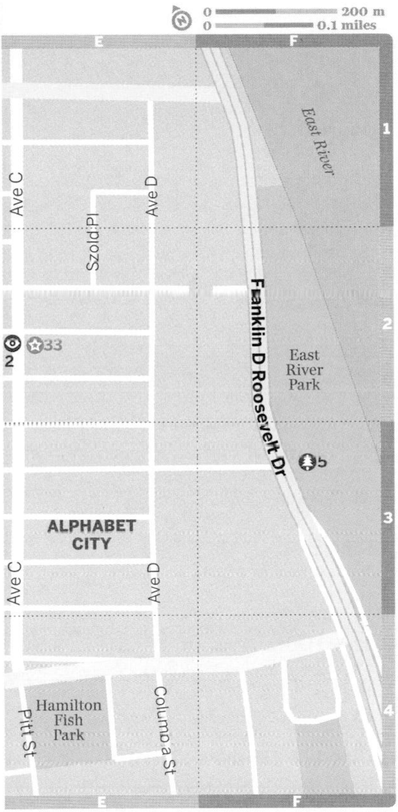
0 200 m
0 0.1 miles
E
F
East River
Ave C
Ave D
Szold Pl
Franklin D Roosevelt Dr
East River Park
2
33
5
ALPHABET CITY
Hamilton Fish Park
Pitt St
Columbia St

Ave, 4/6 to Astor Pl) Market-fresh veggies and mouthwatering mains are the name of the game at Westville, and it doesn't hurt that the cottage-chic surrounds are undeniably charming. The chicken reuben is the ultimate hangover cure-all, though most people opt to take four vegetable side dishes and turn them into a gorgeous meal (the brussel sprouts are heavenly).

Caracas Arepa Bar South American $

Map p106 (☎212-529-2314; www.caracasarepabar.com; 93 1/2 E 7th St btwn First Ave & Ave A; dishes $6-16; 🕒noon-11pm; 🌿; [S]6 to Astor Pl) Cram into this tiny joint and order a crispy, hot *arepa* (corn tortilla stuffed with veggies and meat) such as the Pepi Queen (chicken and avocado) or La Pelua (beef and cheddar). You can choose from 17 types of *arepa* (plus empanadas and daily specials like oxtail soup), served in baskets with a side of *nata* (sour cream) and fried plantains.

ChiKaLicious Dessert $

Map p106 (☎212-995-9511; www.chikalicious.com; 203 E 10th St btwn First & Second Aves; desserts $3-12; 🕒Thu-Sun 3pm-10:30pm; [S]L to 1st Ave, 4/6 to Astor Pl) ChiKaLicious is an East Village favorite taking traditional sweet-tooth standards and transforming them into inspired caloric concoctions. Transcontinental desserts – like green-tea ice cream – are a big hit too. Due to popular demand, ChiKaLicious recently opened a 'dessert club' (more seating space) across the street.

Hearth Italian $$$

Map p106 (☎646-602-1300; www.restauranthearth.com; 403 E 12th St at First Ave; mains $20-40; 🕒6pm-10pm Sun-Thu, to 11pm Fri & Sat; [S]L to 1st Ave; L, N/Q/R/W, 4/5/6 to 14th St-Union Sq) A staple for finicky, deep-pocketed diners, Hearth boasts a warm, brick-walled interior. The seasonal menu includes specials such as roasted sturgeon with lentils and bacon, zucchini ravioli and rabbit papardelle with fava beans.

Redhead Southern $$

Map p106 (☎212-533-6212; www.theredheadnyc.com; 349 E 13th St btwn First & Second Aves; mains $13-25; 🕒Mon-Sun 4pm-2am; [S]L to 1st Ave; L to 3rd Ave; 6 to Astor Pl) Cozy corners of exposed bricks and warm smiles from the staff mirror the home-style comfort food, which has a distinctly Southern bent. There are stacks of fried chicken and rounds of pucker-inducing cocktails on everyone else's table, and you should follow suit. Ask about the 'hoho' for dessert – you won't be sorry.

Prune American $$$

Map p106 (☎212-677-6221; www.prunerestaurant.com; 54 E 1st St btwn First & Second Aves; mains $12-34; 🕒lunch & dinner daily, brunch Sat & Sun; [S]F/V to Lower East Side-2nd Ave) Expect lines around the block on the weekend, when the hungover show up to cure their ills with Prune's brunches and excellent Bloody Marys (in nine

East Village

Top Sights
- St Marks Place ... B2

Sights
- 1 6th and B Garden ... D3
- 2 9th St Garden & La Plaza Cultural ... E2
- 3 All People's Garden ... D4
- 4 Brisas del Caribe ... D4
- 5 East River Park ... F3
- 6 Le Petit Versailles ... D4
- 7 Participant Inc ... D4
- 8 St Mark's in the Bowery ... B2

Eating
- 9 Angelica Kitchen ... B1
- 10 Banjara ... B3
- 11 Cafe Orlin ... B2
- 12 Caracas Arepa Bar ... C2
- 13 ChiKaLicious ... B2
- 14 Hearth ... C1
- 15 Kanoyama ... B1
- 16 Momofuku Noodle Bar ... C2
- 17 Porchetta ... C3
- 18 Prune ... C4
- 19 Redhead ... B1
- 20 Veselka ... B2
- 21 Westville East ... C2

Drinking & Nightlife
- 22 Angel's Share ... A2
- 23 Cherry Tavern ... C3
- 24 Cienfuegos ... C3
- 25 Cock ... B4
- 26 Death + Co ... C3
- 27 Eastern Bloc ... C3
- 28 Immigrant ... B2
- 29 Jimmy's No 43 ... B2
- 30 Mayahuel ... B3
- 31 McSorley's Old Ale House ... A2

Entertainment
- 32 Amore Opera ... C3
- 33 Banjo Jim's ... E2
- 34 Bowery Poetry Club ... A4
- 35 La MaMa ETC ... B3
- 36 New York Theater Workshop ... B3
- 37 Performance Space 122 ... C2
- 38 Sidewalk Café ... C3

Shopping
- 39 Footlight Records ... A1
- 40 John Varvatos ... B4
- 41 Obscura Antiques ... C2
- 42 St Mark's Bookshop ... A2
- 43 Tokio 7 ... C2
- 44 Toy Tokyo ... B2
- 45 Trash & Vaudeville ... A2

Sports & Activities
- 46 Russian & Turkish Baths ... C2

varieties). The small room is always busy as diners pour in for roast suckling pig, rich sweetbreads and sausage-studded concoctions.

Kanoyama — Sushi $

Map p106 (☎212-777-5266; www.kanoyama.com; 175 Second Ave near E 11th St; rolls from $4.50; 🕒dinner; 🥕; [S] L to Third Ave; L, N/Q/R/W, 4/5/6 to 14th St-Union Sq) Providing no-fuss, no-muss sushi with fresh daily specials in the heart of the East Village, Kanoyama is a local favorite that has so far been overlooked by the city's big-name food critics (that might explain its unpretentious air). You can order sushi à la carte or in rolls, or choose from the many tempura plates.

Veselka — Ukrainian $

Map p106 (☎212-228-9682; www.veselka.com; 144 Second Ave at 9th St; mains $6-14; 🕒24hr; [S] L to 3rd Ave, 6 to Astor Pl) A bustling tribute to the area's Ukrainian past, Veselka dishes out borscht and stuffed cabbage amid the usual suspects of greasy comfort food. The cluttered spread of tables is available to loungers and carbo-loaders all night long, though it's a favorite any time of day.

Porchetta — Italian $

Map p106 (☎212-777-2151; 110 E 7th St; dishes from $9; 🕒11:30am-1am Sun-Thu, 11:30am-3am Fri & Sat; [S] 6 to Astor Pl) This white-tiled storefront is short on seating (with just six stools) but long on taste, as renowned chef Sara Jenkins is the talent behind this pork-lovers' takeout haven. The porchetta in question – tender boneless roasted pork that's been wrapped in a pork belly and seasoned with fennel pollen, rosemary, sage, thyme and garlic – is available in sandwich or platter-with-sides versions. For herbivore tag-alongs, there's a mozzarella sandwich on the small menu, too.

Banjara
Indian $$

Map p106 (212-477-5956; 97 First Ave at 6th St; mains $12-18; lunch & dinner; S L to 1st Ave) On 6th St between First and Second Aves you'll find Indian restaurant row. A little more upscale than some of the other options, Banjara has delicious, well-prepared Indian food without all the headache-inducing Christmas lights that festoon many of the other restaurants on the block.

Angelica Kitchen
Vegan, Cafe $$

Map p106 (212-228-2909; www.angelica kitchen.com; 300 E 12th St btwn First & Second Aves; dishes $14-20; lunch & dinner; S L to 1st Ave) This enduring herbivore classic has a calming vibe – candles, tables both intimate and communal, and a mellow, longtime staff – and enough creative options to make your head spin. Some dishes get too-cute names (Sacre-Coeur Basmatica in Paris, Thai Mee Up), but all do wonders with tofu, seitan, spices and soy products, and sometimes an array of raw ingredients.

Lower East Side

Freemans
American $$$

Map p112 (212-420-0012; www.freemans restaurant.com; end of Freeman Alley; mains $24-30; 5pm-11:30pm; S F to 2nd Ave) Tucked down a back alley befitting the metropolitan likes of Paris or London, Freeman's is staunchly reserved for hipster brunch-ophiles who let their chunky jewelry clang on the wooden tables as they lean over to sip overflowing martinis. Potted plants and taxidermic antlers lend an endearing hunting-cabin vibe – a charming escape

---

Art Invasion

It's now been several years since the New Museum has taken hold, inspiring nearby structures to adopt similarly ethereal designs. Perhaps most interestingly the museum has become somewhat of a magnetic force keeping a clutch of small workshops and creative spaces in its orbit.

Though Chelsea may be the heavy hitter when it comes to the New York gallery scene, the Lower East Side has its very own collection of about a dozen quality showplaces. Check out **Participant Inc** (Map p106; 212-254-4334; www. participantinc.org; 253 E Houston St btwn Norfolk & Suffolk Sts; S F to Lower East Side-2nd Ave), which showcases emerging talent and hosts varied performances. It was one of the places hailed as a LES gallery pioneer when it opened several years back. The **Sperone Westwater** (Map p112; www.speronewestwater.com; 257 Bowery; S F to Lower East Side-2nd Ave) gallery represents heavy hitters like William Wegman and Richard Long, and its new home was designed by the famed Norman Foster, who's already made a splash in NYC with his Hearst Building and Avery Fisher Hall designs.

Other popular, contemporary spaces include **Gallery Onetwentyeight** (Map p112; 212-674-0244; www.onetwentyeight.com; 128 Rivington St; call for appointment; S F to Lower East Side-2nd Ave), **Reena Spaulings Fine Art** (Map p112; 212-477-5006; www. reenaspaulings.com; 165 E Broadway), **Lehmann Maupin** (Map p112; 212-254-0054; www. lehmannmaupin.com; 201 Chrystie St; S F to Delancey-Essex Sts) and **Angel Orensanz Foundation** (Map p112; 212-529-7194; www.orensanz.org; 172 Norfolk St; admission price varies; S F to Delancey-Essex Sts).

Community Gardens

After a stretch of arboreal abstinence in New York City, the community gardens of Alphabet City are breathtaking. A network of gardens was carved out of abandoned lots to provide low-income neighborhoods with a communal backyard. Trees and flowers were planted, sandboxes were built, found-art sculptures erected and domino games played – all within green spaces wedged between buildings or even claiming entire blocks. And while some were destroyed – in the face of much protest – to make way for the projects of greedy developers, plenty of green spots have held their ground. You can visit most on weekends, when the gardens tend to be open to the public; many gardeners are activists within the community and are a good source of information about local politics.

Le Petit Versailles (Map p106; www.alliedproductions.org; 346 E Houston St at Ave C) is a unique marriage of a verdant oasis and an electrifying arts organization, offering a range of quirky performances and screenings to the public. The **6th & B Garden** (Map p106; www.6bgarden.org; E 6th St & Ave B; ⏰1-6pm Sat & Sun; 6 to Astor Pl) is a well-organized space that hosts free music events, workshops and yoga sessions; check the website for details. Three dramatic weeping willows, an odd sight in the city, grace the twin plots of **9th St Garden & La Plaza Cultural** (Map p106; www.laplazacultural.com; E 9th St at Ave C). Also check out the **All People's Garden** (Map p106; E 3rd St btwn Aves B & C) and **Brisas del Caribe** (Map p106; 237 E 3rd St), easily located thanks to its surrounding white-picket fence.

from the bustle (when there isn't a crowd inside).

Katz's Delicatessen Deli $

Map p112 (☎212-254-2246; www.katzsdelicatessen.com; 205 E Houston St at Ludlow St; pastrami on rye $15, knockwurst $6; ⏰breakfast, lunch & dinner; [S]F/V to Lower East Side-2nd Ave) Though visitors won't find many remnants of the classic, old-world-Jewish Lower East Side dining scene, there are a few stellar holdouts, among them the famous Katz's Delicatessen, where Meg Ryan faked her famous orgasm in the 1989 Hollywood flick *When Harry Met Sally*, and where, if you love classic deli grub like pastrami and salami on rye, it just might have the same effect on you.

Kuma Inn Pan-Asian $$

Map p112 (☎2120-353-8866; 113 Ludlow St btwn Delancey & Rivington Sts; small dishes $7-11; ⏰dinner Tue-Sun; [S]F, J/M/Z to Delancey-Essex Sts) Reservations are a must at this popular spot in a secretive 2nd-floor location (look for a small red door next to a Chinese deli with 113 painted on the concrete side). The Filipino- and Thai-inspired tapas runs the gamut, from vegetarian summer rolls (with chayote) and edamame (soybean) drizzled with basil-lime oil to an oyster omelet and grilled salmon with mung beans and pickled onions.

Cocoron Noodles $

Map p112 (☎212-925-5220; www.cocoron-soba.com; 61 Delancey St btwn Eldridge & Allen Sts; dishes $9-13; ⏰noon-3pm Tue-Sun, 6pm-11pm Tue-Sat, to 10:30pm Sun; [S]F to Delancey St, B/D to Grand St; J to Bowery) Oh Cocoron, if soba weren't so messy, we'd fill our pockets with your brilliant recipes. A short menu of delicious hot and cold noodle dishes (go for the cold) reads like a haiku dedicated to savory, vegetable-driven fare. Minimalist surrounds and clean wooden tables help offset the cramped quarters, though the tight seating means that you'll have a front-row seat to watch the pan-wielding geniuses.

Meatball Shop
Italian **$**

Map p112 (212-982-8895; www.themeatball shop.com; 84 Stanton St btwn Allen & Orchard Sts; dishes from $9; noon-2am Mon-Wed, Sun, to 4am Thu-Sat; **S** F to 2nd Ave; F to Delancey St; J/M/Z to Essex St) Masterfully executed meatball sandwiches have suddenly spiked in popularity, and the Meatball Shop is riding the wave of success with moist incarnations of the traditional hero. Come early to ensure seating – there's always a line when we swing by.

'Inoteca
Italian **$$**

Map p112 (212-614-0473; 98 Rivington St at Ludlow St; dishes $7-17; lunch & dinner daily, brunch Sat & Sun; **S** F/V to Lower East Side-2nd Ave) It's worth joining the crowd waiting at the cramped bar of this airy, dark-wood-paneled corner haven to choose from tramezzini (small sandwiches on white or whole-wheat bread), panini (pressed sandwiches) and bruschetta options, all delicious and moderately priced.

Prosperity Dumpling
Chinese **$**

Map p112 (212-343-0683; 46 Eldridge St btwn Hester & Canal Sts; dumplings $1-5; Mon-Sun 7:30am-10pm; **S** B/D to Grand St; F to East Broadway; J to Bowery) The Lower East Side's reigning ambassador of cheap eats churns out plump pockets stuffed with a tangy mishmash of chives and pork. Toss a sesame pancake into the mix and you'll still be getting back a chunk of change when you hang the cashier a fiver.

Vanessa's Dumpling House
Chinese **$**

Map p112 (212-625-8008; 118 Eldridge St btwn Grand & Broome Sts; dumplings $1-5; 7:30am-10:30pm; **S** B/D to Grand St, J to Bowery, F to Delancey St) If it weren't for Vanessa, the entire campus of NYU would starve. Tasty dumplings – served steamed, fried or in soup (our favorite) – are whipped together in iron skillets at light speed and tossed into hungry mouths at unbeatable prices. There's a second location at 14th St and Third Ave.

Clinton Street Baking Company
American **$**

Map p112 (646-602-6263; www.clintonstreet baking.com; 4 Clinton St btwn Stanton & Houston Sts; mains from $8.50-17; 8am-4pm Mon-Fri, 6pm-11pm Mon-Sat, 9am-4pm Sat, 9am-6pm Sun; **S** J/M/Z to Essex St, F to Delancey St, F to 2nd Ave) Mom-and-pop shop extraordinaire, Clinton Street Baking Company gets the blue-ribbon in so many categories — best pancakes (blueberry! Swoon!), best muffins, best po'boys (southern-style sandwiches), best biscuits etc – that you're pretty much guaranteed a stellar meal no matter which time of day (or night) you stop by.

Katz's Delicatessen
IMAGESTATE MEDIA PARTNERS LIMITED-IMPACT PHOTOS/ALAMY ©

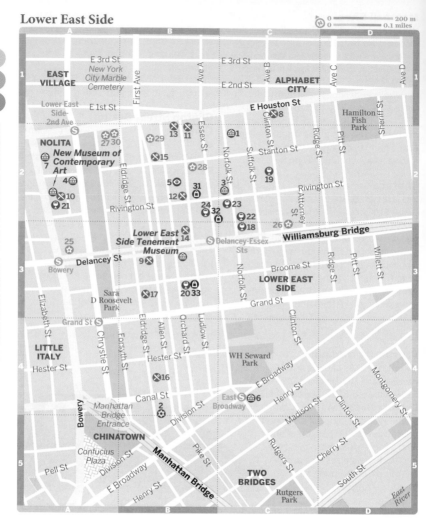

Il Labratorio del Gelato
Ice Cream $

Map p112 (212-343-9922; www.laboratori odelgelato.com; 188 Ludlow St btwn Houston & Stanton Sts; ice cream from $4; 7:30am-10pm Mon-Thu, to midnight Fri, 10am-midnight Sat, 10am-10pm Sun; ; S F to 2nd Ave; F to Delancey St; J/M/Z to Essex St) A fortuitous marriage between cryogenics and farm-fresh bounty, Il Labratorio del Gelato puts the *dolce* in the dolce vita with over 200 varieties of rotating gelato flavors (of which only 20 are on daily display)

created in-house using market-bought ingredients and tried-and-true recipes.

 Drinking & Nightlife

East Village
McSorley's Old Ale House
Bar

Map p106 (212-474-9148; 15 E 7th St btwn Second & Third Aves; S 6 to Astor Pl) Around since 1854, McSorley's feels far removed

Lower East Side

from the East Village veneer of cool: you're more likely to drink with firemen, Wall St refugees and a few tourists. But (didn't you know?) that's become cool again. It's hard to beat the cobwebs and sawdust floors and flip waiters who slap down two mugs of the house's ale for every one ordered.

Angel's Share — Bar

Map p106 (☎212-777-5415; 2nd fl 8 Stuyvesant St near Third Ave & E 9th St; 🕒5pm-midnight; [S]6 to Astor Pl) Show up early and snag a seat at this hidden gem, behind a Japanese restaurant on the same floor. It's quiet and elegant with creative cocktails, but you can't stay if you don't have a table, and they tend to go fast.

Immigrant — Wine Bar

Map p106 (☎212-677-2545; www.theimmigrantnyc.com; 341 E 9th St btwn First & Second Aves; 🕒5pm-1am Mon-Wed & Sun, to 2am Thu, to 3am Fri & Sat; [S]L to 1st Ave, L to 3rd Ave, 4/6 to Astor Pl) Wholly unpretentious, this East Village wine bar – housed in a former tenement (hence the name) – could easily become your *Cheers* if you decide to stick around town.

Cienfuegos — Bar

Map p106 (☎212-614-6818; www.cienfuegosny.com; 95 Ave A btwn 6th & 7th Sts ; [S]F to 2nd Ave, L to 1st Ave, 4/6 to Astor Pl) If Fidel Castro had a stretched Cadillac, its interior would look something like the inside of New York's foremost rum-punch joint. A sampler of tasty Cuban dishes makes the perfect midnight snack.

Jimmy's No 43 — Bar

Map p106 (☎212-982-3006; www.jimmysno43.com; 43 E 7th St btwn Third & Second Aves; 🕒noon-2am Mon-Thu & Sun, to 4am Fri & Sat; [S]N/R to 8th St-NYU, F to 2nd Ave, 4/6 to Astor Pl) Barrels and stag antlers line the walls up to the ceiling as locals chug their drinks. Select from over 50 imported favorites, to go with a round of delectable bar nibbles (betcha didn't think a hot plate could cook pork belly so darn well!).

Mayahuel   Cocktail Bar
Map p106 (☎ 212-253-5888; 304 E 6th St at Second Ave; S L to 3rd Ave; L to 1st Ave; 6 to Astor Pl) Devotees of the fermented agave can seriously indulge themselves experimenting with dozens of varieties (all cocktails $13); in between drinks, snack on tamales and tortillas.

Eastern Bloc   Gay
Map p106 (☎ 222-777-2555; www.easternbloc nyc.com; 505 E 6th St btwn Aves A & B; ☺7pm-4am; S F/V to Lower East Side-2nd Ave) Hang your jacket at the 'Goat Czech' and spring forth into the cramped and crowded sea of boys – some flirting with the topless barkeeps, others pretending not to stare at the retro '70s porno playing on the TVs.

Death + Co   Lounge
Map p106 (☎ 212-388-0882; www.deathand company.com; 433 E 6th St btwn First Ave & Ave A; ☺6pm-1am Mon-Thu & Sun, to 2am Fri & Sat; S F to 2nd Ave, L to 1st Ave, 4/6 Astor Pl) 'Death & Co' is scrawled in ornate cursive on the ground at Death's door, so to speak – the only hint that you're in the right place to try some of the most perfectly concocted cocktails in town. Relax amid dim lighting and thick wooden slatting and let the bartenders – with their PhDs in mixology – work their magic as they shake, rattle and roll your blended poison of choice.

Cock   Gay
Map p106 (☎ 212-777-6254; 29 Second Ave at 2nd St; S F/V to Lower East Side-2nd Ave) A dark, dank spot that's proud of its sleazy-chic reputation, this is the place to join lanky hipster boys and rage until you're kicked out at 4am. Varying theme nights present popular parties with live performers, DJs, drag-queen hostesses, nearly naked go-go boys and porn videos on constant loops.

Cherry Tavern   Bar
Map p106 (☎ 212-777-1448; 441 E 6th St at Ave A; S L to 1st Ave) Not for the 40-year-old virgin – hard-drinking 20- and 30-somethings get their flirt on at this small, dimly lit dive. Arrive before 9pm and you have a shot at the bar or a seat at one of the few tables. Otherwise, clunk your quarters down for a game of pool or sidle up to the jukebox filled with indie/alt songs.

Lower East Side

Whiskey Ward   Bar
Map p112 (☎ 212-477-2998; www.thewhiskey ward.com; 121 Essex St btwn Delancey & Rivington Sts; ☺5pm-4am; S F, J/M/Z to Delancey-Essex Sts) Once upon a time, city officials divided Manhattan into wards, and the Lower East Side was the 'Whiskey Ward,' courtesy of its many drinking establishments. Modern owners of the Whiskey Ward apparently appreciate history as much as they adore single malts, rye whiskey, blended Scotch, Irish whiskey and bourbon.

Back Room   Bar
Map p112 (☎ 212-228-5098; 102 Norfolk St btwn Delancey & Rivington Sts; S F, J/M/Z to Delancey-Essex Sts) Yet another speakeasy-style bar in the LES, the Back Room is entered through a cavern-like alley off Norfolk. The drinks are pricey and served in teacups, and we'd write the whole thing off if it weren't for its undeniable allure. Handsome copper ceilings, art nouveau flourishes, vintage wallpaper, a mirrored bar and an oversized fireplace – all pure eye candy for the not-terribly-sophisticated 20-something crowd.

Nurse Bettie   Cocktail Bar
Map p112 (☎ 917-434-9072; www.nursebettieles. com; 106 Norfolk St btwn Delancey & Rivington Sts; ☺6pm-2am Sun-Tue, to 4am Wed-Sat; S F, J/M/Z to Delancey-Essex Sts) Something a bit new is going on with this pint-sized charmer: plenty of roaming space between slick '00s-modern lounges and '50s-style ice-cream-shop stools and painted pin-ups on the brick walls. Cocktails get freaky: fruity vodka and brandies, plus bubble-gum martinis. You can bring food in, and many won-over locals do.

Barrio Chino   Cocktail Bar
Map p112 (☎ 212-228-6710; 253 Broome St btwn Ludlow & Orchard Sts; S F, J/M/Z to Delancey-Essex Sts) An eatery that spills easily into a party scene, with an airy Havana-meets-Beijing vibe and a focus on fine sipping

RAMIN TALAIE/CORBIS ©

Don't Miss
Lower East Side Tenement Museum

There's no museum in New York that humanizes the city's colorful past quite like the Lower East Side Tenement Museum, which puts the neighborhood's heartbreaking but inspiring heritage on full display in several recreations of turn-of-the-20th-century tenements, including the late-19th-century home and garment shop of the Levine family from Poland, and two immigrant dwellings from the Great Depressions of 1873 and 1929. Always evolving and expanding, the museum has a variety of tours and talks beyond the museum's walls as well – a must for any curious visitor interested in old New York.

At the end of 2011, the museum unveiled its sparkling new visitor center and interpretive space housed at 103 Orchard St. The expansion allowed for the addition of gallery space, an enlarged museum shop, a screening room and plenty of seminar space.

The main portion of your visit is the tenement tour, during which you'll have the opportunity to interact with a guide, but don't forget to check out the one-of-a-kind film in the visitor center that details the difficult life endured by the people who once lived in the surrounding buildings. You'll become very aware of the squalid conditions most tenants faced: no electricity, no running water and a wretched, communal outhouse.

It is well worth stopping by the museum in the evenings when – at least twice a week – the staff hosts 'Tenement Talks,' a lecture and discussion series where a colorful cast of characters from historians through to anthropologists lead small seminars on wide-reaching topics about the city and its people.

NEED TO KNOW

Map p112; ☎212-431-0233; www.tenement.org; 108 Orchard St btwn Broome & Delancey Sts; admission $22; ⏱10am-6pm; Ⓢ B/D to Grand St, J/M/Z to Essex St, F to Delancey St

tequilas (the menu offers 50, some break ing $25 per shot). Or stick with fresh blood-orange or black-plum margaritas, guacamole and chicken tacos.

Welcome to the Johnsons — Bar
Map p112 (☎212-420-9911; 123 Rivington St btwn Essex & Norfolk Sts; Ⓢ F, J/M/Z to Delancey-Essex Sts) Set up like a '70s game room – a bit sleazier than the one on *That '70s Show* – the Johnsons' irony still hasn't worn off for the devoted 20-something crowd. It could have something to do with the $2 Buds till 9pm, the pool table, the blasting garage-rock jukebox or the plastic-covered sofas.

Barramundi — Lounge
Map p112 (☎212-529-6999; 67 Clinton St btwn Stanton & Rivington Sts; Ⓢ F, J/M/Z to Delancey-Essex Sts) This Australian-owned arty place fills an old tenement building with convivial booths, reasonably priced drinks (including some Aussie imports) and some cool tree-trunk tables. Happy hour runs 6pm to 9pm.

Eden @ R Bar — Lesbian
Map p112 (www.myspace.com/edenevents; R Bar, 218 Bowery btwn Rivington & Prince Sts; Ⓢ F/V to Lower East Side-2nd Ave) This weekly lesbian

lounge soiree, held on Wednesdays from 8pm to 3am, is known for drawing sexy, sophisticated ladies with its charming hostess, Maggie C, and music from the oddly named DJ sHErOCK.

 Entertainment

East Village

Performance Space 122 — Theater
Map p106 (PS 122; ☎212-477-5288; www.ps122.org; 150 First Ave at 9th St; Ⓢ R/W to 8th St-NYU, 6 to Astor Pl) This former schoolhouse has been committed to fostering new artists and their far-out ideas since its inception in 1979. Its two stages have hosted such now-known performers as Meredith Monk, Eric Bogosian and the late Spalding Gray, and it's also home to dance shows, film screenings and various festivals for up-and-coming talents.

Banjo Jim's — Live Music
Map p106 (☎212-777-0869; 700 E 9th St at Ave C; Ⓢ L to 1st Ave; 6 to Astor Pl) The latest addition to the nonrock scene on Ave C, Banjo Jim's – a tiny dive with a good jukebox and

Bowery Ballroom

friendly atmosphere – hosts a nightly crew of banjo pickers and lap-steel players.

Sidewalk Café
Country, Folk

Map p106 (212-473-7373; www.sidewalkmusic. net; 94 Ave A at 6th St; S F/V to Lower East Side-2nd Ave; 6 to Astor Pl) Never mind the Sidewalk's burger-bar appearance outside; inside is the home of New York's 'anti-folk' scene, where the Moldy Peaches carved out their legacy before Juno got knocked up. The open-mic 'anti-hootenanny' is Monday night.

La MaMa ETC
Theater

Map p106 (212-475-7710; www.lamama.org; 74A E 4th St; Annex Theater $20, 1st fl Theater $15, the Club $15; hours vary; S F/V to Lower East Side-2nd Ave) A long-standing home for onstage experimentation (the ETC stands for Experimental Theater Club), La MaMa is now a three-theater complex with a cafe, an art gallery and a separate studio building that features cutting-edge dramas, sketch comedy and readings of all kinds.

New York Theater Workshop
Theater

Map p106 (212-460-5475; www.nytw.org; 79 E 4th St btwn Second & Third Aves; S F/V to Lower East Side-2nd Ave) Recently celebrating its 25th year, this innovative production house is a treasure to those seeking cutting-edge, contemporary plays with purpose. It was the originator of two big Broadway hits, Rent and Urinetown, and offers a constant supply of high-quality drama.

Amore Opera
Opera

Map p106 (www.amoreopera.org; Connelly Theater, 220 E 4th St btwn Aves A & B; S F/V to Lower East Side-2nd Ave) This new company, formed by several members of the recently defunct Amato Opera, presents affordable ($35) works. Its inaugural season offerings included La Bohème, The Merry Widow, The Mikado and Hansel and Gretel, performed at its East Village theater.

Bowery Poetry Club
Literary

Map p106 (212-614-0505; www.bowerypoetry. com; 308 Bowery btwn Bleecker & Houston Sts; S 6 to Bleecker St) Just across from the old CBGB site on the East Village/NoHo border, this funky cafe and performance space has eccentric readings of all genres, from plays to fiction, plus frequent themed poetry slams and literary-focused parties that celebrate new books and their authors.

Lower East Side

Bowery Ballroom
Live Music

Map p112 (212-533-2111; www.boweryballroom. com; 6 Delancey St at Bowery St; performance times vary; S J/M/Z to Bowery St) This terrific, medium-sized venue has the perfect sound and feel for more blown-up indie-rock acts (The Shins, Stephen Malkmus, Patti Smith).

Delancey
Live Music

Map p112 (212-254-9920; www.thedelancey. com; 168 Delancey St at Clinton St; S F, J/M/Z to Delancey-Essex Sts) Surprisingly stylish for the Lower East Side, the Delancey hosts some popular indie bands like Clap Your Hands Say Yeah for doting indie-rock crowds. A good early-evening spot to drink too, particularly from the airy 2nd-floor patio deck.

Sapphire
Club

Map p112 (212-777-5153; www.sapphirenyc. com; 249 Eldridge St at E Houston St; admission $5; 7pm-4am; S F/V to Lower East Side-2nd Ave) Fun without attitude! This tiny, hoppin' venue has survived the crowds of the mid-'90s Ludlow St boom with its hip factor intact, and its $5 cover keeps snootiness at a minimum. The tightly packed dance floor gets lit with a mix of R&B, rap, disco and funk.

Pianos
Live Music

Map p112 (212-505-3733; www.pianosnyc.com; 158 Ludlow St at Stanton St; cover charge $8-17; noon-4am; S F/V to Lower East Side-2nd Ave) Nobody's bothered to change the sign at the door, a leftover from the location's previous incarnation as a piano shop. Now it's a musical mix of genres and styles, leaning more toward pop, punk and new wave, but throwing in some hip-hop and indie bands for good measure.

Rockwood Music Hall   Live Music

Map p112 (☎ 212-477-4155; www.rockwoodmu sichall.com; 196 Allen St btwn Houston & Stanton Sts; S F/V to Lower East Side-2nd Ave) Opened by indie rocker Ken Rockwood, this breadbox-sized two-room concert space features a rapid-fire flow of bands and singer/songwriters across the stage. With no cover, and a max of one hour per band (die-hards can see five or more a night), what's to lose? Music kicks off at 3pm on weekends, 6pm on weeknights.

Landmark Sunshine Cinema   Cinema

Map p112 (☎ 212-358-7709; www.landmarkthea tres.com; 143 E Houston St at Forsyth St; S F/V to Lower East Side-2nd Ave) A renovated Yiddish theater, the wonderful Landmark shows foreign and first-run mainstream art films on massive screens. It also has much-coveted stadium-style seating, so it doesn't matter what giant sits in front of you after the lights go out.

🛍 Shopping

East Village

Toy Tokyo   Toys

Map p106 (☎ 212-673-5424; 121 Second Ave btwn St Marks Pl & 7th St; ⏰ 1pm-9pm; S 6 to Astor Pl) The narrow warren of rooms hides all sorts of icons from previous decades. You'll find Superman watches, scowling Godzillas, shiny Transformers, painted toy soldiers and action figures from all genres. As per the name, Japanese toys are particularly well represented – an essential destination for all Japanophiles.

Tokio 7   Consignment Store

Map p106 (☎ 212-353-8443; 83 E 7th St near First Ave; ⏰ noon-8:30pm Mon-Sat, to 8pm Sun; S 6 to Astor Pl) This revered, hip consign-ment shop on a shady stretch of E 7th St, has good-condition designer labels for men and women at some fairly hefty

prices. Best of all is the selection of men's suits – there's nearly always something tip-top in the $100 to $150 range that's worth trying on.

St Mark's Bookshop   Books

Map p106 (☎ 212-260-7853; www.stmarksbook shop.com; 31 Third Ave btwn St Marks Pl & 9th St; ⏰ 10am-midnight Mon-Sat, 11am-midnight Sun; S 6 to Astor Pl) Actually located around the corner from St Marks Pl (it moved long ago), this indie bookshop specializes in political literature, poetry, new nonfic-tion and novels and academic journals. There's also a superior collection of cookbooks, travel guides and magazines, both glossy and otherwise.

Obscura Antiques   Antiques

Map p106 (☎ 212-505-9251; 280 E 10th St btwn First Ave & Ave A; ⏰ 2pm-8:30pm; S L to 1st Ave) Here you'll find taxidermy specimens (like a bear's head), butterfly displays in glass boxes, photos of dead people, a mounted deer-hoof, disturbing little (dental?) instruments, old poison bottles, glass eyes, frock coats, Victorian corsets, miscellaneous beakers and other items not currently available at the local depart-ment store.

John Varvatos   Clothing, Shoes

Map p106 (☎ 212-358-0315; 315 Bowery btwn 1st & 2nd Sts; ⏰ noon-9pm Mon-Sat, to 7pm Sun; S F/V to Lower East Side-2nd Ave, 6 to Bleecker St) Set in the hallowed halls of former punk club CBGB, the John Varvatos Bow-ery store is either a grievous insult to rock history or a creative reconfiguration of the past – depending on which side of the gentrification aisle you happen to stand on. The store goes to great lengths to tie fashion with rock and roll, with records, '70s audio equipment and even electric guitars for sale alongside JV's denim, leather boots, belts and graphic tees.

Footlight Records   Music

Map p106 (☎ 212-533-1572; 113 E 12th St btwn Third & Fourth Aves; ⏰ 11am-7pm Mon-Fri, 10am-6pm Sat, noon-5pm Sun; S R/W to 8th St-NYU; 6 to Astor Pl) Home to a well-chosen collection of out-of-print Broadway and foreign-movie soundtracks, Footlight is a must-visit for vinyl hounds, show-tune lovers and anyone searching for a particular version of a hard-to-find cabaret song.

Trash & Vaudeville
Clothing

Map p106 (4 St Marks Pl; **S** 6 to Astor Pl) Poke your head into Trash & Vaudeville, a landmark goth-and-punk shop where a pre-John Yoko Ono staged happenings in the 1960s.

Lower East Side

Edith Machinist
Vintage

Map p112 (☎212-979-9992, 104 Rivington St at Essex St; ⏰1pm-8pm; **S** F, J/M/Z to Delancey-Essex Sts) To properly strut about the Lower East Side, you've got to dress the part. Edith Machinist can help you get that rumpled but stylish look in a hurry – a bit of vintage glam via knee-high soft suede boots, 1930s silk dresses and ballet-style flats, with military jackets and weather-beaten leather satchels for the gents.

TG170
Clothing

Map p112 (☎212-995-8660; 77 Ludlow St; ⏰noon-8pm; **S** F, J/M/Z to Delancey-Essex Sts) One of the first boutiques to blaze the trail into the Lower East Side way back in 1992, TG170 is still a major destination for downtown style-seekers. Inside the graffiti-covered storefront, you'll find both young and established designers pushing a fashion-forward look.

Essex Street Market
Market

Map p112 (☎212-312-3603; www.essexstreet market.com; 120 Essex St btwn Delancey & Rivington Sts; ⏰8am-7pm Mon-Sat; **S** F/V to Delancey St, J/M/Z to Delancey-Essex Sts) This 60-year-old historic shopping destination is the local place

for produce, seafood, butcher-cut meats, cheeses, Latino grocery items, even a barber. It's a fun place to explore, with snack stands and an attached restaurant when you really want to get down to business.

🌀 Sports & Activities

Russian & Turkish Baths
Bathhouse

Map p106 (☎212-674-9250; www.russianturkish baths.com; 268 E 10th St btwn First Ave & Ave A; per visit $30; ⏰noon-10pm Mon-Tue & Thu-Fri, 10am-10pm Wed, 9am-10pm Sat, 8am-10pm Sun; **S** L to 1st Ave; 6 to Astor Pl) Since 1892, this has been the spa for anyone who wants to get naked (or stay in their swimsuit) and romp in steam baths, an ice-cold plunge pool, a sauna and on the sundeck. The baths are open to both men and women most hours (wearing shorts is required at these times).

Russian & Turkish Baths
DAN HERRICK/LONELY PLANET IMAGES ©

Greenwich Village, Chelsea & the Meatpacking District

There's a good reason why this area is known as the Village. Quaint, quiet lanes carve their way between brown-brick town houses offering endless strolling fodder New York University (NYU) dominates much of the central Village, but the vibe turns mellow west of the park.

Nestled in the few circuitous blocks just below 14th St is the Meatpacking District – once filled with slaughterhouses and now brimming with sleek boutiques and roaring nightclubs.

Chelsea, just a smidge to the north, bridges the gap between the West Village and Midtown, importing bits and bobs from both. It's the de facto neighborhood for the city's sociable gay community, and its broad avenues are lined with breezy cafes, themed bars and sweaty clubs. The neighborhood's massive gallery scene can be found in the West 20s, with starkly contrasting mega-mart retailers orbiting Sixth Ave.

The High Line (p126)

Greenwich Village, Chelsea & the Meatpacking District Highlights

Gallery Hopping (p129)

Chelsea is home to the highest concentration of art galleries in the entire city – and the cluster continues to grow with each season. Most lie in the 20s, on the blocks between Tenth and Eleventh Aves. With hundreds of galleries peppering the area's westernmost avenues and streets it can be difficult to figure out which showcase to visit when; fortunately a casual wander can reveal interesting installations that capture the imagination. Photographs in a Chelsea gallery

② Washington Square Park (p128)

Despite its recent makeover, Washington Sq Park is still the Village's town square. The same odd characters still dance around the fountain, NYU undergrads still flip through used editions of Nietzsche, and shifty amateur chess masters still hustle for games. Only now it's among immaculately landscaped gardens; for better or worse, it's less scruffy and more inviting to strangers.

LEE FOSTER/ALAMY ©

Live Music (p143)

Unofficial headquarters of the world's jazz club scene, some of the city's more prominent ones – Blue Note, Village Vanguard and Smalls Jazz Club – are down in Greenwich Village. Le Poisson Rouge, a relative newcomer, houses a staggering variety of music: jazz, hip-hop, folk, plus global sounds (from Africa, Iceland, Japan) favored by the multiculti-loving crowd. Mos Def performing at Blue Note (p143)

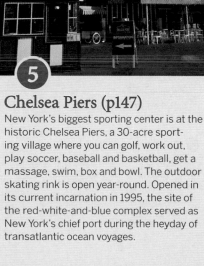

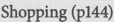

Shopping (p144)

The picturesque streets of the West Village are home to lovely boutiques, with a few antiques dealers, bookstores, record stores, and quirky curio shops adding a bit of eclecticism to an otherwise fashion-focused 'hood. High-end shoppers stick to top-label stores along Bleecker St between Bank and W 10th. The Meatpacking District is all about high-ceiling industrial-chic vibe, with ultra modern designers and expansive boutiques. W 14th St, Meatpacking District

Chelsea Piers (p147)

New York's biggest sporting center is at the historic Chelsea Piers, a 30-acre sporting village where you can golf, work out, play soccer, baseball and basketball, get a massage, swim, box and bowl. The outdoor skating rink is open year-round. Opened in its current incarnation in 1995, the site of the red-white-and-blue complex served as New York's chief port during the heyday of transatlantic ocean voyages.

Greenwich Village Walk

Of all the neighborhoods in New York City, Greenwich Village is the most pedestrian-friendly, with its cobbled corners that stray from the signature gridiron that unfurls across the rest of the island.

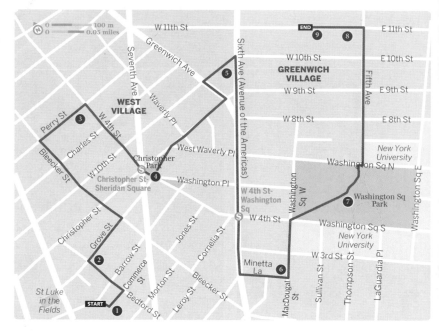

WALK FACTS

- **Start** Cherry Lane Theater
- **Finish** Oscar Wilde's House
- **Distance** 1 mile
- **Duration** One hour and 15 minutes

❶ Cherry Lane Theater

Start your walkabout at the small **Cherry Lane Theater**. Established in 1924, it is the city's longest continuously running off-Broadway establishment and a center of creative activity during the 1940s.

❷ 90 Bedford St

Make a left on Bedford and you'll find **90 Bedford St** on the right hand side at the corner of Grove St. You might recognize the apartment block as the fictitious home of the cast of *Friends*. (Sadly, Central Perk was just a figment of the writers' imaginations.)

❸ 66 Perry St

For another iconic TV landmark, wander up Bleecker St and make a right on Perry St stopping at **66 Perry St**, which was used as the facade and stoop of the city's 'It Girl,' Carrie Bradshaw, in *Sex and the City*.

4 Christopher Park

Make a right on W 4th St until your reach **Christopher Park**, where two white, life-sized statues of same-sex couples stand guard. On the north side is the legendary Stonewall Inn, where a clutch of fed-up drag queens rioted for their civil rights in 1969, signaling the start of the gay revolution.

5 Jefferson Market Library

Follow Christopher St to Sixth Ave to find the **Jefferson Market Library** straddling a triangular plot of land. The 'Ruskinian gothic' spire was once a fire lookout tower; today the structure houses a branch of the public library; in the 1870s it was used as a courthouse.

6 Café Wha?

Stroll down Sixth Ave taking in the flurry of passers-by, then make a left on Minetta Lane to swing by **Café Wha?**, the institution where many young musicians and comedians – like Bob Dylan and Richard Pryor – got their start.

7 Washington Square Park

Wander along MacDougal St until you reach **Washington Sq Park** (p128), the Village's unofficial town square, which plays host to loitering NYU students, buskers and a regular crowd of protestors chanting about various global and municipal injustices. Leave the park through the iconic arch and head up Fifth Ave.

8 Weatherman House

Make a left on W 11th St, where you'll find two notable town houses. First is the infamous **Weatherman house** (18 W 11th St), used in 1970 as a hideout and bomb factory for the radical antigovernment group, Weatherman, until an accidental explosion killed three members and destroyed the house; it was rebuilt in its current angular form in 1978.

9 Oscar Wilde's House

Just a bit further west, is the former, albeit it brief, **home of Oscar Wilde** (48 W 11th St). The famed Irish wit lived here for a few weeks following a US lecture tour in 1882.

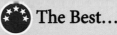

The Best...

PLACES TO EAT

RedFarm Savvy Sino fusion is this cottage-style restaurant's signature on its flavorful dishes. (p134)

Chelsea Market Perfect for a picnic; grab a bottle of wine, cheese, sandwich and gourmet cupcake. (p129)

Babbo Possibly the best of Mario Batali's Italian Manhattan empire. (p135)

Blue Hill A place for Slow Food junkies with deep pockets; an early crusader in the local-is-better movement. (p134)

PLACES TO DRINK

Little Branch No one does speakeasy chic as well as this West Village hideout. (p139)

Boom Boom Room Clink champagne with Vogue photographers and descendants of European royalty. (p139)

Marie's Crisis The ultimate cramped piano bar where no one's afraid to be themselves. (p139)

PERFORMANCE SPACES

Le Poisson Rouge Diverse and exciting line up across musical genres. (p143)

Village Vanguard Venerable institution for jazz stars. (p143)

Upright Citizens Brigade Theatre Improv comedy with occasional big names dropping in. (p143)

Marie's Crisis (p139)

☑ Don't Miss
The High Line

In the early 1900s, the western area around the Meatpacking District and Chelsea was the largest industrial section of Manhattan and a set of elevated tracks were created to move freight off the cluttered streets below. As NYC evolved, the rails eventually became obsolete, and in 1999 a plan was made to convert the scarring strands of metal into a public green space. On June 9, 2009, part one of the city's most beloved urban renewal project opened with much ado, and it's been one of New York's star attractions ever since.

Map p130

☎212-500-6035

www.thehighline.org

Gansevoort St

🕐7am-7pm

S L or A/C/E to 14th St-8th Ave; C/E to 23rd St-8th Ave, 🚌M11 to Washington St; M11, M14 to Ninth Ave M23; M34 to Tenth Ave

More Than Just a Public Space

As the West Village and Chelsea continue to embrace their new-found residential nature, the High Line is making a dedicated move towards becoming more than just a public place but an inspired meeting point. As you walk along the High Line you'll find dedicated staffers wearing shirts with the signature double-H logo who can point you in the right direction or offer additional information about the converted rails. Group tours for children can be organized on a variety of topics from the plant life of the high-rise park to the area's history.

'Spike' level members of the High Line receive a variety of discounts at the establishments in the neighborhood below, from Diane von Furstenberg's boutique under her imaginative geodesic dome, to Amy's Bread, a tasty food outlet in the uberpopular Chelsea Market.

Industrial Past

It's hard to believe that the High Line – a shining example of brilliant urban renewal – was once a dingy rail line that anchored a rather unsavory district of thugs, trannies and slaughterhouses. The tracks were commissioned in the 1930s when the municipal government decided to raise the street-level tracks after years of accidents that gave Tenth Ave the nickname 'Death Avenue.' The project drained more than $150 million in funds (equivalent to about $2 billion by today's dime). After two decades of effective use, a rise in truck transport and traffic led to the decrease in usage, and in the 1980s the rails became obsolete. Petitions were signed by local residents to remove the eyesores, but in 1999 a committee called the Friends of the High Line – founded by Joshua David and Robert Hammond – was formed to save the rusting iron and transform the tracks into a unique elevated green space.

Don't Miss List

ROBERT HAMMOND, COFOUNDER AND EXECUTIVE DIRECTOR OF FRIENDS OF THE HIGH LINE, TALKS ABOUT WHAT MAKES THE 'PARK IN THE SKY' AND ITS SURROUNDING NEIGHBORHOOD SO SPECIAL.

1 HIGH LINE HIGHLIGHTS
To me, the West Village is a reminder of New York's industrial past and residential future. What I love most about the High Line are its hidden moments, like at the Tenth Ave cut-out near 17th St; most people sit on the bleachers, but if you turn the other way you can see the Statue of Liberty far away in the harbor. Architecture buffs will love looking down 18th St, and up on 30th is my favorite moment – a steel cut out where you can see the cars underneath.

2 STOP-OFFS
For lunch near the High Line, I recommend **Hector's Café & Diner**. It's cheap, untouristy and not at all a see-and-be-seen spot – the cookies are great. If you're in the area, you have to visit the galleries in Chelsea – there are over 300, and check out **Printed Matter**, with its artist-made books. Check out the Hôtel Americano (p282) in northern Chelsea – it's very up-and-coming. For an evening out on the town, head to the Boom Boom Room (p139) at the top of the Standard – go early and book ahead.

3 FAMILY FRIENDLY ACTIVITIES
The High Line is also great for kids, with scheduled programming for kids on Saturdays and Wednesdays.

Discover Greenwich Village, Chelsea & the Meatpacking District

⊕ Getting There & Away

○ **Subway** Sixth Ave, Seventh Ave and Eighth Ave are graced with convenient subway stations, but public transportation slims further west. Take the A/C/E or 1/2/3 to reach this colorful clump of neighborhoods – disembark at 14th St (along either service) if you're looking for a good place to make tracks.

○ **Bus** Try M14 or the M8 if you're traveling across town and want to access the westernmost areas of Chelsea and the West Village by public transportation. It's a shame, however, to use the bus or a taxi to get around the West Village – the charming cobblestone streets are perfect for a stroll.

◉ Sights

Greenwich Village & the Meatpacking District

The High Line   Outdoors
See p126.

Washington Square Park   Square
Map p130 (www.washingtonsquareparkcouncil.
org; Fifth Ave at Washington Sq N; S A/C/E,
B/D/F/V to W 4th St-Washington Sq, N/R/W
to 8th St-NYU) A park that began as a potter's field (and, conveniently, a public-
execution ground), this is the town square
of the Village, host to book-toting NYU
students, fire-eating street performers,
dog-run canines and their owners and
speed-chess champs alike. Mint-
condition townhouses and large
modern structures, all belonging
to NYU, surround the space on
all sides. But its biggest claim
to fame is that it's home to
the iconic Stanford White
Arch, colloquially known
as the Washington Square
Arch, which dominates the
park with its 72ft of beaming
white Dover marble. Originally
designed in wood to celebrate
the centennial of George
Washington's inauguration in
1889, the arch proved so popular
that it was replaced with stone six
years later and adorned with statues
of the general in war and peace (the
latter work is by A Stirling Calder, father
of artist Alexander Calder). In 1916 artist
Marcel Duchamp famously climbed to the
top of the arch by its internal stairway and
declared the park the 'Free and Independent Republic of Washington Square.'
    This little republic has just completed
a controversial, $16-million renovation.

Washington Square Park
HENRY WESTHEIM PHOTOGRAPHY/ALAMY ©

And while plenty of change-phobic locals were wary about the plans, most reviews so far have been glowing – which is no wonder, since a new fountain, relocated dog run and lush lawn have added a clean, fresh feel to what had become a ramshackle (though charmingly so) spit of green.

New York University University
Map p130 (NYU; ☎212-998-4636; www.nyu.edu; 50 W 4th St (information center); [S]A/C/E, B/D/F/V to W 4th St-Washington Sq, R/W to 8th St-NYU) In 1831 Albert Gallatin, formerly Secretary of the Treasury under President Thomas Jefferson, founded an intimate center of higher learning open to all students, regardless of race or class background. He'd scarcely recognize the place today, as it's swelled to a student population of more than 54,000, with more than 16,000 employees and schools and colleges at six Manhattan locations. It just keeps growing, too – to the dismay of landmark activists and business owners, who have seen buildings rapidly bought out by the academic giant (or destroyed through careless planning, such as with the historic Provincetown Playhouse) and replaced with ugly dormitories or administrative offices. Still, some of its crevices are charming, such as the leafy courtyard at its School of Law, or impressively modern, like the Skirball Center for the Performing Arts, where top-notch dance, theater, music, spoken-word and other performers wow audiences at the 850-seat theater.

Pier 45 Outdoors
Map p130 (Christopher St at Hudson River; [S]1 to Christopher St-Sheridan Sq) Still known to many as the Christopher Street Pier, this is an 850ft-long finger of concrete, spiffily renovated with a grass lawn, flowerbeds, a comfort station, an outdoor cafe, tented shade shelters and a stop for the New York Water Taxi as part of the ongoing Hudson River Park project. And it's a magnet for downtowners of all stripes, from local families with toddlers in daylight to mobs of young gay kids who flock here at night from all over the city (and beyond) because of the pier's long-established history as a gay cruising hangout.

Top Tip

It's perfectly acceptable to arm yourself with a map (or rely on your smartphone) to get around the West Village's charming-but-challenging side streets. Even some locals have a tricky time finding their way! Just remember that 4th St makes a diagonal turn north – breaking away from usual east–west street grid – and you'll quickly become a Village pro.

Chelsea

Chelsea Galleries Gallery
Map p134 ([S]C/E to 23rd St) Chelsea is home to the highest concentration of art galleries in the entire city – and the number of them just keeps increasing. Most lie in the 20s, on the blocks between Tenth and Eleventh Aves, and wine-and-cheese openings for their new shows are typically held on Thursday evenings. For a complete guide and map, pick up Art Info's Gallery Guide, available for free at most galleries, or visit www.westchelseaarts.com. Among the showcases that create the most buzz in these parts are the so-called 'blue-chip' galleries: the Andrea Rosen Gallery, with gems by Katy Moran, Rita Ackerman and Felix Gonzalez-Torres; the Mary Boone Gallery, whose owner found fame in the '80s with her eye for Jean-Michel Basquiat and Julian Schnabel in SoHo; and the Matthew Marks Gallery, a Chelsea pioneer known for exhibiting big names from Jasper Johns to Ellsworth Kelly. Note that galleries are typically closed on Mondays.

Chelsea Market Market
Map p134 (www.chelseamarket.com; 75 Ninth Ave at 15th St; 🕐7am-9pm Mon-Sat, 10am-8pm Sun; [S]A/C/E to 14th St, L to 8th Ave) In a

CHELSEA

W 15th St

W 14th St

8th Ave-14th St

14th St

Ninth Ave

Tenth Ave

Washington St

W 13th St

W 13th St

Greenwich Ave

W 12th St

Seventh Ave

W 4th St

Eighth Ave

WEST VILLAGE

The High Line

Gansevoort St

MEATPACKING DISTRICT

Washington St

Horatio St

Jane St

Greenwich St

W 12th St

Bethune St

Bank St

Abingdon Sq

Bank St

Hudson St

Bleecker St

W 11th St

W 4th St

Perry St

Charles St

Waverly Pl

W 11th St

W 11th St

West Side Hwy

Perry St

Charles St

Bedford St

Barrow St

Commerce St

Christopher St-Sheridan Square

W 10th St

Christopher St

Barrow St

Morton St

James J Walker Park

St Lukes Pl

Washington St

Clarkson St

Leroy St

W Houston St

Hudson St

Greenwich St

King St

Charlton St

Hudson River

Hudson River Park

Pier 40

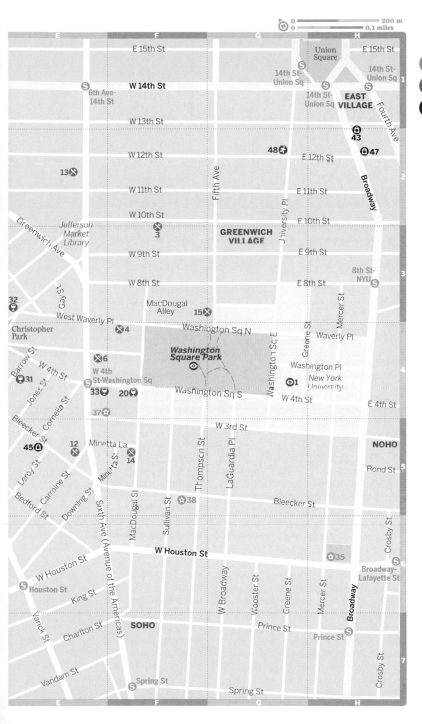

Greenwich Village & the Meatpacking District

Top Sights

The High Line ... A2
Washington Square Park ... F4

Sights

1 New York University ... G4
2 Pier 45 ... A6

Eating

3 Alta ... F3
4 Babbo ... F4
5 Bill's Bar & Burger ... B1
6 Blue Hill ... E4
7 Bonsignour ... C2
8 Buvette ... D4
9 Empellon ... D4
10 Fatty Crab ... B2
11 Hector's Café & Diner ... A2
12 Joe's Pizza ... E5
13 Kin Shop ... E2
14 Minetta Tavern ... F5
15 Otto Enoteca Pizzeria ... F3
16 RedFarm ... C4
17 Spotted Pig ... C3
18 Tartine ... D3

Drinking & Nightlife

19 Art Bar ... C2
20 Bar Next Door ... F4
21 Boom Boom Room ... A2
22 Brass Monkey ... A2
23 Corner Bistro ... C2
24 Cubbyhole ... C2
25 G2 ... B1
26 Henrietta Hudson ... D5
27 Julius Bar ... D3
28 Kettle of Fish ... D4
29 Little Branch ... D5
30 Marie's Crisis ... D4
31 One If By Land, Two If By Sea ... E4
32 Stonewall Inn ... E3
33 Vol de Nuit ... E4
34 White Horse Tavern ... C3

Entertainment

35 Angelika Film Center ... H6
36 Barrow Street Theater ... D4
37 Blue Note ... E4
Duplex ... (see 28)
38 Le Poisson Rouge ... F5
39 Smalls Jazz Club ... D3
40 Village Vanguard ... D2

Shopping

41 Alexander McQueen ... A1
42 DDC Lab ... A1
43 Forbidden Planet ... H2
44 Marc by Marc Jacobs ... C3
45 Murray's Cheese ... E5
46 Stella McCartney ... A1
47 Strand Book Store ... H2

Sports & Activities

48 Bowlmor Lanes ... G2
49 Downtown Boathouse ... B7
50 New York Trapeze School ... B7

shining example of redevelopment and preservation, the Chelsea Market has taken a former factory of cookie giant Nabisco (creator of the Oreo) and turned it into an 800ft-long shopping concourse that caters to foodies. And that's only the lower part of a larger, million-sq-ft space that occupies a full city block, current home of TV channels the Food Network, Oxygen Network and NY1, the local news channel. The prime draw for shoppers, though, are the more than two dozen food shops, including Amy's Bread, Fat Witch Bakery, the Lobster Place, Hale & Hearty Soup, Ronnybrook Dairy and the Nutbox. Live-music shows grace the main public space weekly, and the new High Line passes right by the rear of the building.

Chelsea Hotel Historic Building

Map p134 (☎212-243-3700; 222 W 23rd St btwn Seventh & Eighth Aves; [S]1, C/E to 23rd St) It's probably not any great shakes as far as hotels go – and besides, it mainly houses long-term residents – but as a place of mythical proportions, the Chelsea Hotel is top of the line. The red-brick hotel, featuring ornate iron balconies and no fewer than seven plaques declaring its literary landmark status, has played a major role in pop-culture history. It's where the likes of Mark Twain, Thomas Wolfe, Dylan Thomas and Arthur Miller hung out; Jack Kerouac allegedly crafted *On the Road* during one marathon session here, and it's where Arthur C Clarke wrote *2001: A Space Odyssey*. Dylan Thomas died of alcohol poisoning while staying here in 1953, and Nancy Spungeon died here after being stabbed by her Sex Pistols boyfriend Sid Vicious in 1978. Among the many celebs who have logged time living at the Chelsea are Joni Mitchell, Arthur Miller, Stanley Kubrick, Dennis Hopper, Edith Piaf, Bob Dylan and Leonard Cohen, whose song 'Chelsea Hotel' recalls a romp with Janis Joplin (who spent time here, too). The art-filled lobby is worth a look-see, and its basement-level Star Lounge is a sexy, low-lit spot for a martini.

Rubin Museum of Art Museum

Map p134 (☎212-620-5000; www.rmanyc.org; 150 W 17th St at Seventh Ave; adult/child $10/free, 7pm-10pm Fri free; 🕒11am-5pm Mon & Thu, to 7pm Wed, to 10pm Fri, to 6pm Sat & Sun; [S]1 to 18th St) This is the first museum in the Western world to dedicate itself to the art of the Himalayas and surrounding regions. Its impressive collections include embroidered textiles from China, metal sculptures from Tibet, Pakistani stone sculptures and intricate Bhutanese paintings, as well as ritual objects and dance masks from various Tibetan regions, spanning from the 2nd to the 19th centuries. A small cafe serves traditional Himalayan foods, and the K2 Lounge offers performances and cocktails, and is the perfect nightcap after visiting the galleries on free Friday evenings.

Chelsea Art Museum Museum

Map p134 (☎212-255-0719; www.chelseaartmuseum.org; 556 W 22nd St; adult/child $8/free; 🕒noon-6pm Tue, Wed, Fri & Sat, to 8pm Thu; [S]C/E to 23rd St) Occupying a three-story red-brick building dating from 1850, this popular museum stands on land once owned by writer Clement Clarke Moore (author of the famous poem 'A Visit from St Nicholas'). Its focus is on post-war abstract expressionism, especially by national and international artists, and its permanent collection includes works by Antonio Corpora, Laszlo Lakner, Jean Arp and Ellen Levy.

Chelsea Market (p129)

ALEX SEGRE/ALAMY ©

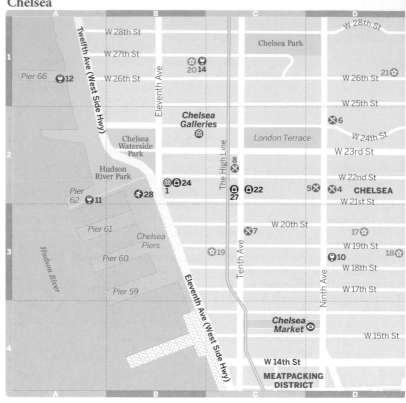

Eating

Greenwich Village & the Meatpacking District

RedFarm   Fusion $$$

Map p130 (📞 212-792-9700; www.redfarmnyc.com; 529 Hudson St btwn 10th & Charles Sts; mains $14-39; 🕒 5pm-12:30am Mon-Thu, to midnight Fri, 11am-2:30pm & 5pm-midnight Sat, 11am-2:30pm & 5-11pm Sun; Ⓢ A/C/E, B/D/F, M to W 4th St, 1/2 to Christopher St-Sheridan Sq, 1/2/3 to 14th St) A recent chart-topper on the best lists of many foodies, RedFarm earns our devotion for preparing mouth-watering mains (rib steak!) without a hint of pretension. Besides the heavily touted mixed-bag recipes, RedFarm also sports

some of the best drinks in town – the Suntory Old-Fashioned is one of the finest scotch cocktails out there.

Blue Hill   American $$$

Map p130 (📞 212-539-1776; 75 Washington Pl btwn Sixth Ave & Washington Sq W; mains $32-36; 🕒 dinner; Ⓢ A/C/E, B/D/F/V to W 4th St-Washington Sq) Gifted chef Dan Barber, who hails from a farm family in the Berkshires, Massachusetts, uses harvests from that land, as well as from farms in upstate New York, to create his widely praised fare. Expect barely seasoned, perfectly ripe vegetables, which serve to highlight centerpieces of cod in almond broth, Berkshire pork stewed with four types of beans, and grass-fed lamb with white beans and new potatoes.

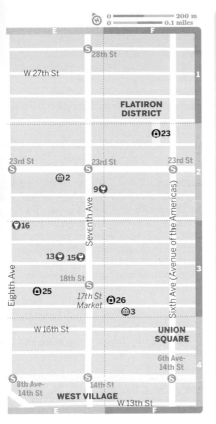

Tartine
French $$

Map p130 (☎212-229-2611; www.tartinecafe nyc.com; 253 W 11th St btwn 4th St & Waverly Pl; mains $10-24; ⊙9am-10:30pm Mon-Sat, to 10pm Sun; Ⓢ1/2/3 to 14th St, 1/2 to Christopher St-Sheridan Sq, L to 8th Ave) Tartine is the corner bistro of your French-ified dreams: wobbly stacks of chairs and tables, pink steaks and escargot, found treasures nailed to wooden walls, and a good-cop-bad-cop duo of waitresses who indiscriminately bounce dishes and diners around the teeny-tiny room.

Babbo
Italian $$$

Map p130 (☎212-777-0303; www.babbonyc. com; 110 Waverly Pl; mains $19-29; ⊙dinner; ⓈA/C/E, B/D/F/V to W 4th St; 1 to Christopher St-Sheridan Sq) Celebrity chef Mario Batali has multiple restaurants in Manhattan, but everyone has a sneaking suspicion that this two-level split town house is his favorite. Whether you order mint love letters, lamb's brain *francobolli* (small, stuffed ravioli) or pig's foot *milanese,* you'll find Batali at the top of his innovative, eclectic game. Reservations are in order.

135

Spotted Pig
Pub $$

Map p130 (📞212-620-0393; www.thespottedpig.com; 314 W 11th St at Greenwich St; mains $14-30; ☺lunch & dinner; 🍴🚻; S A/C/E to 14th St, L to 8th Ave) This Michelin-starred gastropub is a favorite of Villagers, serving a hearty, upscale blend of mains from Italy and the UK. Two floors are bedecked in old-timey souvenirs that serve to make the experience both casual and refined. It doesn't take reservations, so there is often a wait for a table. Brunch and lunch are less packed, so you can usually get a seat straight away.

Minetta Tavern
Bistro $$

Map p130 (📞212-475-3850; www.minettatavernny.com; 113 MacDougal St; mains $17-34; ☺dinner daily, brunch Sat & Sun; S A/C/E, B/D/F/V to W 4th St) Book in advance, or come early to snag a table on a weeknight, because Minetta Tavern is pretty much always packed to the rafters. The snug red-leather banquettes, dark-paneled walls with black-and-white photos, classic checkered floors, tin ceilings and flaring yellow bistro lamps will lure you in. The flavor-filled bistro fare – pan-seared marrow bones, roasted chicken, crisp fries and big burgers, and mustn't-miss French dip sandwiches – will have you wishing you lived upstairs.

Alta
Tapas $$

Map p130 (📞212-505-7777; 54 W 10th St btwn Fifth & Sixth Aves; small plates $5-18.50; ☺dinner; S A/C/E, B/D/F/V to W 4th St-Washington Sq) This gorgeous town house highlights the neighborhood's quaintness, with plenty of exposed brick, wood beams, flickering candles, massive mirrors and romantic fireplace glows. A small-plates menu of encyclopedic proportions cures indecision with the likes of succulent lamb meatballs (butternut-squash foam! Yum!), white-truffle and porcini deviled eggs, warm artichoke salad, fried goat cheese, and blue-crab risotto.

Buvette
French $$

Map p130 (📞212-255-3590; www.ilovebuvette.com; 42 Grove St btwn Bedford & Bleecker Sts; mains $10-15; S1/2 to Christopher St-Sheridan Sq; A/C/E, B/D/F, M to W 4th St; 1/2 to Houston St) The delicate tin tiling on the ceiling is reflected in the swooshing marble countertop at the bar, the perfect place for an early evening glass of wine. For the full dinner experience at this self-proclaimed *gastotèque*, grab a seat at one of the surrounding tables – it's decidedly romantic, with Dutch porcelain hanging from the wooden accents on the walls.

Otto Enoteca Pizzeria
Pizzeria, Italian $$

Map p130 (📞212-995-9559; 1 Fifth Ave near 8th St; mains $8-15; ☺lunch & dinner; S A/C/E, B/D/F/V to W 4th St-Washington Sq) An intimate trattoria in the heart of the Village, this is (a refreshingly affordable) part of Mario Batali's empire, a pizza palace where thin pizzas are cooked on flat iron griddles till they crackle perfectly. They come topped with items far beyond your standard pizza joint – fennel, goat cheese, egg, fresh chilies, capers, the best fresh mozzarella – and sauce that has the perfect balance of smoky and sweet.

Bill's Bar & Burger
Burgers $

Map p130 (📞212-414-3003; www.brguestrestaurants.com; 22 Ninth Ave near 13th St; mains $4.95-10.50; ☺lunch & dinner; S A/C/E, L to 8th Ave-14th St) Classic burgers, bacon-and-cheddar burgers, mushroom-and-swiss burgers, even a short-rib-style burger are what keep the place hopping. There are also 'disco fries' (smothered in gravy and melted cheese), sweet-potato fries, all types of hot dogs (chili dogs, sauerkraut dogs etc), blackened catfish sammies and chicken wings, not to mention apple-crumb pie for dessert.

Kin Shop
Thai $$

Map p130 (📞212-675-4295; www.kinshopnyc.com; 469 Sixth Ave; mains $9-28; ☺11:30am-3pm Mon-Sun, 5:30-11pm Mon-Thu, 5:30-11:30pm Fri & Sat, 5-10pm Sun; S L to 6th Ave; 1/2/3, F/M to 14th St) The second avatar of Top Chef winner Harold Dieterle (the first being Perilla – also a great find – nearby) is this

Thai-inspired joint that finds its place somewhere between neighborhood haunt and forward-thinking fusion kitchen. Curry pastes are crushed in-house – a testament to the from-scratch methods used to craft every item on the colorful menu.

Empellon
Mexican $$

Map p130 (212-367-0999; www.empellon.com; 230 W 4th St btwn Seventh Ave & 10th St; mains $8-19; 5pm-11pm Mon-Wed, 5pm-midnight Thu-Sat; S 1/2 to Christopher St-Sheridan Sq; A/C/E, B/D/F, M to W 4th St; 1/2/3 to 14th St) Chef Alex Stupak has transformed the all-important avocado into the most inventive and flavorful guacamole in town. He's also dropped the 'Tex' from Tex-Mex, creating imaginative south-of-the corner fare that is wholly elegant and beautifully presented.

Fatty Crab
Pan-Asian $$

Map p130 (212-352-3590; www.fattycrab.com; 643 Hudson St btwn Gansevoort & Horatio Sts; mains $16-28; noon-midnight Mon-Wed, to 2am Thu & Fri, 11am-2am Sat, 11am-midnight Sun; S L to 8th Ave; A/C/E, 1/2/3 to 14th St) The Fatty folks have done it again with their small Malaysian-inspired joint in the thick of things on the west side. It's super hip and always teeming with locals who swing by in droves to devour fish curries and pork belly accompanied by a signature selection of cocktails.

Bonsignour
Sandwiches $

Map p130 (212-229-9700; 35 Jane St at Eighth Ave; mains $7-12; breakfast, lunch & dinner; S L to 8th Ave; A/C/E, 1/2/3 to 14th St) Nestled on a quiet Village street, this sandwich shop offers dozens of delicious choices as well as salads, frittatas and a wonderful beef chili. Get

a sandwich or a chicken curry salad to go and wander down the street to Abingdon Square for al fresco dining.

Joe's Pizza
Pizza $

Map p130 (212-366-1182; www.joespizzanyc. com; 7 Carmine St btwn Sixth Ave & Bleecker St; slices from $2.75; 10am-4:30am Mon-Sun; S A/C/E, B/D/F, M to W 4th St, 1/2 to Christopher St-Sheridan Sq, 1/2 to Houston St) Joe's is the Meryl Streep of pizza parlors, collecting dozens of awards and accolades over the last three decades while safely cementing its reputation as one of the top spots for a slice in NYC.

Chelsea

Cookshop
Modern American $$

Map p134 (212-924-4440; www.cookshopny. com; 156 Tenth Ave btwn 19th & 20th Sts; mains $14-33; lunch & dinner; S L to 8th Ave, A/C/E to 14th St, A/C/E to 23rd St) A brilliant brunching pit stop before (or after) tackling the verdant High Line across the street, Cookshop is a lively place that knows its niche and does it oh so well. Excellent service, eye-opening cocktails

Spotted Pig
DAN HERRICK/LONELY PLANET IMAGES ©

(good morning Bloody Maria!), a perfectly baked breadbasket and a selection of inventive egg mains make this a favorite in Chelsea on a Sunday afternoon. Dinner is a sure-fire win as well.

Co
Pizzeria $$

Map p134 (☎212-243-1105; 230 Ninth Ave at 24th St; pizza $9-18; ☺dinner Mon, lunch & dinner Tue-Sun; ⓈC/E to 23rd St) Expect a faithful reproduction of the trademark Neapolitan thin crust pies topped with an assortment of fresh-from-the-farm items like fennel and buffalo mozzarella. Salads of artichoke, beet or radicchio – as well as global wines and a sprinkling of sweets – round out the offerings.

Billy's Bakery
Bakery $

Map p134 (☎212-647-9956; www.billysbakery nyc.com; 184 Ninth Ave btwn 21st & 22nd Sts; cupcakes $3; ☺8:30am-11pm Mon-Thu, to midnight Fri & Sat, 9am-10pm Sun ; ⓈA/C/E, 1/2 to 23rd St, A/C/E to 14th St) New York's *Sex and the City*–fueled cupcake craze has come and gone, but Billy's is still cranking out its four-bite bits of heaven. Red velvet and banana cream top the recipe list, and a

clutch of retro-style pastries are imagined by the I-don't-care-what-I'm-wearing hipsters in the back.

Tía Pol
Tapas $$

Map p134 (☎212-675-8805; www.tiapol.com; 205 Tenth Ave btwn 22nd & 23rd Sts; small plates $2-16; ☺dinner Tue-Sun; ⓈC/E to 23rd St) Wielding Spanish tapas amid closet-sized surrounds, Tía Pol is the real deal, as the hordes of locals swarming the entrance can attest. The red-wine options will have your tongue doing backflips, as will the array of small plates: Spanish tortillas, lemony salad topped with tuna, lima-bean-puree bruschetta and sautéed cockles with razor clams.

Blossom
Vegan $$

Map p134 (☎212-627-1144; 187 Ninth Ave btwn 21st & 22nd Sts; mains $12-22; ☺lunch & dinner; ⓈC/E to 23rd St) This Chelsea veg oasis – with a sinful new wine and chocolate bar attached – is a peaceful, romantic dining room that offers imaginative tofu, seitan and vegetable creations, some raw, all kosher.

Desserts are so rich, you'll swear they're filled with butter and cream. A second

Boom Boom Room

JERRITT CLARK, IMAGEWIRE/GETTY IMAGES ©

Upper West Side location is **Cafe Blossom** (Map p231; ☎ 212-875-2600; 466 Columbus Ave btwn 82nd & 83rd Sts; **S** 1 to 79th St).

🍷 Drinking & Nightlife

Greenwich Village & the Meatpacking District

Little Branch
Cocktail Bar

Map p130 (☎ 212-929-4360; 22 Seventh Ave S at Leroy St; **S** 1 to Houston St) If it weren't for the casual bouncer dressed in slacks and suspenders, you'd never guess that a charming bar lurked behind the boring brown door positioned at the odd triangular intersection. When you get the go-ahead to enter, you'll find a basement bar that feels like a wonder kickback to Prohibition times. Squeaky tunes waft overhead as locals clink glasses and sip inventive, old-timey cocktails.

Boom Boom Room
Lounge

Map p130 (☎ 212-645-4646; 848 Washington St btwn 13th & Little W 12th Sts; ⊙10pm-4am Wed-Thu, 11pm-4am Fri & Sat; **S** L to 8th Ave, 1/2/3, A/C/E to 14th St) Smooth beige surrounds, softer music and plenty of room to swig your top-shelf tipple, the Boom Boom Room is strictly VIP and the favored hangout for the vogue elite (and *Vogue* elite) – expect models, their photographer and the occasional celeb sighting. Come early and book ahead – that's the only way to gain access if you're not a cornerstone of New York's social scene.

Art Bar
Bar

Map p130 (☎ 212-727-0244; 52 Eighth Ave near Horatio St; ⊙4pm-4am, happy hour 4-7pm; **S** L to 8th Ave-14th St, A/C/E to 14th St) A decidedly bohemian crowd favors Art Bar, which doesn't look like much up front (oval booths crowded too close to the wooden bar), but has a bit more going on in the back. Grab your beer or one of the house specials (usually martinis) and head for the couches, placed under a huge *Last*

Supper mural featuring Jimmy Dean and Marilyn Monroe, among others.

Kettle of Fish
Bar

Map p130 (☎ 212-414-2278; www.kettleoffish nyc.com; 59 Christopher St near Seventh Ave; ⊙3pm-4am Mon-Fri, 2pm-4am Sat & Sun; **S** 1 to Christopher St-Sheridan Sq) Step into this dimly lit spot, full of couches and plump chairs, and prepare to stay for a while because the crowd is simply beguiling. It's a dive bar, a sports bar and a gay bar in one, and everyone mixes happily. There are stacks of board games like Monopoly and checkers, which patrons are encouraged to play, as well as darts. And if you get hungry, the barkeeps will offer menus from nearby restaurants that deliver here. The owner is a Packers fan, so expect raucous activity on game days.

Vol de Nuit
Pub

Map p130 (☎ 212-982-3388; 148 W 4th St; **S** A/C/E, B/D/F/V to W 4th St-Washington Sq) Even all the NYU students can't ruin this: a cozy Belgian beer bar, with a few dozen zonkers like Lindemans Framboise (strawberry beer!) and *frites* (fries) to share at the front patio seats, the lounge, the communal wood tables or under the dangling red lights at the bar.

Marie's Crisis
Bar

Map p130 (☎ 212-243-9323; 59 Grove St btwn Seventh Ave S & Bleecker St; ⊙4pm-4am; **S** 1 to Christopher St-Sheridan Sq) Aging Broadway queens, wide-eyed out-of-town gay boys, giggly tourist girls and various other fans of musical theater assemble around the piano here and take turns belting out campy numbers, often joined by the entire crowd. It's old-school fun, no matter how jaded you were when you went in.

Brass Monkey
Bar

Map p130 (☎ 212-675-6686; www.brassmon keybar.com; 55 Little W 12th St at Washington St; ⊙11:30am-4am; **S** A/C/E to 14th St; L to 8th Ave) While most Meatpacking District bars tend toward the chic, the Monkey is more for beer lovers than those worrying about what shoes to wear. The multifloor

GAY RIOTS
OCATE

Monkey is at-ease and down-to-earth, with squeaking wood floors and a nice long list of beers and scotch. The roof deck is a fine destination in warm weather.

Julius Bar   Gay

Map p130 (☎ 212-243-1928; 159 W 10th St at Waverly Pl; Ⓢ A/C/E, B/D/F, M to W 4th St, 1/2/3 to 14th St, 1/2 to Christopher St-Sheridan Sq) One of the infamous originals – in fact, it's the oldest operating gay bar in NYC – Julius is a dive bar through and through. The only hint of its homo roots is the cli-entele, a mixed bag of faithful locals and the occasional newbie. It's refreshingly unpretentious, and just steps away from the better-known Stonewall and Duplex.

G2   Bar

Map p130 (☎ 212-807-8444; www.gaslight nyc.com; 39 Ninth Ave at 14th St; no cover charge; ⊗ 8pm-4am Mon-Sat; Ⓢ A/C/E, L to 8th Ave-14th St) For adult coolness in the hipster-mad Meatpacking District, do

your drinking at G2. G2 is funky, with its crazy potted plants, book shelves, marble-topped tables and distressed velvet couches. A DJ spins house, electronica and hip-hop most nights.

Henrietta Hudson   Lesbian

Map p130 (☎ 212-924-3347; 438 Hudson St; Ⓢ 1 to Houston St) All sorts of cute young dykes, many from neighboring New Jersey and Long Island, storm this sleek lounge, where varying theme nights bring in spirited DJs, who stick to particular genres (hip-hop, house, rock). The owner, Brooklyn native Lisa Canistraci, is a favorite promoter in the world of lesbian nightlife, and is often on hand to mix it up with her fans.

Stonewall Inn   Bar

Map p130 (☎ 212-463-0950; 53 Christopher St; Ⓢ 1 to Christopher St-Sheridan Sq) Site of the Stonewall riots in 1969, this historic bar was losing its fan base to trendier spots until new owners came along several

years back, gave it a facelift and opened it to a new and welcoming crowd. Since then, it's been pulling in varied crowds nightly for parties catering to everyone under the gay rainbow.

One If By Land, Two If By Sea
Bar

Map p130 (212-255-8649; 17 Barrow St; dinner; 1 at Christopher St-Sheridan Sq; A/C/E, B/D/F/V to W 4th St-Washington Sq) Famous for its beef Wellington and graceful, aged location in Aaron Burr's old carriage house, this is quite possibly New York's favorite date restaurant. But it's even better as a quiet watering hole, perfect for a cocktail-hour or late-night libation for those who need a break from the harried streets.

Cubbyhole
Lesbian, Gay

Map p130 (212-243-9041; 281 W 12th St; A/C/E to 14th St, L to 8th Ave) A tiny hideaway festooned with brightly patterned bar stools and strings of colorful lights, this no-attitude neighborhood watering

hole has that truly rare mix of lesbians and gay men who are out to make friends rather than hit the road with the first trick they find. It's got a great jukebox, friendly bartenders and plenty of regulars.

White Horse Tavern
Bar

Map p130 (212-243-9260; 567 Hudson St at 11th St; 1 to Christopher St-Sheridan Sq) It's a bit on the tourist trail, but that doesn't dampen the century-old, pubby dark-wood, tin-ceiling atmosphere of this bar, where Dylan Thomas had his last drink (too many beers led to his 1953 death) and a tipsy Jack Kerouac got kicked out. Sit at the long oak bar inside or on sidewalk tables.

Bar Next Door
Bar

Map p130 (212-529-5945; 129 MacDougal St btwn W 3rd & W 4th Sts; 6pm-2am Sun-Thu, to 3am Fri & Sat; A/C/E, B/D/F/V to W 4th St) One of the loveliest hangouts in the neighborhood, the basement of this restored town house is all low ceilings, exposed brick and romantic lighting. You'll find mellow, live jazz nightly, as well as the tasty Italian menu of the restaurant next door, La Lanterna di Vittorio.

Corner Bistro   Bar
Map p130 (www.cornerbistrony.com; 331 W 4th St btwn Jane & 12th Sts; ⏱11:30am-4am Mon-Sat, noon-4am Sun; 🚇L to 8th Ave; 1/2/3, A/C/E to 14th St) An old-school dive bar with cheap beers on tap – it all sounds pretty standard until you take a mouthwatering bite out of Corner Bistro's bar burger. Nothing beats this juicy meat sandwich with a side scatter of fries.

Chelsea
Bathtub Gin   Bar
Map p134 (📞646-559-1671; www.bathtubgin nyc.com; 132 Ninth Ave btwn 18th & 19th Sts; ⏱6pm-1:30am Sun-Tue, to 3:30am Wed-Sat; 🚇A/C/E to 14th St, L to 8th Ave, A/C/E to 23rd St) Amid New York City's serious obsession with speakeasy-styled hangouts, Bathtub Gin manages to poke its head above the crowd with its super-secret front door, which doubles as a wall for an unassuming cafe. Inside, chill seating, soft

background beats and kindly staff make it a great place to sling back bespoke cocktails with friends.

Frying Pan   Bar
Map p134 (📞212-989-6363; Pier 66 at W 26th St; 🚇C/E to 23rd St) On warm days, the rustic open-air space brings in the crowds, who come to laze on deck chairs, eat burgers off the sizzling grill, drink ice-cold bottles of Corona ($7) and admire the fine views across the water to, uh, New Jersey.

G Lounge   Gay
Map p134 (📞212-929-1085; www.glounge. com; 223 W 19th St btwn Seventh & Eighth Aves; ⏱4pm-4am; 🚇1 to 18th St) Glossy and unpretentious, this gay bar is as straight-friendly as they come, and it's really all about the music. DJs rotate daily, but Tuesday is always BoyBox night. Check out the website to find out who's spinning while you're in town. For heavy drinking and dancing with no cover, you can't beat G – although you may have to wait in line to get in. Dress at G Lounge is refreshingly casual. Cash only.

Chelsea Brewing Company   Pub
Map p134 (📞212-336-6440; West Side Hwy at W 23rd St, Chelsea Piers, Pier 59; ⏱noon-midnight; 🚇C/E to 23rd St) Enjoy a quality microbrew, waterside, in the expansive outdoor area of this way-west beer haven. It's a perfect place to re-enter the world after a day of swimming, golfing or rock climbing as a guest at the Chelsea Piers Complex.

Barracuda   Gay
Map p134 (📞212-645-8613; 275 W 22nd St at Seventh Ave; 🚇C/E to 23rd St) This longtime favorite holds its own even as newer, slicker places come and go. That's because it's got a simple, winning formula: affordable

White Horse Tavern (p141)

cocktails, a cozy rec-room vibe and free entertainment from some of the city's top drag queens.

Peter McManus Tavern
Bar

Map p134 (☎212-929-9691; 152 Seventh Ave at 19th St; ⏱10am-4pm Mon-Sat, noon-4pm Sun; **S**A/C/E to 14th St) Pouring drafts since the 1930s, this family-run dive is something of a museum to the world of the McManuses: photos of yesteryear, an old telephone booth and Tiffany glass. There's also greasy bar food to eat at the cute green booths. Hurrah for the McManus!

Rawhide
Gay

Map p134 (☎212-242-9332; 212 Eighth Ave btwn 20th & 21st Sts; **S**A/C/E, 1/2 to 23rd St, 1/2 to 18th St) Brand your behind with a rainbow flag and jump into Rawhide, one of the last reminders of Chelsea's grittier days. Beefy bartenders serve a mixed bag of queens, though it traditionally attracts a leather crowd.

Home
Club

Map p134 (☎212-273-3700; 532 W 27th St near Tenth Ave; cover charge $20; ⏱10pm-4am Tue-Sun; **S**C/E to 23rd St; 1 to 28th St) Most homes aren't multilevel, cavernous spaces with dark leather couches lining the walls and eerily lit passageways taking you from nook to nook, but maybe that's a growing trend. Either way, there's lots to make you feel comfortable at Home – ample seating and space, and deep electronic, funk and pop coming from the live DJ.

Entertainment

Village Vanguard
Jazz

Map p130 (☎212-255-4037; www.villagevan guard.com; 178 Seventh Ave at 11th St; **S**1/2/3 to 14th St) Possibly the city's most prestig-ious jazz club, the Vanguard has hosted literally every major star of the past 50 years. It started as a home to spoken-word performances and occasionally returns to its roots, but most of the time it's just smooth, sweet jazz all night long.

Upright Citizens Brigade Theatre
Comedy

Map p134 (☎212-366-9176; www.ucbtheatre. com; 307 W 26th St btwn Eighth & Ninth Aves; cover charge $5-8; **S**C/E to 23rd St) Pros of comedy sketches and outrageous improvisations reign at this popular 74-seat venue, which gets drop-ins from casting directors. Getting in is cheap, and so is the beer (from $2 a can). You may recognize pranksters on stage from late-night comedy shows. It's free Wednesdays after 11pm, when newbies take the reins.

Blue Note
Jazz

Map p130 (☎212-475-8592; www.bluenote. net; 131 W 3rd St btwn Sixth Ave & MacDougal St; **S**A/C/E, B/D/F/V to W 4th St-Washington Sq) This is by far the most famous (and expensive) of the city's jazz clubs. Most shows are $20 at the bar, $35 at a table, but can rise for the biggest jazz stars, and a few outside the normal jazz act (um, Doobie Brothers' Michael McDonald, any-one?). Go on an off night, and be quiet – all attention is on the stage!

Le Poisson Rouge
Live Music

Map p130 (☎212-505-3474; www.lepoisson rouge.com; 158 Bleecker St; **S**A/C/E, B/D/F/V to W 4th St-Washington Sq) This newish high-concept art space (complete with dangling fish aquarium) hosts a highly eclectic lineup, with the likes of Deer-hunter, Marc Ribot, Lou Reed and Laurie Anderson performing in past years. Aside from the main (high-tech) concert space, there's also an art gallery and a bar-cafe open during the day.

Smalls Jazz Club
Jazz

Map p130 (☎212-283-9728; www.smallsjazzclub. com; 183 W 10th St at Seventh Ave; cover charge $20; **S**1 to Christopher St-Sheridan Sq) Living up to its name, this cramped but appeal-ing basement jazz den offers a grab-bag collection of jazz acts who take the stage nightly. Cover for the evening is $20 (including a free drink Sunday through Thursday), with a come-and-go policy if you need to duck out for a slice.

Angelika Film Center
Cinema

Map p130 (212-995-2000; www.angelika
filmcenter.com; 18 W Houston St at Mercer St;
tickets $10-14; [ ]; S B/D/F/V to Broadway-
Lafayette St) Angelika specializes in
foreign and independent films and has
some quirky charms (the rumble of
the subway, long lines and occasionally bad sound). But its roomy cafe is a
great place to meet and the beauty of
its Stanford White–designed, beaux arts
building is undeniable.

Atlantic Theater Company
Theater

Map p134 (212-691-5919; www.atlantictheater.
org; 336 W 20th St btwn Eighth & Ninth Aves;
10am-6pm Mon-Fri, 8pm-10pm Tue-Sat, 2pm-
4pm Sat, 3pm-5pm & 7pm-9pm Sun; S A/C/E
to 23rd St, A/C/E to 14th St, 1/2 to 18th St)
Founded by David Mamet and William H
Macy in 1985, the Atlantic Theater is a
pivotal anchor for the off-Broadway community, hosting many Tony Award and
Drama Desk winners over the last 25-plus
years.

Barrow Street Theater
Theater

Map p130 (212-243-6262; www.barrow
streettheatre.com; 27 Barrow St, btwn Seventh
Ave & W 4th St; S 1/2 to Christopher St-Sheridan
Sq; A/C/E, B/D/F, M to W 4th St; 1/2 to Houston
St) A fantastic off-Broadway space in the
heart of the West Village showcasing a
variety of local and international theater.

Duplex
Cabaret, Karaoke

Map p130 (212-255-5438; www.theduplex.
com; 61 Christopher St; cover charge $10-20;
4pm-4am; S 1 to Christopher St-Sheridan
Sq) Cabaret, karaoke and campy dance
moves are par for the course at the
legendary Duplex. Pictures of Joan Rivers
line the walls, and the performers like to
mimic her sassy form of self-deprecation,
while getting in a few jokes about audience members as well.

Kitchen
Dance

Map p134 (212-255-5793; www.thekitchen.
org; 512 W 19th St btwn Tenth & Eleventh Aves;
S A/C/E to 14th St, L to 8th Ave) A loft-like
experimental space in west Chelsea that
also produces edgy theater, readings and

music performances, Kitchen is where
you'll find new, progressive pieces and
works-in-progress from local movers and
shakers.

Joyce Theater
Arts

Map p134 (212-242-0800; www.joyce.org;
175 Eighth Ave; hours vary; S C/E to 23rd
St; A/C/E to 8th Ave-14th St; 1 to 18th St) A
favorite among dance junkies because
of its excellent sight lines and offbeat offerings, this is an intimate venue, seating
470 in a renovated cinema. Its focus is
on traditional modern companies such
as Pilobolus and Parsons Dance, which
make annual apperances.

🅖 Shopping

Greenwich Village & the Meatpacking District

Strand Book Store
Books

Map p130 (212-473-1452; www.strandbooks.
com; 828 Broadway at 12th St; 9:30am-
10:30pm Mon-Sat, 11am-10:30pm Sun; S L,
N/Q/R/W, 4/5/6 to 14th St-Union Sq) Book
fiends (or even those who have casually
skimmed one or two) shouldn't miss New
York's most loved and famous bookstore.
In operation since 1927, the Strand sells
new, used and rare titles, spreading an
incredible 18 miles of books (over 2.5
million of them) among three labyrinthine
floors. Check out the staggering number
of reviewers' copies in the basement, or
sell off your own tomes before you get
back on the plane, as the Strand buys
or trades books at a side counter on
weekdays.

Murray's Cheese
Food & Drink

Map p130 (212-243-3289; www.murray
scheese.com; 254 Bleecker St btwn Sixth &
Seventh Aves; 8am-8pm Mon-Sat, 10am-
7pm Sun; S 1 to Christopher St-Sheridan Sq)
Founded in 1914, this is probably New
York's best cheese shop. Owner Rob
Kaufelt is known for his talent of sniffing
out devastatingly delicious varieties from
around the world. You'll find (and be
able to taste) all manner of *fromage*, be

it stinky, sweet or nutty, from European nations and from small farms in Vermont and upstate New York. There's also prosciutto and smoked meats, freshly baked breads, olives, antipasto, chocolate and all manner of goodies for a gourmet picnic – plus a counter for freshly made sandwiches and melts.

Marc by Marc Jacobs   Fashion
Map p130 (☎212-924-0026; www.marcjacobs. com; 403-405 Bleecker St; ⊙noon-8pm Mon-Sat, to 7pm Sun; Ⓢ A/C/E to 14th St, L to 8th Ave) With five small shops sprinkled around the West Village, Marc Jacobs has established a real presence in this well-heeled neighborhood. Here's the layout: on Bleecker St, you'll find the women's line at No 403-405, women's accessories (fun wallets, rubber boots and T-shirts) at No 385 and the children's line (Little Marc) at No 382. Men should head one block over, where they'll find the men's collection at 301 W 4th St and men's accessories at 208 W 4th. For men's and women's apparel from the Marc Jacobs Collection (the priciest stuff of all), head to the SoHo **Marc Jacobs** (Map p82; ☎212-343-1490; 163 Mercer St; ⊙11am-7pm Mon-Sat, noon-6pm Sun,

Ⓢ B/D/F/V to Broadway-Lafayette St; R/W to Prince St).

Barneys
Co-op   Fashion, Accessories
Map p134 (☎212-593-7800; 236 W 18th St; ⊙11am-8pm Mon-Fri, to 7pm Sat, noon-6pm Sun; Ⓢ 1 to 18th St) The edgier, younger, less expensive version of Barneys has (relatively) affordable deals. At this expansive, loftlike space, with a spare, very selective inventory of clothing for men and women, plus shoes and cosmetics, the biannual warehouse sale (February and August) packs the place, with both endless merchandise and mobs of customers.

Antiques Garage
Flea Market   Antiques
Map p134 (☎212-243-5343; 112 W 25th St at Sixth Ave; ⊙9am-5pm Sat & Sun; Ⓢ 1 to 23rd St) This weekend flea market is set in a two-level parking garage, with more than 100 vendors spreading their wares. Antique-lovers shouldn't miss a browse here, as you'll find clothing, shoes, records, books, globes, furniture, rugs, lamps, glassware, paintings, artwork and many other relics from the past

Strand Book Store

Forbidden Planet
Comics

Map p130 (📞212-473-1576; 840 Broadway; 🕐10am-10pm Mon-Sat, 11am-8pm Sun; Ⓢ L, N/Q/R/W, 4/5/6 to 14th St-Union Sq) Indulge your inner sci-fi nerd. Find heaps of comics, books, manga, video games and figurines (ranging from *Star Trek* to *Where the Wild Things Are*). Fellow Magic and Yu-Gi-Oh! card-game lovers play upstairs in the public sitting area.

Stella McCartney
Fashion

Map p130 (📞212-255-1556; www.stellamccartney.com; 429 W 14th St; 🕐11am-8pm Tue-Sat, noon-6pm Sun; Ⓢ A/C/E, L to 8th Ave-14th St) More showroom than full-fledged store, McCartney's Meatpacking outpost has a minimal selection on hand, but, oh, what a selection it is. Drapy, gauzy, muted in color yet high on femininity, the delicate, ethereal clothes shine in this pared-down setting. Of course, McCartney's clothes are animal-product free, in keeping with her vegan philosophy.

Alexander McQueen
Fashion, Accessories

Map p130 (📞212-645-1797; www.alexandermcqueen.com; 417 W 14th St; 🕐11am-7pm Mon-Sat, noon-6pm Sun; Ⓢ A/C/E, L, 1/2/3 to 8th Ave-14th St) McQueen's rambunctious outfits are shown to perfection in his massive MPD store, and his edgy creations seem made to be worn in this fashion-forward district.

Chelsea

Housing Works Thrift Shop
Fashion, Bric-a-Brac

Map p134 (📞212-366-0820; 143 W 17th St; 🕐10am-6pm Mon-Sat, noon-5pm Sun; Ⓢ 1 to 18th St) This shop, with its swank window displays, looks more boutique than thrift, but its selections of clothes, accessories, furniture and books are great value. All proceeds benefit the charity serving the city's HIV-positive and AIDS homeless communities. There are 10 other branches around town.

Balenciaga
Fashion, Accessories

Map p134 (📞212-206-0872; 522 W 22nd St at Eleventh Ave; 🕐10am-7pm Mon-Sat, noon-5pm Sun; Ⓢ C/E to 23rd St) Come and gaze at this cool, gray, Zen-like space. It's the gallery district's showcase, appropriately enough, for the artistic, post-apocalypse, avant-garde styles of this French fashion house. Expect strange lines, goth patterns and pants for very skinny (and deep-pocketed) gals.

192 Books
Books

Map p134 (📞212-255-4022; www.192books.com; 192 Tenth Ave btwn 21st & 22nd Sts; 🕐11am-7pm Tue-Sat, noon-6pm Sun & Mon; Ⓢ C/E to 23rd St) Located right in the gallery district is this small indie bookstore, with sections on literature, history, travel, art and criticism. A special treat

Alexander McQueen
ALEX SEGRE/ALAMY ©

is its offerings of rotating art exhibits, during which the owners organize special displays of books that relate thematically to the featured show or artist.

Sports & Activities

Chelsea Piers Complex
Sports

Map p134 (☎212-336-6000; www.chelseapiers. com; Hudson River at end of W 23rd St; S C/E to 23rd St) This massive waterfront sports center caters to the athlete in everyone. You can set out to hit a bucket of golf balls at the four-level driving range, ice skate on the complex's indoor rink or rent in-line skates to cruise along the new bike path on the Hudson River Park – all the way down to Battery Park. The complex has a jazzy bowling alley, Hoop City for basketball, a sailing school for kids, batting cages, a huge gym facility with an indoor pool (day passes for nonmembers are $50), indoor rock-climbing walls – the works. There's even waterfront dining and drinking at the Chelsea Brewing Company, which serves great pub fare and delicious home brews for you to carb-load on after your workout.

Bowlmor Lanes
Bowling

Map p130 (☎212-255-8188; www.bowlmor.com; 110 University Pl; individual games from $10, shoe rental $6; ⊙4pm-1am Mon-Thu, 11am-3:30am Fri & Sat, 11am-midnight Sun; S L, N/Q/R/W, 4/5/6 to 14th St-Union Sq) Open since 1938, Bowlmor has Manhattan's go-to-lanes for stars, bar mitzvah parties and beer-slug-

ging NYU students. After 9pm Monday, it goes DJ-blasting glow-in-the-dark, with unlimited bowling for $24 including shoe rental (age 21 and up).

New York Trapeze School
Sports

Map p130 (www.newyork.trapezeschool.com; Pier 40 at West Side Hwy; classes $47-65, 5-week course $270; S 1 to Houston St) Fulfill your circus dreams, like Carrie did on *Sex and the City*, flying trapeze to trapeze in this open-air tent by the river. It's open from May to September, on top of Pier 40. The school also has an **indoor facility** (Map p188; 518 W 30th St btwn Tenth & Eleventh Aves; S A/C/E to 34th St-Penn Station) open year-round. Call or check the website for daily class times. There's a one-time $22 registration fee.

Downtown Boathouse
Kayaking

Map p130 (☎646-613-0740; www.downtown boathouse.org; Pier 40, near Houston St; tours free; ⊙9am-6pm Sat & Sun mid-May–mid-Oct, some weekday evenings mid-Jun–mid-Sep; S 1 to Houston St) New York's most active public boathouse offers free walk-up 20-minute kayaking (including equipment) in the protected embayment in the Hudson River on weekends and some weekday evenings. Longer rides (eg to Governors Island) usually go from the Midtown location at **Clinton Cove** (Pier 96, W 56th St; ⊙9am-6pm Sat & Sun, 5-7pm Mon-Fri mid-Jun-Aug; S A/C, B/D, 1 to 59th St-Columbus Circle); there's another boathouse at **Riverside Park** (Map p231; W 72nd St; ⊙10am-5pm Sat & Sun; S 1/2/3 to 72nd St) on the Upper West Side.

Union Square, Flatiron District & Gramercy

This trio of neighborhoods boasts lovely architecture and diverse public spaces. Although Union Sq earned its moniker from rather practical and prosaic roots, it is much more than the junction of two roads. In many ways the neighborhood is the union of disparate parts of the city, acting as veritable urban glue linking unlikely cousins. Shops and eateries surround the park, whose interior hops with activity.

To the northwest is the Flatiron District, loaded with loft buildings and boutiques, and doing a good imitation of SoHo without the pretensions, prices or crowds. The neighborhood takes its name from the Flatiron Building – a thin, gorgeous work of architecture that sits just south of Madison Square Park. The Gramercy area, loosely comprising the 20s blocks east of Park Ave South, is named after one of New York's loveliest parks and is primarily a residential area.

Union Square, Flatiron District & Gramercy Highlights

Flatiron Building (p156)

At the intersection of Broadway, Fifth Ave and 23rd St, the famous (and absolutely gorgeous) 1902 Flatiron Building has a distinctive triangular shape to match its site. It was New York's first iron-frame high-rise, and the world's tallest building until 1909. The surrounding district is a fashionable area of boutiques and loft apartments.

Good Eats (p157)

This area is on the discerning diner's map for two widely respected restaurants, Gramercy Tavern and Craft, both of which bear the stamp of celebrity chef Tom Colicchio. The Union Square Greenmarket, the largest of the nearly 50 greenmarkets throughout the five boroughs, is ideal for preparing a picnic. And Union Sq and Flatiron have designated parking spaces for some of the best food trucks and carts in town. Craft (p158)

WENDY CONNETT/ALAMY ©

Classic Bars (p161)

3

For a memorable, turn-of-the-century vibe, you can't do better than to pull up a stool or grab a hard bench at Pete's Tavern or the Old Town Bar & Restaurant. These neighborhood watering holes, open since 1864 and 1892 respectively, will have you feeling wistful for a time gone by. Both also serve food, including good burgers.

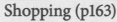

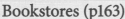

Bookstores (p163)

4

Bibliophiles beware of stimulation overload. Armchair travelers can browse their way around the world at Idlewild Books, and kids can let their imaginations wander during story time at Books of Wonder. And of course there's the flagship Barnes & Noble at the northern end of the park, a virtual living room for the neighborhood's residents. Barnes & Noble, Union Square

Shopping (p163)

5

Huge chain stores flank Union Sq park to the north and south. Fourteenth St, more to the west than to the east, has store upon store hawking discount electronics, cheap linens and a great range of shoes and clothing, from bargain indies as well as chains like Urban Outfitters and Diesel. You'll find more upmarket chain stores heading up Fifth Ave, with Paul Smith, BCBG, Anthropologie, Zara and Intermix among others. ABC Carpet & Home (p163)

151

Union Square & Gramercy Walk

*There's not a lot of ground to cover – Madison Square Park and Union Sq are your
anchors. You'll feel the Village vibe spilling over with quirky cafes, crowded lunch
spots, after-work watering holes, funky storefronts and dreadlocked buskers.*

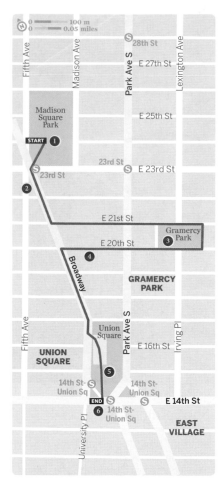

➊ Madison Square Park

Start off in **Madison Square Park** (p156);
this peaceful green space is dotted with
19th-century statues of folks including
Senator Roscoe Conkling (who froze to
death in a brutal 1888 blizzard) and Civil
War admiral David Farragut. Between 1876
and 1882 the torch-bearing arm of the
Statue of Liberty was on display here, and in
1879 the first Madison Square Garden arena
was constructed at Madison Ave and 26th
St. If you'd like to eat before the walk, hit up
Shake Shack (p156) for a gourmet burger
and fries.

➋ Flatiron Building

Take in lovely views of the beaux arts
triangular masterpiece, the **Flatiron
Building** (p156), before exiting the park at
its southwest corner. Cross the street to
stand up close and admire the city's oddest
skyscraper from a whole new angle at Fifth
Ave and Broadway. The building's construction (originally known as the Fuller Building)
coincided with the proliferation of mass-
produced picture postcards – the partner-
ship was kismet. Even before its completion,
there were images of the soon-to-be tallest
tower circulating the globe, creating much
wonder and excitement.

➌ Gramercy Park

Follow Broadway south to 21st St and take
a left. Past Park Ave S you'll find yourself
alongside **Gramercy Park**, which was
created by Samuel Ruggles in 1831 after
he drained the swamp in this area and laid
out streets in an English style. You can't
enter the park, as it's private, but go ahead
and peer through the gate. Just across the
street from the southwestern corner of the

WALK FACTS

- **Start** Madison Square Park
- **Finish** DSW
- **Distance** 2 miles
- **Duration** Two hours

park is the **National Arts Club**. Calvert Vaux, who was one of the creators of Central Park, designed the building, originally the private residence of Samuel J Tilden, governor of New York and failed presidential candidate in 1876.

4 Theodore Roosevelt's Birthplace

Head back west along 20th St, stopping at the reconstructed version of **Theodore Roosevelt's birthplace**, run by the National Parks Service; hourly tours offered.

5 Union Square

Once back on Broadway continue south and you'll soon find yourself at the northwest corner of **Union Square** (p154). Check out the produce, cheese, baked goods and flowers of the Greenmarket farmers market or amuse yourself by watching the skateboarders, visiting the Gandhi statue near the southwest corner, or grabbing some food at one of the surrounding eateries for a picnic in the park.

6 DSW

Standing like a beacon of retail on Union Sq South (14th St) is the massive warehouse, **DSW**, dedicated to heavily discounted designer shoes and accessories. Shop if you wish, but the real attraction is the store's massive, north-facing window, which lets you look down over the park and across to the top of the Empire State Building from a 4th-floor perch.

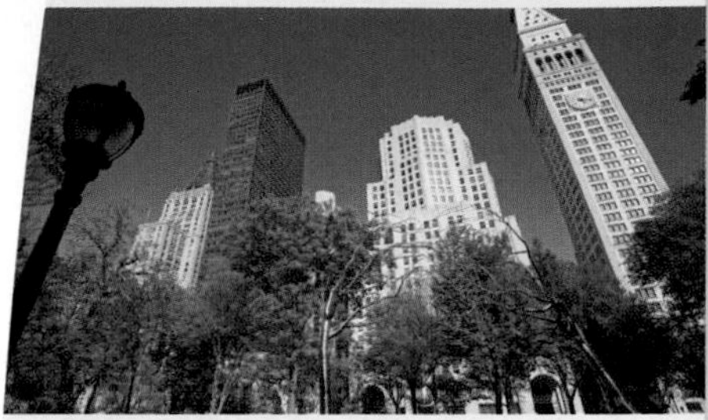

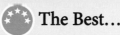

The Best...

PLACES TO EAT

Craft Copycats sprang up around town, but this spot still reigns – and still feels fresh – as ingredients change seasonally. (p158)

Pure Food & Wine For fresh, creative and alarmingly delicious vegetarian cuisine. (p160)

Eataly The Macy's of food courts with a handful of specialty dining halls, all with a different focus. (p163)

PLACES TO DRINK

Raines Law Room Walk through the unassuming entrance and let Raines Law Room transport you to a far more sumptuous era. (p161)

Old Town Bar & Restaurant The classic, preserved decor here offers a turn-of-the-century vibe. (p161)

Crocodile Lounge Williamsburg comes to Manhattan! (p162)

PLACES FOR VIEWS

Birreria Amazing roof deck. (p159)

Madison Square Park The south side offers a full-frontal of the Flatiron Building. (p156)

Madison Square Park (p156)

Don't Miss
Union Square

Union Sq is like the Noah's Ark of New York, rescuing at least two of every kind from the curling seas of concrete. In fact, one would be hard-pressed to find a more eclectic cross-section of locals gathered in one public place. Here, amid the tapestry of stone steps and fenced-in foliage, it's not uncommon to find denizens of every ilk: suited business-folk gulping fresh air during their lunch breaks; dreadlocked loiterers tapping beats on their tabla; skateboarding punks flipping tricks on the southeastern stairs; rowdy college kids guzzling student-priced eats; and throngs of protesting masses chanting fervently for various causes.

Map p158

www.union
squarenyc.org

17th St btwn
Broadway &
Park Ave S

S L, N/Q/R/W,
4/5/6 to 14th St-
Union Sq

Riches & Rags

Opened in 1831, Union Sq quickly became the central gathering place for those who lived in the mansions nearby. Concert halls and artist societies further enhanced the cultured atmosphere, and high-end shopping quickly proliferated along Broadway, which was dubbed 'Ladies' Mile.'

When the Civil War broke out, the vast public space was center stage for protestors of all sorts – from union workers to political activists. By the height of the WWI, the area had fallen largely into disuse, allowing politically and socially driven organizations like the American Civil Liberties Union, the Communist and Socialist Parties and the Ladies' Garment Workers Union to move in. The square is still the site for political and social protests today.

Public Art

A walk around Union Sq will reveal almost a dozen notable pieces of art – there's Rob Pruitt's 10ft homage to Andy Warhol (erected on the exact spot where he was shot by Valerie Solanas), and the imposing equestrian statue of George Washington. On the south side of the square sits a massive art installation meant to be a symbolic representation of the passage of time. The winking orange digits of *Metronome's* digital clock denote the following: the 14 numbers are split into two groups of seven – the seven from the left tell the current time (hour, minute, second, tenth-of-a-second) and the seven from the right, read in reverse order, show the remaining time in the day.

Greenmarket

The Union Square Greenmarket (pictured), a sprawling sensory delight held Monday, Wednesday, Friday and Saturday, is arguably the most famous of the city's farmers markets, and attracts many of the city's top chefs to its stalls to finger aromatic greens, fresh yellow corn and deep orange squashes.

Don't Miss List

BY MICHAEL HURWITZ,
GREENMARKET DIRECTOR AT
GROW NYC

1 SEASONAL SPECIALITIES

You know it's spring when you see ramps and signs advertising 'wintered-over greens.' This basically means plants spend winter months in the ground, but the flavors are so sweet and crisp, not bitter; my favorite is broccoli rabe. A few other specialties are foraged fiddlehead ferns and garlic scapes – the edible flower stalks of hardneck garlic plants.

2 VARIETIES

There are more than 600 varieties of greens and 100 varieties of apples alone from upstate New York, which represents nearly 28,000 acres of farmland.

3 SUNDAYS

Sundays are the most popular day, and we average a couple hundred thousand visitors. On Mondays there are the fewest number of vendors – around 65 to 70 – but on Sundays there is the most variety with more than 100 vendors. On Fridays, look out for the Tundra Brewery stand – it's the first 100% locally produced beer. All of its barley and hops come from a family farm in Stamford, NY.

4 LOCAVORE LESSONS

Some of the city's best chefs from the most critically acclaimed restaurants get their produce from here. There are tastings every day, guest chefs give cooking demonstrations, and there are regular speakers, book signings and classes. Not to mention, you can talk to the farmers and ask for recipes and recommended ways of preparing food.

5 OTHER MARKETS

The Wednesday market at Dag Hammarskjold Plaza near the UN is another favorite; there are great producers and the park is pretty. On Thursdays and Saturdays, check out the market in Tucker Square across from Lincoln Plaza and look for quince, a pear-like fruit, and heirloom varieties of apples.

Discover Union Square, Flatiron District & Gramercy

Getting There & Away

- **Subway** A slew of subway lines converge below Union Square shuttling passengers up Manhattan's East Side on the 4, 5 and 6 lines straight across to Williamsburg on the L or up and over to Queens on the N, Q and R lines. The L also travels across to the West Side, although when there's no traffic it costs about the same to take a cab (if you're two or more people).

- **Bus** Easy to remember, the M14 and the M23 provide crosstown service along 14th St and 23rd St respectively. Go for the bus over the subway if you're traveling between two eastern points in Manhattan – it's not worth traveling over to Union Sq to walk back to First Ave.

◉ Sights

Union Square   Square
See p154.

Flatiron Building   Landmark
Map p158 (Broadway cnr Fifth Ave & 23rd St; S N/R, 6 to 23rd St) Built in 1902, the 20-story Flatiron Building, designed by Daniel Burnham, has a uniquely narrow triangular footprint that resembles the prow of a massive ship, and a traditional beaux arts limestone facade, built over a steel frame, that gets more complex and beautiful the longer you stare at it. Best viewed from the traffic island north of 23rd St between Broadway and Fifth Ave, this unique structure dominated the plaza back in the skyscraper era of the early 1900s. In fact, until 1909 it was the world's tallest building. Like many of New York City's monumental homages to civic progress, the Flatiron building is still fully functional and houses an assortment of private businesses. The famed structure is therefore best appreciated from the exterior. Plans are underway to transform the building into a luxurious five-star hotel, but progress is on permanent hold until the final tenants willingly vacate the premises.

Madison Square Park   Park
Map p158 (www.nycgovparks.org; 23rd to 26th Sts btwn Fifth & Madison Aves; ☺6am-1am; S N/R, 6 to 23rd St) This park defined the northern reaches of Manhattan until the island's population exploded after the Civil War. It has enjoyed a rejuvenation in the past few years thanks to a renovation and re-dedication project, and now locals

Union Square (p154)

unleash their dogs here in the popular dog-run area, as workers enjoy lunches – which can be bought from the hip, on-site **Shake Shack** (212-989-6600; www.shakeshack.com; cnr 23rd St & Madison Ave; hamburgers from $3.50; ☺lunch & dinner; **S** R/W to 23rd St) – while perched on the shaded benches or sprawled on the wide lawn. These are perfect spots from which to gaze up at the landmarks that surround the park, including the Flatiron Building (p156) to the southwest, the art deco **Metropolitan Life Insurance Tower** to the southeast and the **New York Life Insurance Building**, topped with a gilded spire, to the northeast. In warm months, various park programs feature readings and music performances, many for kids, while eclectic sculptures are shown year-round. And, at the southeast corner of the park, you'll find one of the city's few self-cleaning, coin-operated toilets, which lets you do your business for only 25¢.

Theodore Roosevelt's Birthplace
Historic Site

Map p158 (☎212-260-1616; www.nps.gov/thrb; 28 E 20th St btwn Park Ave S & Broadway; adult/child $3/free; ☺9am-5pm Tue-Sat; **S** N/R/W, 6 to 23rd St) This National Historic Site is a bit of a cheat, since the physical house where the 26th president was actually born was demolished in his own lifetime. But this building is a worthy reconstruction by his relatives, who joined it with another family residence next door. If you're interested in Roosevelt's extraordinary life, which has been somewhat overshadowed by the enduring legacy of his younger cousin Franklin D, visit here – especially if you don't have the time to see his spectacular summer home in Long Island's Oyster Bay. Included in the admission price are half-hour house tours, offered on the hour from 10am to 4pm.

Tibet House
Cultural Center

Map p158 (☎212-807-0563; www.tibethouse.org; 22 W 15th St btwn Fifth & Sixth Aves; suggested donation $5; ☺noon-5pm Mon-Fri; **S** F to 14th St, L to 6th Ave) With the Dalai Lama as the patron of its board, this nonprofit cultural

space is dedicated to presenting Tibet's ancient traditions through art exhibits, a research library and various publications, while programs on offer include educational workshops, open meditations, retreat weekends and docent-led tours to Tibet, Nepal and Bhutan.

National Arts Club
Cultural Center

Map p158 (☎212-475-3424; www.nationalartsclub.org; 15 Gramercy Park S; **S** 6 to 23rd St) This club, founded in 1898 to promote public interest in the arts, boasts a beautiful, vaulted, stained-glass ceiling above the wooden bar in its picture-lined front parlor. The club holds art exhibitions, ranging from sculpture to photography, that are sometimes open to the public from 1pm to 5pm (check the website for schedules).

🍴 Eating

ABC Kitchen
Modern American **$$**

Map p158 (☎212-475-5829; www.abckitchennyc.com; 35 E 18th St btwn Broadway & Park Ave; small plates $9-15; ☺Sun-Thu 5:30pm-10pm, to 11:30pm Fri & Sat, last reservations half-hour prior; **S** L, N/Q/R, 4/5/6 to Union Sq) A culinary avatar of the wildly wonderful home goods department store, ABC Kitchen's trim, cottage-like surrounds is neatly tucked behind the ballroom chandeliers and oriental drapery out front. Plates are as eclectic as the fairy-tale decor – though you'll never go wrong with an organic app and one of the scrumptious whole-wheat pizzas.

Eleven Madison Park
French **$$$**

Map p158 (☎212-889-0905; www.elevenmadisonpark.com; 11 Madison Ave btwn 24th & 25th Sts; 4-course dinner $125; ☺lunch & dinner; **S** N/R, 6 to 23rd St) An art deco wonder often overlooked in this star-studded town, Eleven Madison Park is welcoming enough to bring children into fine dining, and delicious enough to please even the most discerning diner. Dishes include muscovy duck with honey sauce, wild salmon with horseradish crust and fennel risotto, halibut *mi-cuit* (half-cooked) with carrots, and seasonal surprises.

Union Square, Flatiron District & Gramercy

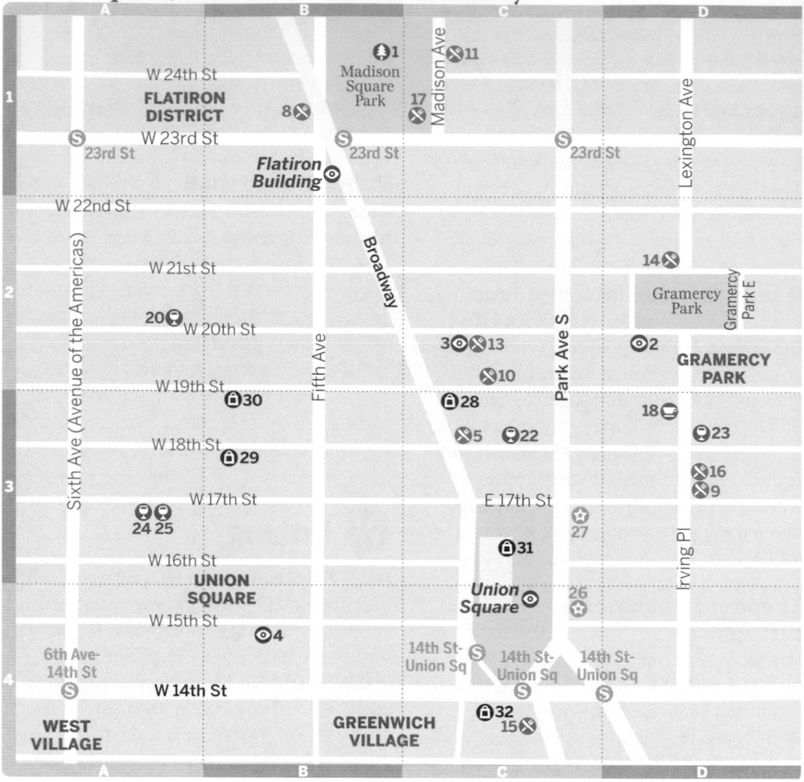

Gramercy Tavern American **$$$**

Map p158 (☎212-477-0777; www.gramercytavern.com; 42 E 20th St btwn Broadway & Park Ave S; tasting menu lunch/dinner $58/116; 🕒lunch & dinner; [S]6 to 23rd St) This country-chic restaurant, aglow with copper sconces, bright murals and dramatic floral arrangements, is still in the spotlight – perhaps now more than ever. That's thanks to the lighter fish-and-vegetable menu that has replaced what was meat-heavy and hearty. Smoked lobster, Spanish mackerel, blackfish and tuna-and-beet tartare are packed with punches, as are the heavenly desserts and excellent wine options.

Casa Mono Tapas **$$**

Map p158 (☎212-253-2773; www.casamononyc.com; 52 Irving Pl btwn 17th & 18th Sts; small plates $9-20; 🕒noon-midnight; [S]4/5/6, N/R/Q, L to Union Sq) Another winner from Mario Batali and Chef Andy Nusser, Casa Mono has a great, long bar where you can sit and watch your *pez espada a la plancha* and *gambas al ajillo* take a grilling. Or grab one of the wooded tables and nosh on tapas with *jerez* (sherry) from the bottles lining the walls. For a cheese dessert, hop next door to Bar Jamon, also owned by Batali; you may have to squeeze in – the place is communal and fun.

Craft American **$$$**

Map p158 (☎212-780-0880; www.craftrestaurantsinc.com/craft-new-york; 43 E 19th btwn Park Ave S & Broadway; mains $18-50; 🕒dinner; [S]L, N/Q/R/W, 4/5/6 to 14th St-Union Sq) When super chef Tom Colicchio opened this fine-food palace in a sweeping architectural

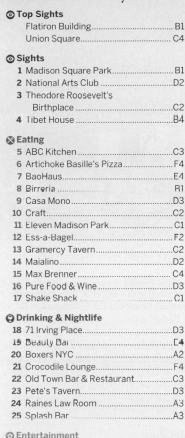

space several years ago, the concept was completely new: create your own meal with à la carte items, and enjoy the feeling that not a plate on your table was cookie cutter. Menu items can be found under their appropriate subject headings – fish, 'farm egg,' meat, vegetables, salad – and it's up to you to make the matches (or ask for some expert direction).

Birreria   American $$
Map p158 (www.eatalyny.com; 200 Fifth Ave at 23rd St; mains $15-24; ⏰11:30am-midnight Sun-Wed, to 1am Thu-Sat ; Ⓢ F, N/R, 6 to 23rd St) The crown jewel of Italian gourmet market Eataly is its rooftop beer garden tucked betwixt the Flatiron's corporate towers. A beer menu of encyclopedic proportions offers drinkers some of the best brews on the planet (watch out though – some bottles cost more than a main!).

Oh, and if you can find the hidden access elevator without asking an Eataly employee then congrats – you have better hunting skills than a foxhound.

DENNIS JOHNSON/LONELY PLANET IMAGES ©

Ess-a-Bagel
Deli $

Map p158 (212-260-2252; www.ess-a-bagel. com; 359 First Ave at 21st St; bagels from $1; 6am-9pm Mon-Fri, to 5pm Sat & Sun; S L, N/Q/R, 4/5/6 to Union Sq) It's simply impossible to resist the billowy tufts of sesame-scented smoke that waft out onto First Ave. Inside, crowds of lip-smacked locals yell at the bagel mongers for their classic New York snack topped with generous gobs of cream cheese.

Maialino
Italian $$

Map p158 (212-777-2410; www.maialinonyc. com; 2 Lexington Ave at 21st St; mains $15-36; breakfast, lunch & dinner; S 4/5, N/R to 23rd St) Danny Meyer's done it again – take your taste buds on a Roman holiday and sample exquisite iterations of Italian peasant fare created from the green-market produce from down the street in Union Sq. You can come for a fresh cup of breakfast brew, but the lunchtime prix fixe (at a reasonable $35) should not be passed up.

Pure Food & Wine
Vegetarian $$$

Map p158 (212-477-1010; www.oneluckyduck. com/purefoodandwine; 54 Irving Pl btwn 17th & 18th Sts; mains $19-26; dinner; S L,

N/Q/R/W, 4/5/6 to 14th St-Union Sq) The 'chef' (there's no oven in the kitchen) at this gem achieves the impossible: churning out not just edible but also extremely delicious and artful concoctions, made completely from raw organics that are put through blenders, dehydrators and the capable hands of Pure's staff. The dining room is sleek and festive, but in warmer months don't miss a chance to settle into a table in the shady oasis of a backyard.

BaoHaus
Taiwanese $

Map p158 (646-669-8889; www.baohausnyc. com; 238 E 14th St near Second Ave; bao from $3; 11am-midnight Sun-Thu, 11.30am-4am Fri & Sat; S L, N/Q/R, 4/5/6 to Union Sq) Blink and you'll miss this hole-in-the-wall and bastion of food-related pun-dom. Three-bite bao (Taiwanese pocket sandwiches) are whipped up in seconds by the sociable staffers.

Artichoke Basille's Pizza
Pizza $

Map p158 (212-228-2004; www.artichokepizza. com; 328 E 14th St btwn First & Second Aves; slice from $4.50; lunch & dinner; S L, N/Q/R/W, 4/5/6 to 14th St-Union Sq) Run by two Italian guys from Staten Island, the pizza here is authentic, tangy and piled high with all sorts of toppings. The signature pie is a rich, cheesy treat with artichokes and spinach; the plain Sicilian is thinner, with emphasis solely on the crisp crust and savory sauce.

Max Brenner · Dessert $

Map p158 (Chocolate By the Bald Man ; 📞 212-388-0030; www.maxbrenner.com; 841 Broadway btwn 13th & 14th Sts; desserts from $7; 🕐 9am-midnight Mon-Thu, to 2am Fri & Sat, to 11pm Sun; S L, N/Q/R/W, 4/5/6 to 14th St-Union Sq) Sweet-toothed Aussie Max Brenner has brought his chocolate empire to Union Sq, and his wildly popular cafe-cum-chocolate-bar, looking from the outside like a gingerbread house, is all the rage. Besides the sweets he's got a full menu (great breakfast) and also does low-cal variations mixed by hand on the spot.

 Drinking & Nightlife

Old Town Bar & Restaurant · Bar

Map p158 (📞 212 529 6732; www.oldtownbar. com; 45 E 18th St btwn Broadway & Park Ave S; S L, N/Q/R/W, 4/5/6 to 14th St-Union Sq) It still looks like 1892 in here, with the original tile floors and tin ceilings – the Old Town is an 'old world' drinking-man's classic (and woman's: Madonna lit up at the bar here, when lighting up was still legal, in her 'Bad Girl' video). There are cocktails around, but most come for an afternoon beer and burger (around $10), both very good.

Pete's Tavern · Bar

Map p158 (📞 212-473-7676; www.petestavern. com; 129 E 18th St at Irving Pl; 🕐 noon-2am; S L, N/Q/R/W, 4/5/6 to 14th St-Union Sq) This dark and atmospheric watering hole has all the earmarks of a New York classic – pressed tin, carved wood and an air of literary history. You can get a respectable burger here, and choose from more than 15 draft beers. The pub draws in everyone from post-theater couples and Irish expats to no-nonsense NYU students.

Raines Law Room · Cocktail Bar

Map p158 (www.raineslawroom.com; 48 W 17th St btwn Fifth & Sixth Aves; S F, M to 14th St, L to 6th Ave, 1/2 to 18th St) A sea of velvet drapes and overstuffed leather lounge chairs, tin-tiled ceilings, the perfect amount of exposed brick, and expertly crafted cocktails using perfectly aged spirits – these guys are about as serious as a mortgage payment when it comes to amplified atmosphere.

Beauty Bar · Theme Bar

Map p158 (📞 212-539-1389; 531 E 11th St btwn Second & Third Aves; 🕐 5pm-4am Mon-Fri, 7pm-4am Sat-Sun; S L to 3rd Ave) A kitschy favorite since the mid-90s, this homage to old-fashioned beauty parlors pulls in a cool local crowd with its gritty soundtrack, nostalgic vibe and around US$10 manicures (with a free Blue Rinse margarita thrown in) from Wednesday to Sunday.

71 Irving Place · Cafe

Map p158 (Irving Farm Coffee Company; www. irvingfarm.com; 71 Irving Pl btwn 18th & 19th Sts; 🕐 7am-10pm Mon-Fri, 8am-10pm Sat & Sun; S 4/5/6, N/Q/R to 14th st-Union Sq, 4/6 to 23rd

Curry Hill

It's not exactly politically correct, but a small four-block section north of Union Sq and Gramercy, traditionally known as Murray Hill, is sometimes also referred to as Curry Hill – a nod to the numerous Indian restaurants, shops and delis that proliferate here. Starting around E 28th St and flowing north on Lexington Ave to about E 33rd St, you'll find some of the finest Indian eateries in town – and most at bargain prices. The all-time local fave? **Curry in a Hurry** (Map p178; 📞 212-683-0900; www.curryhurry.net; 119 Lexington Ave at E 28th St; 🕐 lunch & dinner; S 6 to 28th St). It's not fancy, but even Bono of U2 fame has been spotted having a nosh here.

St) No one takes their coffee more seriously than Irving Farm – a quaint cafe just steps away from the peaceful Gramercy Park. Hand-picked beans are lovingly roasted on a farm in the Hudson Valley (about 90 miles from NYC), and imbibers can tell – this is one of the smoothest cups of joe you'll find in Manhattan.

Crocodile Lounge — Lounge

Map p158 (☎212-477-7747; 325 E 14th St btwn First & Second Aves; [S] L to 1st Ave) The Brooklyn success story Alligator Lounge – 20-something hideout with free pizza – has set up a 14th St outpost hauling in East Villagers seeking free dinner, some Skee-Ball and a few unusual microbrews on tap.

Boxers NYC — Gay

Map p158 (☎212-255-5082; www.boxersnyc.com; 37 W 20th St, btwn Fifth & Sixth Aves; [S] F, N/R, 6 to 23rd St) Dave & Busters meets David Bowie at this self-proclaimed gay sports bar in the heart of the Flatiron District. There's football on the TV, buffalo wings at the bar, and topless wait staff keeping the pool cues polished. Monday's drag theme keeps everyone keenly aware that Boxers has a different definition of 'bromance'.

Splash Bar — Gay

Map p158 (☎212-691-0073; www.splashbar.com; 50 W 17th St btwn Fifth & Sixth Aves; 🕐5pm-4am Wed-Sat; [S] L to 6th Ave, F/V to 14th St) As megaclubs come and go, this staple (found near Chelsea's eastern border with the Flatiron District) has become hotter than ever. It's a multilevel club that balances both a lounge and dance-club vibe, thanks to a mix of hang-out spaces, an unrivaled lineup of DJs, great special events and performances, and some of the most smokin' bartenders around.

☆ Entertainment

Union Square Theater — Theater

Map p158 (☎212-674-2267; www.nytheater.com; 100 E 17th St at Union Sq; [S] L, N/Q/R/W, 4/5/6 to 14th St-Union Sq) The coolest thing about this theater is that it's built in what used to be Tammany Hall, seat of the most corrupt Democratic political machine that's ever ruled the city. Now the theater outrages the public in other ways, by hosting searing works like *The Laramie Project*, and the side-splittingly funny (and un-PC) puppet show *Stuffed and Unstrung* (not for children). Campy musicals also pop up sometimes.

Fuerza Bruta — Performing Arts

Map p158 (Daryl Roth Theatre, 101 E 15th St at Union Sq; tickets $79-89, rush tickets $27; 🕐shows Wed-Fri 8pm, Sat 7pm & 10pm, Sun 7pm; [S] L, N/Q/R/W, 4/5/6 to 14th St-Union Sq) Defying

Lavazza coffee bar, Eataly
RICHARD LEVINE/ALAMY ©

the laws of gravity and the theater-going experience in general, Fuerza Bruta is sensory overload on steroids as a visceral world of sound and fury is unleashed upon unwitting audience members. You've gotta see it to believe it.

Shopping

Union Square Greenmarket
Market

Map p158 (17th St btwn Broadway & Park Ave S; ◷10am-6pm Mon, Wed, Fri & Sat; Ⓢ L, N/Q/R/W, 4/5/6 to 14th St-Union Sq) The Union Square Greenmarket is arguably the most famous greenmarket in NYC.

ABC Carpet & Home
Homewares

Map p158 (🖊212-473-3000; www.abccarpetandhome.com; 888 Broadway at 19th St; ◷10am-7pm Mon-Wed & Fri, to 8pm Thu, 11am-7pm Sat, noon-6pm Sun; Ⓢ L, N/Q/R/W, 4/5/6 to 14th St-Union Sq) Set up like a museum on six floors, ABC is filled with all sorts of furnishings, small and large, including easy-to-pack knickknacks, designer jewelry, global gifts and more bulky antique furnishings and carpets. Come Christmas season the shop is a joy to behold: the decorators here go all out with lights and other wondrous touches.

Eataly
Food & Drink

Map p158 (www.eatalyny.com; 200 Fifth Ave at 23rd St; Ⓢ F, N/R, 6 to 23rd St) A 50,000-sq-ft tribute to the *dolce vita*, Mario Batali's food-filled wonderland is a New York-ified version of those dreamy Tuscan markets you find in Diane Lane films. Decked stem to the stern with gourmet edibles, Eataly

is a must for a picnic lunch – though make sure to leave room for some pork shoulder at the rooftop beer garden, Birreria (p159).

Idlewild Books
Books

Map p158 (🖊212-414-8888; www.idlewildbooks.com; 12 W 19th St btwn Fifth & Sixth Aves; ◷11:30am-8pm Mon-Fri, noon-7pm Sat & Sun; Ⓢ L, N/Q/R/W, 4/5/6 to 14th St-Union Sq) One of the best new indie bookshops to open in recent years, Idlewild is a great shopping destination when planning or even daydreaming about travel. Books are divided by region, and cover guidebooks as well as fiction, travelogues, history, cookbooks and other stimulating fare for delving into a country.

Books of Wonder
Books

Map p158 (🖊212-989-3270; www.booksofwonder.com; 18 W 18th St btwn Fifth & Sixth Aves; ◷10am-7pm Mon-Sat, 11am-6pm Sun; 🚻; Ⓢ F/V, L to 6th Ave-14th St) Folks adore this small, fun-loving bookstore devoted to children's and young-adult titles. It's a great place to take the kids on a rainy day, especially when a kids' author is giving a reading, or a storyteller is on hand.

Whole Foods
Food & Drink

Map p158 (🖊212-673-5388; 4 Union Sq S; ◷8am-11pm; Ⓢ L, N/Q/R/W, 4/5/6 to 14th St-Union Sq) One of several locations of the healthy food chain that is sweeping the city, this is an excellent place to shop for a picnic. Find endless rows of gorgeous produce, both organic and non-organic, plus a butcher, a bakery, a health and beauty section, and aisles packed with natural packaged goods.

Midtown

This is, in many ways, the heart of Manhattan. It's the New York most outsiders thrill over in films or daydream about before they ever set foot in the city. It's classic NYC, home to Broadway and larger-than-life billboards, crushing crowds, skyscraping icons and an inimitable, frenzied energy.

Midtown West is a general term that refers to any part of Midtown (between 34th and 59th Sts) that lies west of Fifth Ave. Its collection of neighborhoods includes the trendy far-west reaches of Hell's Kitchen, the office-worker crush of harried suit-wearers along Sixth Ave, and the bustle of Times Square.

From the sophisticated shops of storied Fifth Ave to a handful of iconic sights, Midtown East is the quieter side of Manhattan's full belly. It's where you'll find the Chrysler Building, the UN Building, St Patrick's Cathedral and the beaux arts–style Grand Central train station – plus iconic stores such as Tiffany & Co and Saks Fifth Avenue.

Radio City Music Hall (p193)
COREY WISE/LONELY PLANET IMAGES ©

Midtown Highlights

Rockefeller Center (p187)

A ritzy enclave full of media companies and wine bars, Rockefeller Center also doubles as a public art plaza: *Prometheus* overlooks the famous skating rink; there's *Atlas*, carrying the world on Fifth Ave; and the aptly named *News*, an installation by Isamu Noguchi, sits not far from NBC studios. Inside, you can zip up to its observation deck, Top of the Rock, for absolutely amazing views. Ice skating rink, Rockefeller Center

Skyline (p184)

No matter where you are in the city, the Empire State Building's jutting silhouette is the perfect landmark. Its legendary observation decks, although encased in safety wire, are not for the faint of heart. The Chrysler Building, an art deco masterpiece, is magnificent when viewed from a distance. However, Midtown's skyline has enough modernist and post modern beauties to satisfy the wildest of high-rise dreams. Empire State Building (p184)

VERONICA GARBUTT/LONELY PLANET IMAGES ©

Madison Square Garden (p194) 3

Typical of New York braggadocio and despite the local teams' recent travails, Madison Square Garden is still known as the 'World's Greatest Arena.' Most famously home to the NBA's New York Knicks and the New York Rangers hockey team, catching a game here is a chance to immerse yourself in the city's passionate sports culture.

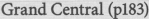

4 Grand Central (p183)

New York's most breathtaking beaux arts building, Grand Central, more than just a station, is an enchanted time machine; its swirl of chandeliers, marble, and historic bars and restaurants are a porthole into an era where train travel and romance were not mutually exclusive. While the underground electric tracks serve only commuter trains en route to northern suburbs and Connecticut, Grand Central is one stop you cannot afford to miss.

5 Midtown Shopping (p194)

It's here that you'll find fabled department stores like Fifth Ave's Bergdorf & Goodman, Madison Ave's Barneys and Herald Square's Macy's, the planet's largest store. Rockstars pick up pedals on W 48th St, while gem hunters scour the Diamond District on W 47th St. Self-made style mavens hit the Garment District (around Seventh Ave in the 30s), and a handful of trend-sensitive boutiques dot Ninth Ave in hip Hell's Kitchen.

Macy's (p197)

Midtown Walk

This walk takes you through Bryant Park, a famed green refuge, then the Diamond District, a world unto itself and a bit like Harry Potter's Diagon Alley; play spot the landmark at Top of the Rock, then hang with Picasso and Warhol at MoMA.

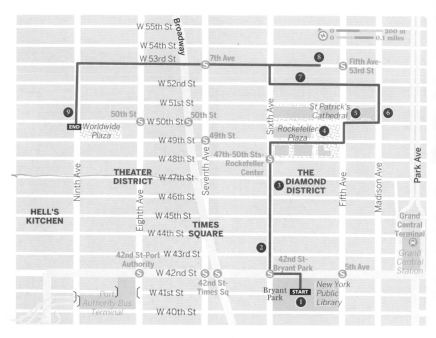

WALK FACTS

- **Start** Bryant Park
- **Finish** Hell's Kitchen
- **Distance** 1.5 miles
- **Duration** 2½ hours

❶ Bryant Park

Start at **Bryant Park** (p180), the Midtown oasis that sits just west of the New York Public Library on Fifth Ave. It's a perfect place to sit and watch the swirl of people passing through – or to create your own swirl, by going for a spin on the carousel.

❷ International Center of Photography

Head up and across Sixth Ave to find the **International Center of Photography** (p181) at 43rd St. Head in to explore the two airy levels of top-notch images.

❸ Diamond District

Continue north up Sixth Ave to 47th St, which features the **Diamond District** (p182) between Sixth and Fifth Aves. Take a stroll up one side and back along the other and head inside some of the shops, rubbing elbows with folks seeking engagement rings and aggressive hawkers looking to make you a deal.

4 Rockefeller Center & Top of the Rock

Walk a few more blocks north on Sixth Ave and turn right onto 49th St to reach **Rockefeller Center** (p187), an art deco–inspired center of commerce and industry, where you can explore the plazas, outdoor sculptures, shops and jumble of architecture. Also here is **Top of the Rock** (p187), an observatory with views to rival the Empire State Building, including stellar eyefuls of Central Park below.

5 St Patrick's Cathedral

Continue on to Fifth Ave and turn left – on 50th St is the Gothic stunner, **St Patrick's Cathedral** (p180), that looks as if it's been there a million years while this modern city has popped up around it. Head in for a look at the heavenly ceilings.

6 Villard Houses

Head around behind the cathedral, onto Madison Ave, and take a gander at the lovely **Villard Houses**, a collection of six townhouses built by financier Henry Villard in 1881.

7 Paley Center for Media

Continuing north from here, turn left on 52nd St and walk until you pass Fifth Ave. You'll soon come to the **Paley Center for Media** (p180), where you might catch a film screening or choose to hunker down with some old-school TV shows.

8 Museum of Modern Art

Head up Sixth Ave and turn right on 53rd St to find the **Museum of Modern Art** (p174), home to more than 100,000 pieces of heavy hitting modern artwork.

9 Hell's Kitchen

Wind up your tour by walking west to Ninth Ave and heading downtown, which will take you through **Hell's Kitchen**. Though there's not a specific sight to seek out, it's a great neighborhood for strolling and exploring – and noshing, as this stretch of Ninth down to about 42nd St is chock-full of eateries from all over the world. Pick the place that looks best and chow down.

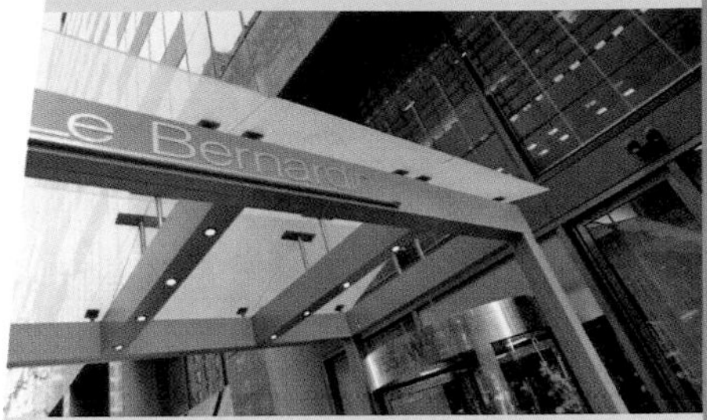

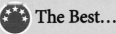

The Best...

PLACES TO EAT

Le Bernardin Triple-Michelin starred luxe, fine-dining holy grail. (p185)

Danji Masterfully prepared and wildly inventive 'Korean tapas'. (p185)

Burger Joint A hard-to-find no-fuss, no-bull buger, fries and beer place. (p185)

PLACES TO DRINK

Campbell Apartment A delightful throwback to the roaring '20s in a hidden corner of Grand Central Station. (p186)

Rum House A refreshed slice of old New York with a pianist every night. (p191)

Terroir An injection of a little cred in Murray Hill's drinking scene with the third branch of this acclaimed wine bar. (p190)

PLACES FOR VIEWS

Top of the Rock Jaw-dropping observation deck with possibly the most expansive views in the city. (p187)

Empire State Building Iconic viewing deck from one of the city's highest profile landmarks. (p184)

Top of the Strand For that 'Oh my God, I'm in New York' feeling, head to the Strand hotel's rooftop bar. (p190)

Robert Floor-to-ceiling picture windows look out on Central Park from the Museum of Arts & Design. (p191)

Le Bernardin (p185)
TIMOTHY A. CLARY/AFP/GETTY IMAGES ©

Don't Miss
Times Square

Love it or hate it, the intersection of Broadway and Seventh Ave (better known as Times Square) is New York City's hyperactive heart. It's not hip, fashionable or in-the-know, and it couldn't care less. It's too busy pumping out iconic, mass-marketed NYC – yellow cabs, golden arches, soaring skyscrapers and razzle-dazzle Broadway marquees. This is the New York of collective fantasies – the place where Al Jolson 'makes it' in the 1927 film The Jazz Singer, where photojournalist Alfred Eisenstaedt famously captured a lip-locked sailor and nurse on V-J Day in 1945, and where Alicia Keys and Jay-Z waxed lyrically about this 'concrete jungle where dreams are made.'

Map p188

www.timessquare.
com

Broadway at
Seventh Ave

S N/Q/R, S, 1/2/3, 7
to Times Sq-42nd St

Cleaning the Square

For several decades, the dream here was a sordid, wet one. The economic crash of the early 1970s led to a mass exodus of corporations from Times Square. Billboard niches went dark, stores shut and once-grand hotels were converted into SROs (single-room occupancy) dives, attracting the poor and the destitute. What was once an area bathed in light and showbiz glitz became a dirty den of drug dealers and crime. While the adjoining Theater District survived, its respectable playhouses shared the streets with porn cinemas, strip clubs and adult bookstores. That all changed with tough-talking mayor Rudolph Giuliani, who, in the 1990s, forced out the skin flicks, boosted police numbers and lured a wave of 'respectable' retail chains, restaurants and attractions. By the new millennium, Times Square had gone from 'X-rated' to 'G-rated,' drawing almost 40 million annual visitors and raking in more than $1.8 billion annually from its 17,000 hotel rooms.

A Subway, a Newspaper & a Very Famous Dropping Ball

At the turn of 20th century, Times Sq was known as Longacre Sq, an unremarkable intersection far from the city's commercial epicenter of Lower Manhattan. This would change with one deal between friends: subway pioneer August Belmont and *New York Times* publisher Adolph Ochs. Heading construction of the city's first subway line (from Lower Manhattan to the Upper West Side and Harlem), Belmont astutely realized that a Midtown business hub along 42nd St would maximize profit and patronage on the route. On his mission to draw business into the area, Belmont approached Ochs, who had recently turned around the fortunes of the *New York Times*. Belmont argued that moving the newspaper's operations to the intersection of Broadway and 42nd St would be a win-win for Ochs, for not only would an in-house subway station

Broadway Don't Miss List

BROADWAY'S BIGGEST NAME – TONY AWARD WINNER NIKKI M JAMES, STAR OF *THE BOOK OF MORMON* – GIVES US HER TOP PICKS FOR A PERFECT NIGHT OUT ON THE TOWN.

1 BEST PLACES TO GO PRE-SHOW

The Book of Mormon has a 7pm curtain, which means I get to the theater around 6pm, and that makes for a rather awkward time to eat. I usually swing by **Thalia's Kitchen** – the take-away offshoot of Thalia – for a delicious salad. Thalia Kitchen is where all the Broadway types go – from actors to crew members – before taking the stage.

2 A PERFECT NIGHT OUT ON BROADWAY

I definitely recommend eating dinner after the show and having a little snack beforehand. It's always a bummer when people fill up on giant bowls of pasta and then fall into a food coma while watching the show. And we see a lot more in the audience than people think.

Afterwards it's fun to swing by Don't Tell Mama (p194) to check out some fun, offbeat cabaret – the gypsies, tramps and thieves of Midtown.

3 BEST PLACE TO CHECK OUT THE CITY'S LATEST PERFORMANCES

Sleep No More is this choose-your-adventure kind of experience; like a crazy cool '60s 'happening.'

4 TIPS & TRICKS FOR SCORING TICKETS

Show up around two hours before the show and put your name in the lottery to score front-row seats. *The Book of Mormon* gives away about 20 tickets every night for $32. It's not easy to get tickets, but it can be a lot of fun hanging out with other fans.

As told to Brandon Presser

Below: Metal bas-relief with statue of Alan E Lefcourt, Brill Building; **Right:** TKTS Booth

mean faster distribution of the newspaper around town, but also the influx of commuters to the square would mean more sales right outside its headquarters. Belmont even convinced New York mayor George B McClellan Jr to rename the square in honor of the broadsheet. It was an offer too good to resist and in the winter of 1904–05, both subway station and the *Times'* new headquarters at One Times Sq made their debut. In honor of the move, the *Times* hosted a New Year's Eve party in 1904, setting off fireworks from its skyscraper rooftop. By 1907, however, the square had become so built-up that fireworks were deemed a safety hazard, forcing the newspaper to come up with alternative crowd-puller. It came in the form of 700-pound wood-and-iron ball, lowered from the roof of One Times Sq to herald the arrival of 1908.

Brill Building

At the northwest corner of Broadway and 49th St, the **Brill Building** might look unassuming, but this 1930s veteran

is widely considered the most important generator of popular songs in the western world. By 1962, more than 160 music businesses were based here, from songwriters, managers and publishers, to record companies and promoters. It was a one-stop shop for artists, who could craft a song, hire musicians, cut a demo and (hopefully) convince a producer without ever leaving the building. Among the legends who did were Carol King, Bob Dylan, Joni Mitchell and Paul Simon. A few legacies from that gilded era live on, from on-site sheet-music megastore Colony (p197) to music outfitter Rudy's Music (p197) on nearby W 48th St, a street once dubbed Music Row.

Broadway Classics

The Broadway of the 1920s was well-known for its lighthearted musicals, commonly fusing vaudeville and music hall traditions, and producing classic tunes like George Gershwin's *Rhapsody in Blue* and Cole Porter's *Let's Misbehave*. At the same time, Midtown's

theater district was evolving as a platform for new American dramatists. One of the greatest was Eugene O'Neill. Born in Times Sq at the long-gone Barrett Hotel (1500 Broadway) in 1888, the playwright debuted many of his works here, including Pulitzer Prize winners *Beyond the Horizon* and *Anna Christie*. O'Neill's success on Broadway paved the way for other American greats like Tennessee Williams, Arthur Miller and Edward Albee – a surge of serious talent that led to the establishment of the annual Tony Awards in 1947, Broadway's answer to Hollywood's Oscars.

Theater Tickets

These days, New York's Theater District covers an area stretching roughly from 40th St to 54th St between Sixth and Eighth Aves, with dozens of Broadway and off-Broadway theaters spanning blockbuster musicals to new and classic drama. Unless there's a specific show you're after, the best – and most affordable – way to score tickets in the area is at the **TKTS Booth**, where you can line up and get same-day half-price tickets for top Broadway and off-Broadway shows. Smart phone users can download the free TKTS app, which offers rundowns of both Broadway and off-Broadway shows, as well as real-time updates of what's available on that day. Always have a back-up choice in case your first preference sells out, and never buy tickets from scalpers on the street.

The TKTS Booth is an attraction in its own right: its illuminated roof of 27 ruby-red steps rises a panoramic 16ft 1in above the 47th St sidewalk. Needless to say, the view across Times Sq from the top is a crowd pleaser, so good luck finding a spot to park your booty.

Don't Miss
Museum of Modern Art

Superstar of the modern art scene, MoMA's booty makes many other collections look... well... endearing. You'll find more A-listers here than at an Oscars after party: Van Gogh, Matisse, Picasso, Warhol, Lichtenstein, Rothko, Pollock, Bourgeois. Since its founding in 1929, the museum has amassed more than 150,000 artworks, documenting the emerging creative ideas and movements of the late 19th century through to those that dominate today. For art buffs, it's Valhalla. For the uninitiated, it's a thrilling crash course in all that is beautiful and addictive about art.

MoMA

Map p188

www.moma.org

11 W 53rd St btwn Fifth & Sixth Aves, Midtown West

adult/child $25/ free, 4pm-8pm Fri free

⏱10:30am-5:30pm Sat-Mon, Wed & Thu, to 8pm Fri, to 8:30pm the first Thu of every month

Ⓢ E/M to Fifth Ave-53rd St

Collection Highlights

It's easy to get lost in MoMA's vast collection. To maximize your time and create a plan of attack, download the museum's floor plan and visitor guide from the website beforehand. MoMA's permanent collection spans four levels, with prints, illustrated books and the unmissable Contemporary Galleries on level two; architecture, design, drawings and photography on level three; and painting and sculpture on levels four and five. Many of the big hitters are on these last two levels, so tackle the museum from the top down before the fatigue sets in. Must-sees include Van Gogh's *The Starry Night*, Cézanne's *The Bather*, Picasso's *Les Demoiselles d'Avignon*, and Henri Rousseau's *The Sleeping Gypsy*, not to mention iconic American works like Warhol's *Campbell's Soup Cans* and *Gold Marilyn Monroe*, and Lichtenstein's equally poptastic *Girl With Ball*.

Abstract Expressionism

One of the greatest strengths of MoMA's collections is abstract expressionism, a radical movement that emerged in New York in the 1940s and boomed a decade later. Defined by its penchant for irreverent individualism and monumentally scaled works, this 'New York School' helped turn the metropolis into the epicenter of western contemporary art. Among the stars are Rothko's *Magenta, Black, Green on Orange*, Pollock's *One (Number 31, 1950)* and de Kooning's *Painting*.

Abby Aldrich Rockefeller Sculpture Garden

With architect Yoshio Taniguchi's acclaimed reconstruction of the museum in 2004 came the restoration of the Sculpture Garden to the original, larger vision of Philip Johnson's 1953 design. Johnson described the space as a 'sort of outdoor room,' and on warm, sunny days it's hard not to think of it as a soothing, alfresco lounge. One resident who can't seem to get enough of it is Aristide Maillol's *The River*, a larger-than-life female sculpture that featured in Johnson's original garden. She's in fine company too, with fellow works from greats including Auguste Rodin, Alexander Calder and Henry Moore. Sitting above the garden's eastern end is possibly MoMA's least noticed work, *Water Tower*, a translucent resin installation by British artist Rachel Whiteread.

Modern Eats

MoMA's eateries have a stellar reputation. For communal tables and a super-casual vibe, nosh on Italian-inspired panini, pasta, salumi and cheeses at **Cafe 2**. For table service, à la carte options and Danish design, opt for **Terrace Five**, whose terrace overlooks the Sculpture Garden. If you're after a luxe feed, book a table at fine-dining **Modern**, whose Michelin-starred menu serves up decadent, French-American creations like 'pralines' of foie gras terrine with mango puree and balsamic vinegar. Fans of *Sex and the City* will be keen to know that it was here that scribe-about-town Carrie announced her impending marriage to Big. (If you're on a *real* writer's wage, you can always opt for simpler, cheaper Alsatian-inspired grub in the adjacent Bar Room.)

Gallery Conversations

To delve a little deeper into MoMA's collection, join one of the museum's daily 'Gallery Conversations,' which sees lecturers, graduate students and the odd curator offer expert insight into specific works and exhibitions. Talks take place each day at 11:30am and 1:30pm (except on Tuesdays).

Film Screenings

MoMA screens an incredibly well-rounded selection of celluloid gems from its collection of more than 22,000 films, including the works of the Maysles Brothers and every Pixar animation film ever produced. Expect anything from Academy-nominated documentary shorts and Hollywood classics to experimental works and retrospectives. And your museum ticket gets you in for free.

Discover Midtown

Getting There & Away

- **Subway** A/C/E and 1/2/3 lines run north to south through Midtown West. The 4/5/6 lines run north to south through Midtown East. The central B/D/F/M lines run up Sixth Ave, while N/Q/R lines follow Broadway. The 7, E and M lines offer some crosstown service.
- **Bus** Routes include the 11 (running northbound on Tenth Ave and southbound on Ninth Ave), the M101, M102 and M103 (running northbound along Third Ave and southbound along Lexington Ave) and the M15 (running northbound on First Ave and southbound on Second Ave). Crosstown buses run along 34th and 42nd Sts.

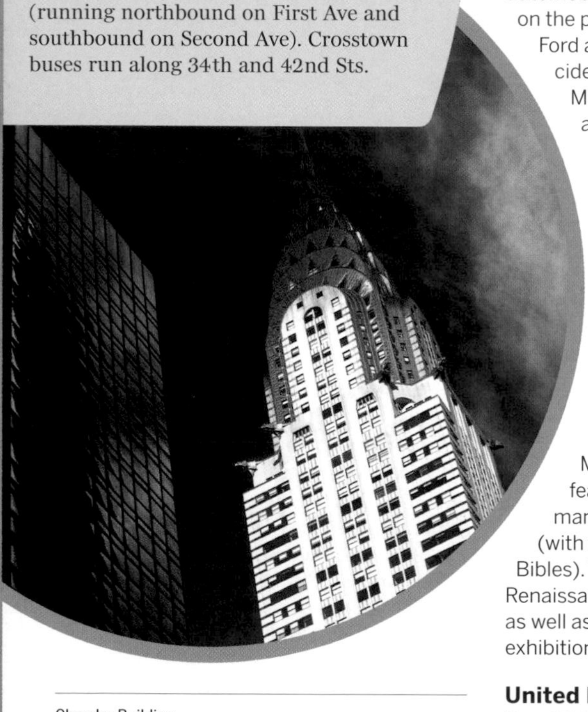

Chrysler Building

Sights

Midtown East

Chrysler Building Notable Building
Map p178 (Lexington Ave at 42nd St; 🕐 lobby 8am-6pm Mon-Fri; [S] S, 4/5/6, 7 to Grand Central-42nd St) The 77-floor Chrysler Building makes most other skyscrapers look like uptight geeks. Designed by William Van Alen in 1930, it's a dramatic fusion of art deco and Gothic aesthetics, adorned with stern steel eagles and topped by a spire that screams Bride of Frankenstein. The building was constructed as the headquarters for Walter P Chrysler and his automobile empire. Unable to compete on the production line with bigger rivals Ford and General Motors, Chrysler decided to trump them on the skyline. More than 80 years on, Chrysler's ambitious $15 million statement remains one of New York's most poignant symbols.

Pierpont Morgan Library Cultural Building
Map p178 (www.morganlibrary.org; 29 E 36th St at Madison Ave; adult/child $15/10; 🕐 10:30am-5pm Tue-Thu, to 9pm Fri, 10am-6pm Sat, 11am-6pm Sun; [S] 6 to 33rd St) Part of the 45-room mansion once owned by steel magnate JP Morgan, this sumptuous library features a phenomenal array of manuscripts, tapestries and books (with no fewer than three Gutenberg Bibles). There's a study filled with Italian Renaissance artwork, a marble rotunda, as well as a program of top-notch rotating exhibitions.

United Nations Notable Building
Map p178 (☎ 212-963-8687; www.un.org/tours; First Ave at 46th St; guided tour adult/

Midtown

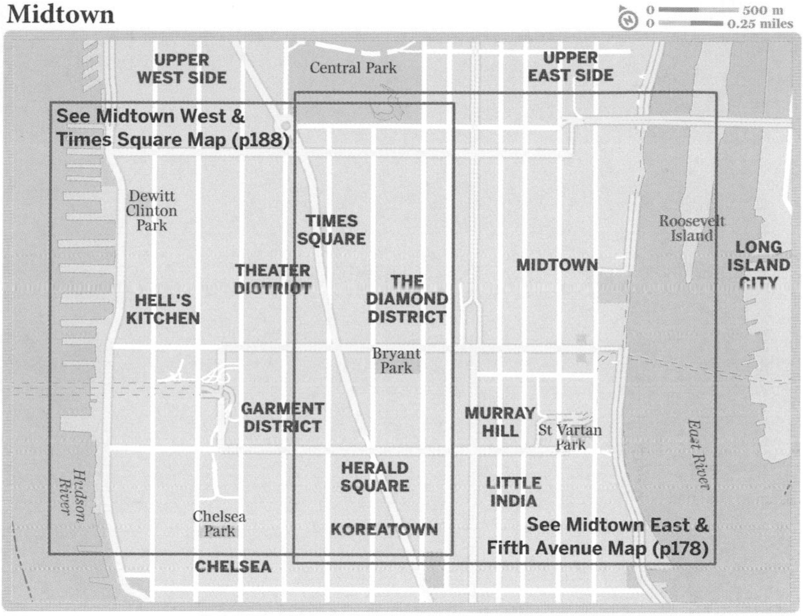

child $16/11, children under 5yr not admitted; 🕒tours 9:45am-4:45pm Mon-Fri, 10am-4:15pm Sat & Sun, closed Sat & Sun Jan & Feb; 📶; [S]S, 4/5/6, 7 to Grand Central-42nd St) Welcome to the headquarters of the UN, a worldwide organization overseeing international law, international security and human rights. While the soaring, Le Corbusier–designed Secretariat building is off-limits, 60-minute guided tours do take in the General Assembly, where the annual convocation of member nations takes place every fall, as well as exhibitions about the UN's work and artworks given by member states.

Museum of Sex — Museum

Map p178 (www.museumofsex.com; 233 Fifth Ave at 27th St; adult/child $17.50/$15; 🕒11am-8pm Sun-Thu, to 9pm Fri & Sat; [S]N/R to 23rd St) From vintage condoms to Japanese Shunga prints, 'MoSex' explores the world of sex in culture and nature. One long-running exhibition, 'Action: Sex and the Moving Image,' examines representations of sex in mainstream cinema and pornography, while the permanent collection showcases plenty of racy sex-related paraphernalia. The in-house bar serves 'stimulating' drinks with names like New Orleans Brothel and Frida Calor.

Fifth Avenue

New York Public Library — Cultural Building

Map p178 (Stephen A Schwarzman Building; www.nypl.org; Fifth Ave at 42nd St; 🕒10am-6pm Mon & Thu-Sat, to 8pm Tue & Wed, 1-5pm Sun, guided tours 11am & 2pm Mon-Sat, 2pm Sun; 📶; [S]B/D/F, M to 42nd St-Bryant Park, 7 to Fifth Ave) Loyally guarded by 'Patience' and 'Fortitude' (the famous marble lions overlooking Fifth Ave), this beaux arts show-off is one of NYC's best free attractions. When dedicated in 1911, New York's flagship library ranked as the largest marble structure ever built in the US, and to this day, its Rose Main Reading Room will steal your breath with its lavish, coffered ceiling.

The library's Exhibition Hall contains precious manuscripts by just about every author of note in the English language, including an original copy of the Declaration of Independence and a Gutenberg Bible. To properly explore this

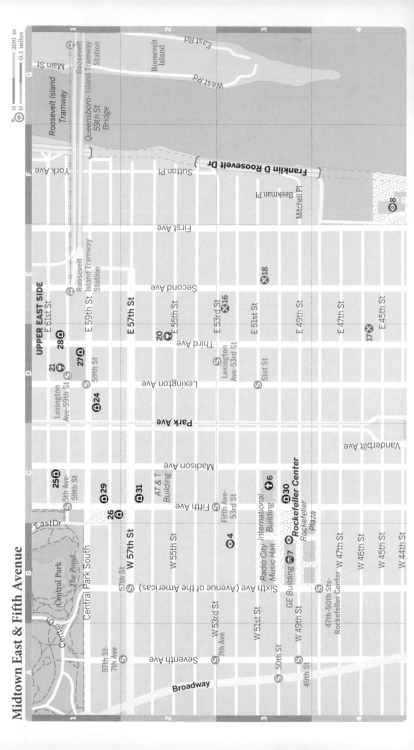

Midtown East & Fifth Avenue

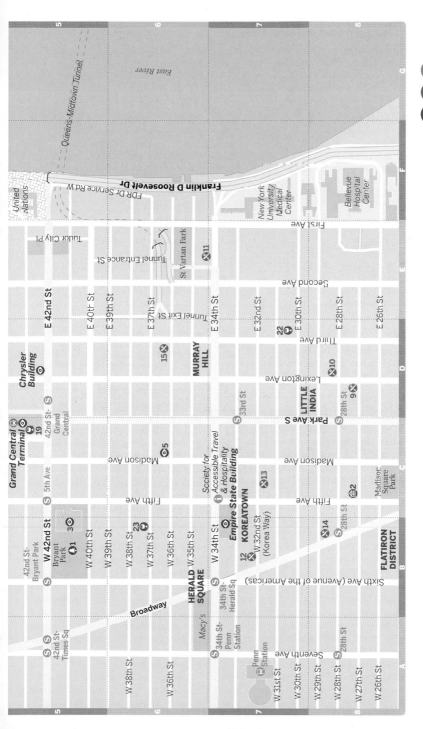

East River

Queens-Midtown Tunnel

FDR Dr Service Rd W
Franklin D Roosevelt Dr

United Nations

Tudor City Pl

Tunnel Entrance St

St Vartan Park

New York University Medical Center

Bellevue Hospital Center

First Ave

Second Ave

Tunnel Exit St

E 42nd St
E 40th St
E 39th St
E 37th St
E 34th St
E 32nd St
E 30th St
E 28th St
E 26th St

Chrysler Building

Grand Central Terminal

42nd St-Grand Central

5th Ave

MURRAY HILL

Third Ave

Lexington Ave

Park Ave S

LITTLE INDIA

28th St

Madison Ave

Madison Ave

33rd St

Society for Accessible Travel & Hospitality

Empire State Building

KOREATOWN

W 32nd St (Korea Way)

Fifth Ave

Fifth Ave

Madison Square Park

Sixth Ave (Avenue of the Americas)

FLATIRON DISTRICT

42nd St-Bryant Park

Bryant Park

W 42nd St
W 40th St
W 39th St
W 38th St
W 37th St
W 36th St
W 35th St
W 34th St

HERALD SQUARE

34th St-Herald Sq

Broadway

Macy's

34th St-Penn Station

Penn Station

Seventh Ave

42nd St-Times Sq

W 38th St
W 36th St
W 31st St
W 30th St
W 29th St
W 28th St
W 27th St
W 26th St

28th St

179

Midtown East & Fifth Avenue

mini-universe of books, art, chandeliers and porticoes, join a free guided tour, which leaves from the information desk in Astor Hall.

Bryant Park — Park
Map p178 (www.bryantpark.org; 42nd St btwn Fifth & Sixth Aves; ⏱7am-midnight Mon-Sat, to 11pm Sun May-Sep, 7am-10pm Sun-Thu, to midnight Fri & Sat Nov-Feb, 7am-7pm Mar, 7am-10pm Apr & Oct; 📶; Ⓢ B/D/F/M to 42nd St-Bryant Park, 7 to Fifth Ave) European coffee kiosks, alfresco chess games, summer film screenings and winter ice-skating: it's hard to believe that this leafy oasis was dubbed 'Needle Park' in the '80s. Nestled behind the show-stopping New York Public Library building, it's a handy spot for a little time-out from the Midtown madness.

It's a shamelessly charming place, complete with a Brooklyn-constructed, French-inspired Le Carrousel offering rides for $2, and frequent special events, from readings to concerts. And it becomes a winter wonderland at Christmastime, with holiday gift vendors lining the park's edge and a popular ice-skating rink sprouting in its middle.

Paley Center for Media — Cultural Building
Map p178 (www.paleycenter.org; 25 W 52nd St btwn Fifth & Sixth Aves; adult/child $10/5; ⏱noon-6pm Wed & Fri-Sun, to 8pm Thu; Ⓢ E/M to Fifth Ave-53rd St) Heaven for pop-culture fans, the Paley Center offers more than 150,000 TV and radio programs from around the world on its computer catalog. While reliving your favorite TV shows on one of the museum's consoles is sheer bliss on a rainy day, the radio-listening room is an unexpected pleasure – as are the excellent, regular screenings, festivals, speakers and performers.

St Patrick's Cathedral — Church
Map p178 (www.saintpatrickscathedral.org; Fifth Ave btwn 50th & 51st Sts; ⏱6.30am-8.45pm; Ⓢ B/D/F, M to 47th-50th Sts-Rockefeller Center) America's largest Catholic cathedral is a vision in neo-Gothic. Highlights include the Louis Tiffany–designed altar and Charles Connick's stunning Rose Window, the latter gleaming above a 7000-pipe church organ.

A basement crypt behind the altar contains the coffins of every New York cardinal and the remains of Pierre

Touissant, a champion of the poor and the first black American up for sainthood (he emigrated from Haiti).

Midtown West & Times Square

Times Square   Landmark
See p170.

Museum of Modern Art   Gallery
See p174.

International Center of Photography   Gallery
Map p188 (ICP; www.icp.org; 1133 Sixth Ave at 43rd St; admission $12, by donation Fri 5 8pm; ⏱10am-6pm Tue, Wed, Sat & Sun, to 8pm Thu & Fri; Ⓢ B/D/F, M to 42nd St-Bryant Park) ICP is New York's paramount showcase for photography, with a strong emphasis on photojournalism and changing exhibitions focused on a wide range of creative themes. Past shows in its two-floor space have included work by Henri Cartier-Bresson, Man Ray and Robert Capa The center is also a school, offering course-work (for credit) and a public lecture series.

Intrepid Se... Museum
Map p188 (www. Twelfth Ave at 4... ⏱10am-6pm da... Nov-Mar; Ⓢ A/C Bus Terminal, ... Intrepid surviv... kamikaze atta... aircraft carrie... ing host to a ... tive military m... through videos, historical artifacts and frozen-in-time living quarters. The flight deck features fighter planes and military helicopters, which might inspire you try the museum's high tech flight simulators.

The museum is also home to the guided-missile submarine Growler, (not for the claustrophobic), a decommissioned Concorde, and from summer 2012 the former NASA space shuttle Orbiter Enterprise. Come May, the Intrepid is also the nexus for the Fleet Week celebrations, when thousands of the world's sailors descend on Manhattan for shore leave.

Museum of Arts & Design
Map p188 (MAD... Columbus Cir... adult/chi... & Sun... St-...

Bryant Park

Museum

www.madmuseum.org; 2
...le btwn Eighth Ave & Broadway;
...$15/free; 🕙11am-6pm Tue, Wed, Sat
to 9pm Thu & Fri; Ⓢ A/C, B/D, 1 to 59th
...olumbus Circle) MAD offers four floors of
superlative design and handicrafts, from
blown glass and carved wood to elaborate
metal jewelry. Its temporary exhibitions
are nothing short of innovative, with past
shows exploring anything from American
Modernism to art made from dust, ash,
dirt and sand. Stock up on contemporary
jewelry and design objects in the gift
shop, or sip cocktails at the ninth-floor
restaurant/bar.

Diamond District   Street
Map p188 (www.diamonddistrict.org; 47th St
btwn Fifth & Sixth Aves; Ⓢ B/D/F, M to 47th-50th
Sts-Rockefeller Center) Like Diagon Alley in
Harry Potter, the Diamond District is a
world unto itself. A frenetic whirl of Hasidic Jewish traders, aggressive hawkers
and love-struck couples looking for the
perfect rock, its 2600-plus businesses
peddle all manner of diamonds, gold,
pearls, gemstones and watches. In fact,
the strip handles approximately 90% of
the cut diamonds sold in the country.

Herald Square   Square
Map p188 (cnr Broadway, Sixth Ave & 34th St;
Ⓢ B/D/F, M, N/Q/R to 34th St-Herald Sq) This
crowded convergence of Broadway, Sixth
Ave and 34th St is best known as the
home of the gigantic Macy's department
store, where you can still ride some of the
original wooden elevators.

The square gets its name from a
long-defunct newspaper, the New York
Herald (1835–1924), and the small, leafy
park here bustles during business hours
thanks to a much-needed facelift.

Garment District   Neighborhood
Map p188 (Seventh Ave btwn 34th St & Times
Sq; Ⓢ N/Q/R, S, 1/2/3 & 7 to Times Sq-42nd St)
Otherwise known as the Fashion District,
this thread-obsessed area might look like
an unremarkable-looking stretch of designers' offices and wholesale and retail

shops, but it's where you'll find a huge
selection of fabrics, sequins, lace and,
chances are, those day-glo velvet buttons
you've been missing since 1986.

 Eating

Midtown East & Fifth Avenue

Hangawi   Korean $$
Map p178 (📞 212-213-0077; www.hangawirestau
rant.com; 12 E 32nd St btwn Fifth & Madison Aves;
mains $17-25; 🕙 lunch Mon-Sat, dinner daily;
Ⓢ B/D/F, M, N/Q/R to 34th St-Herald Sq) Sublime, flesh-free Korean is the draw at high-
achieving Hangawi. Leave your shoes
at the entrance and slip into a soothing,
zen-like space of meditative music, soft
low seating and clean, complexly-flavored
dishes. Show-stoppers include the leak
pancakes and a seductively smooth tofu
claypot in ginger sauce.

The Smith   American $$
Map p178 (www.thesmithnyc.com; 956 Second
Ave at 51st St; mains $17-29; 🕙 Mon-Wed 7:30am-
midnight, Thu-Fri to 1am, Sat 10am-1am, Sun to
midnight; Ⓢ 6 to 51st St) Its name aglow in
bold red neon, the Smith has sexed-up
dining in the far eastern throws of Midtown with its industrial-chic interior, buzzing bar and well-exectued brasserie grub.
With much of the food made from scratch
on-site, the emphasis is on regional produce, retro American and Italian-inspired
flavors, and slick and personable service.

John Dory
Oyster Bar   Seafood $$
Map p178 (www.thejohndory.com; 1196 Broadway
at 29th St; small plates $9.50-25 ; 🕙 noon-
midnight; Ⓢ N/R to 28th St) This loud, vibey
seafood favorite sits just off the Ace Hotel
(p284) lobby. Only hotel guests can book,
so head in early for clever, tapas-style creations like sea urchin with pomegranate
and black pepper, or chorizo stuffed squid
with smoked tomato. Between 5pm and
7pm, $15 gets you six oysters or clams
and a glass of sparkling vino or ale.

Don't Miss
Grand Central Terminal

Threatened by the debut of rival Penn Station (the majestic original, not the current eyesore), shipping and railroad magnate Cornelius Vanderbilt set to work transforming his 19th-century Grand Central Depot into a 20th-century showpiece. The fruit of his envy is Grand Central Terminal, New York's most breathtaking beaux arts building. More than just a station, this is an enchanted time machine, its swirl of chandeliers, marble, and historic bars and restaurants a porthole into an era where train travel and romance were not mutually exclusive.

For better or worse, there are no teary good-byes for people traveling across the country from here today, as Grand Central's underground electric tracks serve only commuter trains en route to northern suburbs and Connecticut. Whether or not you're traveling, Grand Central is one stop you cannot afford to miss.

The vaulted landing directly below the bridge linking the Main Concourse and Vanderbilt Hall harbors one of Grand Central's quirkier features, the so-called Whispering Gallery. If you're in company, stand facing the walls diagonally opposite each other and whisper something. If your partner proposes (it happens a lot down here), chilled champagne is just through the door at the station's oldest nosh spot, Grand Central Oyster Bar & Restaurant. Hugely atmospheric (with a vaulted tiled ceiling by Catalan-born Rafael Guastavino), stick to what it does exceptionally well: oysters. An elevator beside the restaurant leads up to another historic gem: Campbell Apartment (p186).

NEED TO KNOW

Map p178; www.grandcentralterminal.com; 42nd St at Park Ave, B4; ⊙5:30am–2am; S S, 4/5/6, 7 to Grand Central-42nd St

DENNIS JOHNSON/LONELY PLANET IMAGES ©

Don't Miss
Empire State Building

The Chrysler Building may be prettier and the One World Trade Center may now be taller, but the Queen Bee of the New York skyline remains the Empire State Building. It's Hollywood's tallest star, enjoying more than its fair share of close-ups in around one hundred films, from King Kong to Independence Day. No other building screams New York quite like it, and heading up to the top is a quintessential experience.

The statistics are astounding: 10 million bricks, 60,000 tons of steel, 6400 windows and 328,000 sq ft of marble. Built on the original site of the Waldorf-Astoria, construction took a record-setting 410 days, using seven million hours of labor and costing a mere $41 million. Coming in at 102 stories and 1472ft from top to bottom, the limestone phallus opened for business on May 1, 1931.

There are two observation decks. The open-air 86th-floor deck offers an alfresco experience, with coin-operated telescopes for close-up glimpses of the metropolis. The enclosed 102nd-floor deck is New York's highest – at least until the opening of the observation deck at One World Trade Center in mid-2014. The views over the city's five boroughs (and five neighboring states, weather permitting) are quite simply exquisite. Alas, the passage to heaven will involve a trip through purgatory: the queues are notorious. Getting here very early or very late will help avoid delays – as will buying your tickets online, ahead of time; the $2 purchase charge is well worth the hassle it will save you.

NEED TO KNOW

Map p178; www.esbnyc.com; 350 Fifth Ave at 34th St; 86th-floor observation deck adult/child $22/16, incl 102nd-floor observation deck $37/31; 🕐8am-2am, last elevators up 1.15am; [S] B/D/F, M, N/Q/R to 34th St-Herald Sq

Social Eatz
Fusion $

Map p178 (www.socialeatz.com; 232 E 53rd St btwn Second & Third Aves, Midtown East; burgers $8-11, salads $6-7; S E, M to Lexington Ave-53rd St) American comfort food gets an Asian twist at this hip, '70s-inspired diner. Celebrate inter-racial harmony with Korean beef tacos, St Louis pork ribs with gochujang-spiked BBQ sauce, or Korean spiced slaw. Topping them all is the mighty Bibimbap Burger, voted America's best by prolific foodie website Eater.

Gahm Mi Oak
Korean $$

Map p178 (43 W 32nd St btwn Broadway & Fifth Ave; dishes $10-22; ⊙24hr; S N/Q/R, B/D/F, M to 34th St-Herald Sq) If you're craving *yook hwe* (raw beef and Asian pear matchsticks) at 3am, this K-Town savior has you covered. The shtick here is authenticity; try the house speciality *sul long tang* (a milky broth of ox bones, boiled for 12 hours, and pimped with brisket and scallion).

Sparks
Steakhouse $$$

Map p178 (www.sparkssteakhouse.com; 210 E 46th St btwn Second & Third Aves, Midtown East; ⊙lunch & dinner Mon-Fri, dinner Sat; S S, 4/5/6, 7 to Grand Central-42nd St) Get an honest-to-goodness New York steak-house experience at this classic joint, a former mob hangout that's been around for nearly 50 years, and still packs 'em in for a juicy carnivorous feed.

Sarge's Deli
Deli $$

Map p178 (www.sargesdeli.com; 548 Third Ave btwn 36th & 37th Sts, Midtown East; mains $15-26; ⊙24hr; S 6 to 33rd St) It's like a scene from a '70s sitcom: brown vinyl booths filled with weathered cabbies, loud-mouthed businessmen and neurotic couples. Eavesdrop 24/7 over a pastrami sandwich, blintzes and matza ball chicken soup, but leave room for the pornographically good strawberry cheesecake.

Bhatti
Indian $$

Map p178 (www.bhattinyc.com; 100 Lexington Ave at 27th St ; dishes $7-21; S 6 to 28th St) One of your best options in 'Curry Hill' (Murray Hill), well-priced Bhatti has no shortage of Indian families tucking into expat-approved

north Indian dishes. Service may be patchy but the food more than compensates.

El Parador Cafe
Mexican $$

Map p178 (☎212-679-6812; www.elparadorcafe. com; 325 E 34th St; mains $18-29; ⊙noon-midnight, closed Sun Aug; S 6 to 33rd St) Back in the day, the far-flung location of this Mexican stalwart (serving here since 1970) was much appreciated by philandering husbands. The shady regulars may have gone, but the old-school charm remain, from the beveled candleholders and dapper Latino waiters, to the satisfying south-of-the-border standbys.

Midtown West & Times Square

Le Bernardin
Seafood $$$

Map p188 (☎212-554-1515; www.le-bernardin. com; 155 W 51st St btwn Sixth & Seventh Aves; prix fixe lunch/dinner $75/125, tasting menus $145-190; ⊙lunch Mon-Fri, dinner Mon-Sat; S 1 to 50th St, B/D/E to 7th Ave) At the helm is celebrity chef Eric Ripert, whose deceptively simple-looking seafood often borders on the transcendental. The menu works simply: four lunch courses for $75, or four dinner courses for $125, with ample choices per course, and two tastings menus for those with more time and money. Book at least three weeks ahead for dinner, and one week ahead for lunch.

Danji
Korean $$

Map p188 (www.danjinyc.com; 346 W 52nd St, Midtown West; plates $7-20; ⊙lunch Mon-Fri, dinner Mon-Sat; S C/E to 50th St) Young-gun chef Hooni Kim has captured tastebuds with his Michelin-starred Korean 'tapas.' Served in a snug-and-slinky contemporary space, his drool-inducing creations are divided into 'traditional' and 'modern' options. Though the highlights are many, the celebrity dish is the sliders, a duo of *bulgogi* beef and spiced pork belly, each dressed with scallion vinaigrette and served on butter-grilled buns.

Burger Joint
Burgers $

Map p188 (www.parkermeridien.com/eat4.php; Le Parker Meridien, 119 W 56th St, Midtown West; burgers $7; S F to 57th St) With only a small neon burger as your clue, this speakeasy burger hut loiters behind the curtain in the lobby of the Le Parker Meridien hotel. Find it and you'll stumble onto a thumping scene of graffiti-strewn walls, retro booths, and attitude-loaded staff slapping up beef-n-patty brilliance.

It gets packed, so head in early, late or wait.

Totto Ramen Japanese **$**

Map p188 (www.tottoramen.com; 366 W 52nd St, Midtown West; ramen $9.50-12.50; ⏰lunch Mon-Sat, dinner Mon-Sun; [S]C/E to 50th St) Write your name and number of guests on the clipboard by the door and wait for your (cash-only) ramen revelation. Skip the chicken and go for the pork, which sings in dishes like miso ramen (with fermented soybean paste, egg, scallion, bean sprouts, onion and homemade chili paste).

Marseille French, Mediterranean **$$**

Map p188 (www.marseillenyc.com; 630 Ninth Ave at 44th St; mains $19-28.50; ⏰lunch & dinner; [S]A/C/E to 42nd St-Port Authority) A nostalgic fusion of theatrical lighting, sweeping curves and mirrored panels, this Hell's Kitchen gem looks somewhere between an old cinema lobby and an art deco brasserie. At once buzzing and romantic, it's a fabulous spot to kick back with a spiced pear martini and nibble on flavor-packed French-Med fare.

Bocca di Bacco Italian **$$**

Map p188 (☎212-265-8828; www.boccadibacconyc.com; 828 Ninth Ave btwn 54th & 55th Sts, Midtown West; mains $16-24; ⏰dinner Mon-Sun; [S]A/C, B/D, 1 to 59th St-Columbus Circle) With its art-slung walls and rustic interior, this electric restaurant/wine bar combo is Hell's Kitchen's take on the classic Italian enoteca. Fueling the conversation is a repertoire of beautifully prepared Italian dishes, from soulful *zuppe* (soups) to sublime meats and seafood mains.

El Margon Cuban **$**

Map p188 (136 W 46th St btwn Sixth & Seventh Aves, Midtown West; sandwiches from $4, mains $9; [S]B/D/F, M to 47-50th Sts-Rockefeller Center) It's still 1973 at this ever-packed Cuban lunch counter, where orange Laminex and greasy goodness never went out of style. Go for gold with their legendary cubano sandwich (a pressed panino jammed with rich roast pork, salami, cheese, pickles, mojo and mayo).

🍷 Drinking & Nightlife

Midtown East & Fifth Avenue

Campbell Apartment Bar

Map p178 (www.hospitalityholdings.com; 15 Vanderbilt Ave at 43rd St; ⏰noon-1am Mon-Thu, to 2am Fri, 2pm-2am Sat, 3pm-midnight Sun; [S]S, 4/5/6, 7 to Grand Central-42nd St) This sublime,

Campbell Apartment

AA WORLD TRAVEL LIBRARY/ALAMY ©

DAN HERRICK/LONELY PLANET IMAGES ©

Don't Miss Rockefeller Center

The Rockefeller Center – a 22-acre 'city within a city' – debuted at the height of the Great Depression. Taking nine years to build, it was America's first multiuse retail, entertainment and office space – a modernist sprawl of 19 buildings, outdoor plazas and big-name tenants. Developer John D Rockefeller Jr may have sweated over the cost (a mere $100 million), but it was all worth it, the center was declared a National Landmark in 1987.

There are views, and then there is the view from the Top of the Rock (**Map p178; www.topoftherocknyc.com; 30 Rockefeller Plaza at 49th St, entrance on W 50th St btwn Fifth & Sixth Aves; adult/child $25/16, sunrise & sunset $38/20; 🕗8am-midnight, last elevator at 11pm; [S] B/D/F, M to 47th-50th Sts-Rockefeller Center**). Crowning the GE Building, 70 stories above Midtown, its jaw-dropping vista includes one icon that you won't see from atop the Empire State Building – the Empire State Building.

TV comedy *30 Rock* gets its name from the GE Building, and the tower is the real-life home of NBC TV. NBC Studio Tours leave from inside the NBC Experience Store every 15 minutes, and include a sneak peek of the legendary *Saturday Night Live* set. Advanced phone bookings are strongly recommended. Across 49th St, opposite the plaza, is the glass-enclosed NBC Today show studio, broadcasting live, 7am to 10am daily.

Come the festive season, Rockefeller Plaza is where you'll find NYC's most famous Christmas tree. In its shadow, Rink at Rockefeller Center is the famous ice-skating rink.

NEED TO KNOW

Map p178; www.rockefellercenter.com; Fifth to Sixth Aves & 48th to 51st Sts; 🕗24hr, times vary for individual businesses; [S] B/D/F, M to 47th-50th Sts-Rockefeller Center

Midtown West & Times Square

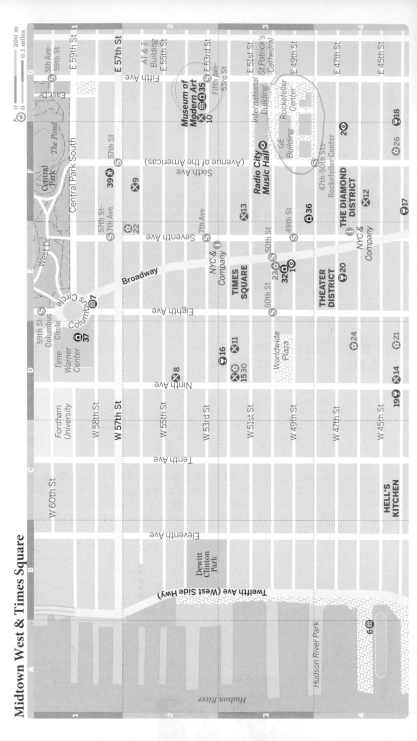

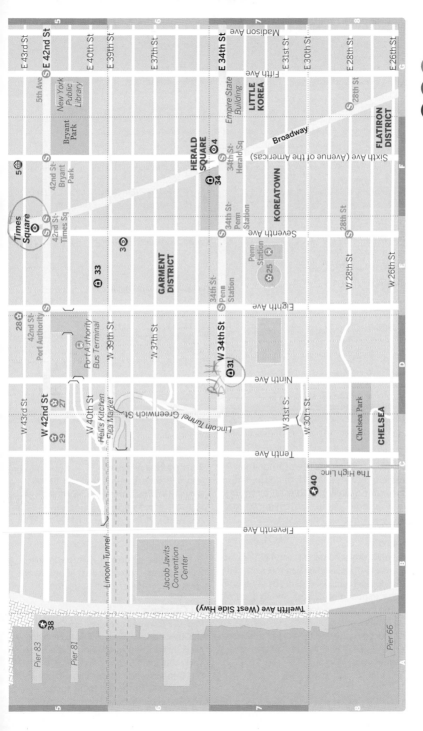

Midtown West & Times Square

deliciously snooty bar was once the home of a '20s railroad magnate. The Euro-chic detailing includes Florentine-style carpets, decorative ceiling beams and a soaring leaded glass window.

Terroir
Wine Bar

Map p178 (www.wineisterroir.com; 439 Third Ave, Midtown East; ⊙5pm-1am Mon-Thu, to 2am Fri & Sat, to 11pm Sun; Ⓢ6 to 28th St) Low-slung bulbs, exposed brickwork and long communal tables ooze downtown cool, while the well-versed, well-priced wine list features a mind-boggling array of drops by the glass. The vino-friendly grub is inspired and delicious.

Top of the Strand
Cocktail Bar

Map p178 (www.topofthestrand.com; Strand Hotel, 33 W 37th St btwn Fifth & Sixth Aves; ♿; Ⓢ B/D/F, M to 34th St) Sporting slinky cabanas and a sliding glass roof, this cocktail bar's view of the Empire State Building is unforgettable.

Expect DJ-spun tunes Thursday to Sunday and a mixed crowd of post-work locals and international hotel guests.

PJ Clarke's
Bar

Map p178 (www.pjclarkes.com; 915 Third Ave at 55th St, Midtown East; ⓈE, M to Lexington Ave-53rd St) Another bastion of old New York, this lovingly worn wooden saloon has been straddling the scene since 1884; Buddy Holly proposed to his fiancée here and Old Blue Eyes pretty much owned

table 20. Choose a jukebox tune, order a round of crab cakes, and settle in with a come-one-and-all crowd of collar-and-tie colleagues, college students and nostalgia-longing urbanites.

Subway Inn
Bar

Map p178 (143 E 60th St btwn Lexington & Third Aves; S 4/5/6 to 59th St, N/Q/R to Lexington Ave-59th St) Occupying its own world across from Bloomingdale's, this old-geezer watering hole is a vintage cheap-booze spot that, despite the classic rock and worn red booths, harkens to long-past days when Marilyn Monroe would drop in.

Midtown West & Times Square

Rum House
Cocktail Bar

Map p188 (www.edisonrumhouse.com; 228 W 47th St btwn Broadway & Eighth Ave, Midtown West; ◷ 11am-4am Mon-Sun; S N/Q/R to 49th St) Not along ago, this was Hotel Edison's crusty old piano bar. Enter the capable team from Tribeca bar Ward III, who ripped out the green carpet, polished up the coppertop bar and revived this slice

of old New York. You'll still find a nightly pianist, but he's now accompanied by well-crafted drinks and an in-the-know medley of whiskeys and rums.

Lantern's Keep
Cocktail Bar

Map p188 (☎ 212-453-4287; www.thelanterns keep.com; Iroquois Hotel, 49 W 44th St, Midtown West; ◷ 5pm-midnight Tue-Sat; S B/D/F, M to 42nd St-Bryant Park) Can you keep a secret? If so, cross the lobby of the **Iroquois Hotel** (☎ info 000-332-7220, info 212-840-3080; www. iroquoisny.com; 49 W 44th St, Midtown West; d $230-500; ☎; S B/D/F, M to 42nd St-Bryant Park) and slip into this dark, intimate cocktail salon. Its speciality is pre-Prohibition libations, shaken and stirred by passionate, personable mixologists. Reservations are recommended.

Robert
Cocktail Bar

Map p188 (www.robertnyc.com; Museum of Arts & Design, 2 Columbus Circle btwn Eighth Ave & Broadway; S A/C, B/D, 1 to 59th St-Columbus Circle) Perched on the ninth floor of the Museum of Arts & Design, '60s-inspired, pink-tastic Robert is technically a high-end, Modern-American restaurant. While the food is satisfactory, it's a little

PJ Clarke's

overpriced, so head in late afternoon or post-dinner, find a sofa and gaze out over Central Park with a MAD Manhattan (Bourbon, Blood Orange Vermouth and liquored cherries).

Jimmy's Corner — Dive Bar

Map p188 (140 W 44th St btwn Sixth & Seventh Aves, Midtown West; 🕑10am-4am; [S]N/Q/R, 1/2/3, 7 to 42nd St-Times Sq, B/D/F, M to 42nd St-Bryant Park) This skinny, welcoming, completely unpretentious dive off Times Square is run by an old boxing trainer, as if you wouldn't guess by all the framed photos of boxing greats (and lesser-known fighters too). The jukebox covers Stax to Miles Davis (plus Lionel Ritchie's most regretful moments), kept low enough for post-work gangs to chat away.

Industry — Gay

Map p188 (www.industry-bar.com; 355 W 52nd St btwn Eighth & Ninth Aves, Midtown West; 🕑4pm-4am; [S]C/E, 1 to 50th St) What was once a parking garage is now the hottest gay bar in Hell's Kitchen – a slick 4000-sq-ft watering hole with handsome lounge areas, a pool table and a stage for top-notch drag divas. Head in between 4pm and 9pm for the two-for-one drinks special, or squeeze in later to party with the eye-candy party hordes.

Rudy's — Dive Bar

Map p188 (www.rudysbarnyc.com; 627 Ninth Ave at 44th St; [S]A/C/E to 42nd St-Port Authority Bus Terminal) The big pantless pig in a red jacket out front marks Hell's Kitchen's best divey mingler, with cheap pitchers of Rudy's two beers, half-circle booths covered in red duct tape, and free hot dogs. A mix of folks come to flirt or watch muted Knicks games as classic rock plays.

★ Entertainment

Jazz at Lincoln Center — Jazz

Map p188 (☎tickets to Dizzy's Club Coca-Cola 212-258-9595, tickets to Rose Theater & Allen Room 212-721-6500; www.jazzatlincolncenter.org; Time Warner Center, Broadway at 60th St; [S]A/C, B/D, 1 to 59th St-Columbus Circle) Perched high atop the Time Warner Center, Jazz at Lincoln Center consists of three state-of-the-art venues: the mid-sized Rose Theater; the panoramic, glass-backed Allen Room; and the intimate, atmospheric Dizzy's Club Coca-Cola. It's the last one you're likely to visit given its regular, nightly shows. The talent is often exceptional, as are the dazzling Central Park views.

Signature Theatre — Theater

Map p188 (☎tickets 212-244-7529; www.signaturetheatre.org; 480 W 42nd St btwn Ninth & Tenth Aves; [S]A/C/E to 42nd St-Port Authority Bus Terminal) Now in its new Frank Gehry–designed home – complete with three theaters, bookshop and cafe – Signature Theatre devotes entire seasons to the body of work of its playwrights-in-residence. To date, featured dramatists have included Tony Kushner, Edward Albee, Athol Fugard and Kenneth Lonergan.

Carnegie Hall — Live Music

Map p188 (☎212-247-7800; www.carnegiehall.org; W 57th St & Seventh Ave; [S]N/Q/R to 57th St-7th Ave) This legendary music hall may not be the world's biggest, nor grandest, but it's definitely one of the most acoustically blessed venues around. Opera, jazz and folk greats feature in the Isaac Stern Auditorium, with edgier jazz, pop, classical and world music in the hugely popular Zankel Hall.

Birdland — Jazz, Cabaret

Map p188 (☎212-581-3080; www.birdlandjazz.com; 315 W 44th St btwn Eighth & Ninth Aves, Theater District; admission $10-50; 🕑club from 7pm, shows around 8:30pm & 11pm; 📶; [S]A/C/E to 42nd St-Port Authority Bus Terminal) Off Times Square, it's got a slick look, not to mention the legend – its name dates from bebop legend Charlie Parker (aka 'Bird'), who headlined at the previous location on 52nd St, along with Miles, Monk and just about everyone else (you can see their photos on the walls). Covers run from $20 to $50 and the lineup is always stellar.

Don't Miss
Radio City Music Hall

A spectacular art deco diva, this 5901-seat movie palace was the brainchild of vaudeville producer Samuel Lionel 'Roxy' Rothafel. Never one for understatement, Roxy launched his venue on December 23, 1932 with an over-the-top extravaganza that included a Symphony of the Curtains (starring, you guessed it, the curtains), and the high-kick campness of dance troupe the Roxyettes (mercifully renamed the Rockettes).

By the 1940s, Radio City had become the greatest single attraction in New York, its red carpet well-worn with a string of movie premieres. Alas, the good times didn't last, dwindling popularity and soaring rents forcing the theater's closure in 1978. True to Hollywood form, however, the venue escaped demolition with a last-minute reprieve, its interior declared a landmark worthy of a $5 million restoration.

While the original, wood-paneled elevators are sublime, the pièce de résistance is the main auditorium, its radiating arches evoking a setting sun. It's here that you'll see Radio City Music Hall's legendary pipe organ (the biggest built for a movie palace) and the landmark-listed Great Stage, famed for its still-sophisticated hydraulics.

As far as catching a show here goes, be warned: these days the vibe doesn't quite match the theater's splendor; latecomers are allowed, disrupting performances, and glow-in-the-dark cocktails create an ugly sea of purple drinks more akin to a stadium rock concert. And while the word 'Rockettes' can provoke eye rolling, fans of glitz and kitsch might get a thrill from the troupe's annual Christmas Spectacular.

NEED TO KNOW

Map p188; www.radiocity.com; 1260 Sixth Ave at 51st St; tours adult/child $22.50/16; ⏱tours 11am-3pm; **S** B/D/F, M to 47th-50th Sts-Rockefeller Center

Playwrights Horizons — Theater

Map p188 (☏ tickets 212-279-4200; www.
playwrightshorizons.org; 416 W 42nd St btwn Ninth
& Tenth Aves, Midtown West; S A/C/E to 42nd St-
Port Authority Bus Terminal) An excellent place
to catch what could be the next big thing,
this veteran 'writers' theater' is dedicated to
fostering contemporary American works.

Caroline's on Broadway — Comedy

Map p188 (☏ 212-757-4100; www.carolines.
com; 1626 Broadway at 50th St, Midtown West;
S N/Q/R to 49th St, 1 to 50th St) You may
recognize this big, bright, mainstream
classic from comedy specials filmed here
on location. It's a top spot to catch US
comedy big guns and sitcom stars, but
for something a little more subversive,
don't miss the late-late Friday night show
The Degenerates.

Don't Tell Mama — Cabaret

Map p188 (☏ 212-757-0788; www.donttellma
manyc.com; 343 W 46th St; 2-drink minimum;
⏰ 4pm-1am; S N/Q/R, S, 1/2/3, 7 to Times
Sq-42nd St) Piano bar and cabaret venue
extraordinaire, Don't Tell Mama is an unpretentious little spot that's been around
for more than 25 years and has the talent
to prove it. Its regular roster of performers aren't big names, but true lovers of
cabaret who give each show their all and
don't mind a little singing help from the
audience sometimes.

Oak Room — Cabaret

Map p188 (www.algonquinhotel.com; Algonquin
Hotel, 59 W 44th St btwn Fifth & Sixth Aves,
Midtown West; S B/D/F/V to 42nd St-Bryant Park)
Glam up, order a martini and get the Dor-
othy Parker vibe at this famous piano bar.
Famed for launching the careers of Harry
Connick Jr, Diana Krall and Michael Fein-
stein, its Sunday brunch often sees jazz
veteran Barbara Carroll grace the piano.

Second Stage Theatre — Theater

Map p188 (Tony Kiser Theatre; ☏ tickets 212-246-
4422; www.2st.com; 305 W 43rd St at Eighth Ave,
Midtown West; S A/C/E to 42nd St-Port Authority Bus Terminal) If you're after top-notch
contemporary American theater, this is a
good place to find it.

Therapy — Gay

Map p188 (www.therapy-nyc.com; 348 W 52nd
St btwn Eighth & Ninth Aves; S C/E, 1 to 50th
St) Industry may be the street's new hot
shot, but this multilevel, contemporary
space was the first gay man's lounge/club
to draw throngs to Hell's Kitchen. It still
draws the crowds with its nightly shows
(from music to comedy) and decent fare
Sunday to Friday (burgers, hummus,
salads).

Madison Square Garden — Live Music

Map p188 (www.thegarden.com; Seventh Ave btwn
31st & 33rd Sts; S 1/2/3 to 34th St-Penn Station)
NYC's major performance venue – part
of the massive complex housing Penn
Station and the WaMu Theater – hosts
big-arena performers, from Kanye West
to Madonna. It's also a sports arena, with
New York Knicks (Map p188; ☏ 212-465-
6073, tickets 866-858-0008; www.nyknicks.
com; Madison Square Garden, Seventh Ave btwn
31st & 33rd Sts, Midtown West; tickets $13-330;
S A/C/E, 1/2/3 to 34th St-Penn Station), **New
York Liberty** (Map p188; ☏ 212-564-9622,
tickets 212-465-6073; www.nyliberty.com;
Madison Square Garden, Seventh Ave btwn 31st &
33rd Sts, Midtown West; tickets $10-85; A/C/E,
1/2/3 to 34th St-Penn Station) and **New York
Rangers** (Map p188; ☏ 212-465-6000, tickets
212-307-7171; www.nyrangers.com; Madison
Square Garden, Seventh Ave btwn 31st & 33rd Sts,
Midtown West; tickets from $50; A/C/E, 1/2/3 to
34th St-Penn Station) games, as well as box-
ing matches and events like the Annual
Westminster Kennel Club Dog Show.

🅰 Shopping

Midtown East & Fifth Avenue

Barneys — Department Store

Map p178 (www.barneys.com; 660 Madison Ave
at 61st; S N/Q/R to 5th Ave-59th St) Serious
fashionistas shop at Barneys, well-known
for its spot-on collections of in-the-know
labels like Holmes & Yang, Kitsuné, Miu
Miu and Derek Lam. For less expensive

deals (geared to a younger market), check out Barneys Co-op on the 7th and 8th floors, or on the Upper West Side, in Chelsea, SoHo or Brooklyn.

MoMA Design & Book Store — Books, Gifts

Map p188 (www.momastore.org; 11 W 53rd St btwn Fifth & Sixth Aves; $\boxed{S}$ E, M to 5th Ave-53rd St) The flagship store at the Museum of Modern Art is a savvy spot to souvenir shop in one fell swoop. Aside from stocking must-have books (from art and architecture tomes to pop culture readers and kids' picture books), you'll find art prints and posters, edgy homewares, jewelry, bags and one-of-a-kind knickknacks.

Bloomingdale's — Department Store

Map p178 (www.bloomingdales.com; 1000 Third Ave at E 59th St; ⏱10am-8:30pm Mon Fri, to 7pm Sat, 11am-7pm Sun; 📶; $\boxed{S}$ 4/5/6 to 59th St, N/Q/R to Lexington Ave-59th St) Fresh from a major revamp, epic 'Bloomie's' is something like the Metropolitan Museum of Art to the shopping world: historic, sprawling, overwhelming and packed with bodies, but you'd be sorry to miss it. Raid the racks for clothes and shoes from

a who's who of US and global designers, including an increasing number of 'new-blood' collections. Refuel pitstops include a branch of cupcake heaven Magnolia Bakery.

Bergdorf Goodman — Department Store

Map p178 (📞w; www.bergdorfgoodman.com; 754 Fifth Ave btwn 57th & 58th Sts; $\boxed{S}$ N/Q/R to 5th Ave-59th St, F to 57th St) Not merely loved for its Christmas windows (the city's best), BG gets the approval of the fashion cognoscenti for its exclusive labels and all-round fabulousness. Reinvent yourself with threads from the likes of John Varvatos, Marc Jacobs and Etro, then complete the picture with a lust-inducing booty of handbags, shoes, jewelery, cosmetics and homewares. The men's store is across the street.

Saks Fifth Ave — Department Store

Map p178 (www.saksfifthavenue.com; 611 Fifth Ave at 50th St; $\boxed{S}$ B/D/F, M to 47th-50th Sts-Rockefeller Center, E, M to 5th Ave 53rd St) Complete with beautiful vintage elevators, Saks' 10-floor flagship store fuses old-world glamor with solid service and must-have

Barneys

labels. Go luxe with the likes of Escada, Kiton and Brunello, or opt for younger, edgier, more affordable labels like Scotch & Soda, Vince and Rag & Bone.

Tiffany & Co   Jewelry, Homewares

Map p178 (www.tiffany.com; 727 Fifth Ave; S F to 57th St) This fabled jeweler, with its trademark clock-hoisting Atlas over the door, has won countless hearts with its luxe diamond rings, watches, silver Elsa Peretti heart necklaces, crystal vases and glassware. Swoon, drool, but whatever you do, don't harass the elevator attendants with tired 'Where's the breakfast?' jokes.

FAO Schwarz   Children

Map p178 (www.fao.com; 767 Fifth Ave; S 4/5/6 to 59th St, N/Q/R to 5th Ave-59th St) The toy store giant, where Tom Hanks played footsy piano in the movie *Big,* is number one on the NYC wish list of most visiting kids. The magical (over-the-top consumerist) wonderland, with dolls up for 'adoption,' life-size stuffed animals, gas-powered kiddie convertibles, air-hockey sets and much more, might even thrill you, too.

Dylan's Candy Bar   Food & Drink

Map p178 (www.dylanscandybar.com; 1011 Third Ave at 60th St; ⏱10am-9pm Mon-Thu, to 10pm Fri & Sat, 11am-9pm Sun; S N/Q/R to Lexington Ave-59th St) Willy Wonka has nothing on this three-level feast of giant swirly lollipops, crunchy candy bars, glowing jars of jelly beans, softball-sized cupcakes and a luminescent staircase embedded with scrumptious, unattainable candy. There's a cafe for hot chocolate, espresso, ice cream and other pick-me-ups on the second floor.

Argosy   Books

Map p178 (www.argosybooks.com; 116 E 59th St; ⏱10am-6pm Mon-Fri year-round, to 5pm Sat Sep–mid-May; S 4/5/6 to 59th St, N/Q/R to Lexington Ave-59th St) Since 1925, this landmark used-book store has stocked fine antiquarian items such as leatherbound books, old maps, art monographs and other classics picked up from high-class estate sales and closed antique shops.

Midtown West & Times Square

B&H Photo-Video   Electronics

Map p188 (www.bhphotovideo.com; 420 Ninth Ave btwn 33rd & 34th Sts; ⏱9am-7pm Mon-Thu, to 1pm Fri, 10am-6pm Sun; S A/C/E to 34th St-Penn Station) Visiting NYC's most popular camera shop is an experience in itself – it's massive and crowded, and bustling with black-clad (and tech-savvy) Hasidic Jewish salesmen bused in from communities in distant Brooklyn neighborhoods.

It's all very orderly and fascinating, and the selection of cameras, camcorders, computers and other electronics is outstanding.

FAO Schwarz

Macy's
Department Store

Map p188 (www.macys.com; 151 W 34th St at Broadway; $\boxed{S}$ B/D/F, M, N/Q/R to 34th St-Herald Sq) The world's largest department store covers most bases, with clothing, furnishings, kitcheware, sheets, cafes, hair salons and even a branch of the Metropolitan Museum of Art gift store. It's more 'mid-priced' than 'exclusive', with affordable mainstream labels and big-name cosmetics. Plus, riding the creaky wooden elevators between the eighth and ninth floors on the Broadway side is a must-do NYC experience.

Colony
Music

Map p188 (www.colonymusic.com; 1619 Broadway; ⏰9am-1am Mon-Sat, 10am-midnight Sun; $\boxed{S}$ N/Q/R to 49th St) Located in the Brill Building (onetime home of Tin Pan Alley song crafters), historic Colony once sold sheet music to the likes of Charlie Parker and Miles Davis. Its collection remains the city's largest. Extras include a 60,000-strong LP collection, karaoke CDs and an eclectic booty of memorabilia (Beatles gear, unused Frank and Sammy tickets, Jimmy Osmond dolls), all for sale.

Drama Book Shop
Books

Map p188 (www.dramabookshop.com; 250 W 40th St btwn Seventh & Eighth Aves; ⏰11am-7pm Mon-Wed, Fri & Sat, to 8pm Thu; $\boxed{S}$ A/C/E to 42nd St-Port Authority Bus Terminal) Broadway fans will find treasures in print at this expansive bookstore, which has taken its theatre (both plays and musicals) seriously since 1917. Staffers are good at recommending worthy selections, which span the classics to current hits.

Time Warner Center
Mall

Map p188 (www.shopsatcolumbuscircle.com; Time Warner Center, 10 Columbus Circle; $\boxed{S}$ A/C, B/D, 1 to 59th St-Columbus Circle) A great add-on to an adventure in Central Park, the swank Time Warner Center have a fine booty of largely upscale vendors including Coach, Stuart Weitzman, Williams-Sonoma, True Religion, Hugo Boss, Godiva, Sephora, J Crew, Armani Exchange and Tourneau. For delectable picnic fare, visit the enormous **Whole Foods** (www.wholefoodsmarket.com; Time Warner Center, 10 Columbus Circle; ⏰8am-11pm; $\boxed{S}$ A/C, B/D, 1 to 59th St-Columbus Circle) in the basement for ready-to-go salads, sandwiches, sushi and hot foods.

Rudy's Music
Music

Map p188 (www.rudysmusic.com; 169 W 48th St at Seventh Ave; ⏰closed Sun; $\boxed{S}$ N/Q/R to 49th St) The stretch of 48th St just off Times Square was known as Music Row, and it's where rock royals like the Beatles, Jimi Hendrix and the Stones dropped in for acoustic essentials. Rudy's is one of the last vestiges of this venerable block, particularly for high-end acoustic and classical guitars.

Upper East Side

The Upper East Side has New York's greatest concentration of cultural centers. A long section of Fifth Ave north of 79th St has even been officially designated 'Museum Mile' and includes the grande dame that is the Metropolitan Museum of Art.

But it's not *all* highbrow museums: you'll also find plenty of seriously high-end shops. The neighborhood – whose residents, by the way, are in a never-ending contest with those of the Upper West Side just across the park – also includes many of the city's most exclusive hotels and residences (not to mention many of the city's most moneyed celebrities, from Woody Allen to Shirley MacLaine).

The side streets from Fifth Ave to Third Ave between 57th and 86th Sts feature some stunning town houses and brownstones. Walking through this area at night offers opportunities to see how the other half lives.

199

Upper East Side Highlights

Frick Collection (p212)

The wily and wealthy Henry Clay Frick, a Pittsburgh steel magnate, established a trust to open his private art collection as a museum. On display are paintings by Titian and Johannes Vermeer, and portraits by Gilbert Stuart, El Greco, Goya and John Constable. Perhaps the best asset here is that it is never crowded, providing a welcome break from the swarms of gawkers at larger museums. Courtyard garden, Frick Collection

1

2

Shopping (p217)

The Upper East Side isn't for amateurs. Madison Ave (from 60th St to 72nd St) features one of the globe's glitziest stretches of retail: the flagship boutiques of some of the world's top designers, including Gucci, Prada and Cartier. The neighborhood is also a good spot to hunt down designer deals at consignment shops. Ralph Lauren, Madison Ave

Neue Galerie (p209)

This showcase for German and Austrian art is a small gem among the Fifth Ave biggies, as it's an intimate but well-hung collection, featuring impressive works by Gustav Klimt, Paul Klee and Egon Schiele, housed in a former Rockefeller mansion with winding staircases and wrought-iron banisters. It also boasts a lovely, street-level eatery, Café Sabarsky, serving Viennese meals, drinks and to-die-for pastries on a corner that overlooks Central Park.

Cooper-Hewitt National Design Museum (p209)

This museum is in the 64-room mansion built by billionaire Andrew Carnegie in 1901 in what was, in those days, way uptown. A must for anyone interested in architecture, engineering, jewelry or textiles. Exhibitions have examined everything from advertising campaigns to Viennese blown glass. Even if none of this grabs you, the mansion is stunning and the museum's garden and terrace are well worth a visit.

Roosevelt Island (p215)

Not exactly part of the Upper East Side, Roosevelt Island, in the middle of the East River, is really nothing more than a planned residential community that looks like an Olympic village from the 1960s. However, zipping across the river via the four-minute aerial tram is worth it for the stunning views. Bring along a picnic or a bike. Roosevelt Island tram

Upper East Side Walk

Take a stroll around the Upper East Side – especially the area that covers the blocks from 60th to 86th Sts between Park and Fifth Aves – for a chance to see all things luxurious, as well as some of Manhattan's most filmed locations.

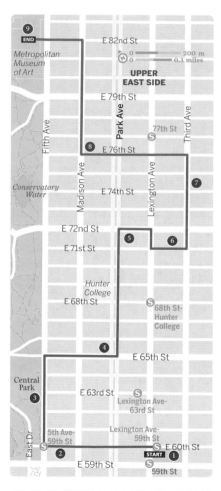

1 Bloomingdale's

Start outside the iconic department store, **Bloomingdale's**, where Darryl Hannah and Tom Hanks shattered televisions in *Splash* (1984) and Dustin Hoffman hailed a cab in *Tootsie* (1982). Pop in to raid the racks for clothes and shoes from a who's who of US and global designers.

2 Copacabana

West of here, 10 60th St is the site of the now defunct **Copacabana** nightclub (now a health food restaurant) that hosted Ray Liotta and Lorraine Bracco in *Goodfellas* (1990) and a coked-up lawyer played by Sean Penn in *Carlito's Way* (1993).

3 Central Park

Continue down 60th St until you hit **Central Park**. The park has appeared in *The Royal Tenenbaums* (2001), *Ghostbusters* (1983), *The Muppets Take Manhattan* (1983), *Barefoot in the Park* (1967) and the cult classic *The Warriors* (1979).

4 John Malkovich's Apartment

Head up Fifth Ave and then turn right into E 65th St and walk until you reach Park Ave. At 620 Park Ave, on the corner of 65th St, you'll find the building that served as **John Malkovich's apartment** in Charlie Kaufman's *Being John Malkovich* (1999).

5 High-Rise

To the north at 114 72nd St is the **high-rise** where Sylvia Miles lured Jon Voight in *Midnight Cowboy* (1969).

WALK FACTS

- **Start** Bloomingdale's
- **Finish** The Met
- **Distance** 1.5 miles
- **Duration** Two hours

6 Holly Golightly's Apartment

One block to the east and south is 171 E 71st St, a townhouse featured in one of the most famous movies to star New York: this was **Holly Golightly's apartment** in *Breakfast at Tiffany's* (1961).

7 JG Mellon

Continuing east to Third Ave, you'll find the restaurant **JG Mellon** at the corner of 74th St, a good spot for beer and burger – plus the site of a meeting between Dustin Hoffman and Meryl Streep in *Kramer vs. Kramer* (1979).

8 Carlyle

Heading west to Madison Ave, the tony **Carlyle** hotel stands at 35 76th St where Woody Allen and Dianne Wiest had a date from hell in *Hannah and Her Sisters* (1986). Notable guests in real life have included John and Jacqueline Kennedy, as well as Princess Diana.

9 Metropolitan Museum of Art

From the Carlyle, it's a short jaunt north and west to the **Met** (p204) at 82nd St and Fifth Ave, where Angie Dickinson had a fatal encounter in *Dressed to Kill* (1980) and Billy Crystal chatted up Meg Ryan in *When Harry Met Sally* (1989). End the tour by getting lost inside the museum's priceless collections.

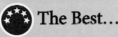 The Best...

PLACES TO EAT

Earl's Beer & Cheese Tiny spot that reinvents traditional American cuisine for today's finicky foodie. (p213)

Café Sabarsky Well-rendered Austrian specialties are worth the wait. (p213)

Sandro's Pasta prices are linked to the stock market: 'When the Dow goes down, your value goes up!' (p214)

PLACES TO DRINK

Metropolitan Museum Roof Garden Café & Martini Bar The sort of setting you can't get enough of (even if you are a jaded local). (p215)

Heidelberg Homey restaurant and German beer garden serving sauerbraten and other traditional goodies. (p216)

Bemelmans Bar Listen to the piano man tickle the ivories in the glorious 1940s elegance of this fabled bar. (p216)

FORMER MANSIONS

Frick Collection Henry K Frick's flamboyantly opulent home-cum-museum. (p212)

Neue Galerie Once a Rockefeller abode near the Met. (p209)

Cooper-Hewitt National Design Museum Billionaire Andrew Carnegie's 64-room home. (p209)

Bemelmans Bar (p216)

Don't Miss
Metropolitan Museum of Art

This sprawling encyclopedic museum, founded in 1870, houses one of the biggest art collections in the world. Its permanent collection has more than two million individual objects, from Egyptian temples to American paintings. Known colloquially as 'The Met,' the museum attracts almost six million visitors a year to its 17 acres of galleries – making it the largest single-site attraction in New York City. (Yup, you read that right: 17 acres.) In other words, plan on spending some time here. It is B-I-G.

Map p210

☎ 212-535-7710

www.met museum.org

1000 Fifth Ave at 82nd St

suggested donation adult/ child $25/free

⏲ 9:30am-5:30pm Tue-Thu & Sun, to 9pm Fri & Sat

🚻

Ⓢ 4/5/6 to 86th St

Egyptian Art

The museum has an unrivaled collection of ancient Egyptian art, some of which dates back to the Paleolithic era. Located to the north of the Great Hall, the 39 Egyptian galleries open dramatically with one of the Met's prized pieces: the Mastaba Tomb of Perneb (c 2300 BC), an Old Kingdom burial chamber crafted from limestone. From here, a web of rooms is cluttered with funerary stele, carved reliefs and fragments of pyramids. (Don't miss the irresistible quartzite sculpture of a lion cub in Gallery 103.) These eventually lead to the Temple of Dendur (Gallery 131), a sandstone temple to the goddess Isis that resides in a sunny atrium gallery with a reflecting pool – a must-see for the first-time visitor.

European Paintings

Want Renaissance? The Met's got it. On the museum's second floor, the European Paintings' galleries display a stunning collection of masterworks. This includes more than 1700 canvases from the roughly 500-year-period starting in the 13th century, with works by every important painter from Duccio to Rembrandt. In fact, everything here is, literally, a masterpiece. On the north end, in Gallery 615, is Vermeer's tender 17th-century painting A Maid Asleep. Gallery 608, to the west, contains a luminous 16th-century altar by Renaissance master Raphael. And in a room stuffed with works by Zurbarán and Murillo (Gallery 618), there is an array of paintings by Velázquez, the most extraordinary of which depicts the dashing Juan de Pareja. And that's just the beginning. You can't go wrong in these galleries.

Art of the Arab Lands

The newly renovated second-floor space comes with a very unwieldy name. The 'New Galleries for the Art of the Arab Lands, Turkey, Iran, Central Asia, and Later South Asia' are comprised of 15 incredible rooms that showcase the museum's extensive collection of art from the Middle East and Central and South Asia. In addition to garments, secular decorative objects and manuscripts, you'll find treasures such as a 12th-century ceramic chess set from Iran (Gallery 453) that is downright Modernist in its simplicity. There is also a superb array of Ottoman textiles (Gallery 459), a medieval-style Moroccan court (Gallery 456) and an 18th-century room from Damascus (Gallery 461).

American Wing

In the northwest corner, the recently revamped American galleries showcase a wide variety of decorative and fine art from throughout US history. These include everything from colonial portraiture to Hudson River School masterpieces to John Singer Sargent's unbearably sexy Madame X (Gallery 771) – not to mention Emanuel Leutze's massive canvas of Washington Crossing the Delaware (Gallery 760). The galleries are stacked around an interior sculpture court abutted by a pleasant cafe.

Rooftop

One of the best spots in the entire museum is the roof garden, which features rotating sculpture installations by contemporary and 20th-century artists. (Sol Lewitt, Jeff Koons and Andy Goldsworthy have all shown here.) But its best feature is the views it offers of the city and Central Park. It is also home to the Roof Garden Café & Martini Bar (p215), the best place in the museum for a sip – especially at sunset. The roof garden is open from April to October.

Seeing the Museum

A desk inside the Great Hall has audio tours in several languages ($7), while docents offer guided tours of specific galleries. These are free with admission. Check the website or information desk for details. If you can't stand crowds, avoid weekends.

Don't Miss
Guggenheim Musuem

A sculpture in its own right, architect Frank Lloyd Wright's building almost overshadows the collection of 20th-century art it houses. Completed in 1959, the inverted ziggurat structure was derided by some critics, but it was hailed by others who welcomed it as a beloved architectural icon. Since it first opened, this unusual structure has appeared on countless postcards, TV programs and films.

Map p210

☎ 212-423-3500

www.guggen
heim.org

1071 Fifth Ave
at 89th St

adult/child $18/
free, by donation
5:45-7:45pm Sat

🕐 10am-5:45pm
Sun-Wed & Fri, to
7:45pm Sat

👫

S 4/5/6 to 86th St

Abstract Roots

The Guggenheim came out of the collection of Solomon R Guggenheim, a New York mining magnate who began acquiring abstract art in his 60s at the behest of his art adviser, an eccentric German baroness named Hilla Rebay. In 1939, with Rebay serving as director, Guggenheim opened a temporary museum on 54th St titled Museum of Non-Objective Painting. (Incredibly, it had grey velour walls, piped in classical music and burning incense.) Four years later, the pair commissioned Wright to construct a permanent home for the collection.

A Pink Guggenheim

Wright made hundreds of sketches and pondered the use of various materials for the construction of the museum. At one point, he considered using red marble for the exterior facade – a 1945 model sketch shows a pink building – but the color scheme was rejected.

Years in the Making

Like any development in New York City, the project took forever to come to fruition. Construction was delayed for almost 13 years due to budget constraints, the outbreak of WWII and outraged neighbors who weren't all that excited to see an architectural spaceship land in their midst. Construction was completed in 1959, after both Wright and Guggenheim had passed away.

Bring on the Critics

When the Guggenheim opened its doors in October 1959, the ticket price was 50 cents and the works on view included pieces by Kandinsky, Alexander Calder and abstract expressionists Franz Kline and Willem De Kooning.

The structure was savaged by the *New York Times*, which lambasted it as 'a war between architecture and painting in which both come out badly maimed.' But others quickly celebrated it as 'the most beautiful building in America.' Whether Wright intended to or not, he had given the city one of its most visible landmarks.

To the Present

The Guggenheim's vast collection includes works by Kandinsky, Picasso, Chagall and Jackson Pollock. In 1976, Justin Thannhauser donated a major trove of impressionist and modern works that included paintings by Monet, Van Gogh and Degas. Three years later, Guggenheim's niece Peggy left the museum key surrealist works, including pieces by René Magritte and Yves Tanguy. In 1992, the Robert Mapplethorpe Foundation bequeathed 200 photographs to the museum, making the Guggenheim the single-most important public repository of his work.

Only a tiny fraction of the Guggenheim's collection is on view at any given time.

Visiting the Museum

The museum's ascending ramp is occupied by rotating exhibitions of modern and contemporary art. Though Wright intended visitors to go to the top and wind their way down, the cramped, single elevator doesn't allow for this. Exhibitions, therefore, are installed from bottom to top.

There are two good on-site food options: **The Wright**, at ground level, a space-age eatery serving steamy risotto and classic cocktails, and **Cafe 3**, on the third floor, which offers sparkling views of Central Park and excellent coffee and light snacks.

The line to get in to the museum can be brutal. You'll save time if you purchase tickets online in advance.

Discover Upper East Side

Getting There & Away

- **Subway** The sole subway lines here are the 4/5/6 which travel north and south on Lexington Ave. Note that this train gets packed to sardine levels at rush hour, which means that if you're just traveling one or two stops, you'll be better off walking. A new stretch of subway track underneath Second Ave is expected to be completed by late 2016.

- **Bus** The M1/2/3/4 buses all make the scenic drive down Fifth Ave along the eastern edge of Central Park. The M15 can be handy for getting around the far east side, traveling up First Ave and down Second. Crosstown buses at 66th, 72nd, 79th, 86th and 96th Sts take you across the park and into the Upper West Side.

Metropolitan Museum of Art

LEESNIDERP/DREAMSTIME.COM ©

Sights

Metropolitan Museum of Art Museum

See p204.

Guggenheim Museum Museum

See p206.

Whitney Museum of American Art Museum

Map p210 (☎212-570-3600, 800-944-8639; www.whitney.org; 945 Madison Ave cnr 75th St; adult/child $18/free; 🕐11am-6pm Wed, Thu, Sat & Sun, 1-9pm Fri; [S]6 to 77th St) The Whitney makes no secret of its mission to provoke, which starts with its imposing Brutalist building, a structure that houses works by 20th-century masters Edward Hopper, Jasper Johns, Georgia O'Keeffe and Mark Rothko. In addition to rotating exhibits, there is a biennial on even years, an ambitious survey of contemporary art that rarely fails to generate controversy.

The museum was opened in 1931 by society doyenne Gertrude Vanderbilt Whitney, who was known for her lively Greenwich Village salons. During her lifetime, she collected more than 600 works of art, including canvases by painters such as Thomas Hart Benton and George Bellows. These works comprise the core of the museum's permanent collection, which is beautifully displayed on the fifth floor.

After inhabiting various locations downtown, the Whitney moved to its current Marcel Breuer–designed building in 1975. But, having outgrown these digs, it is set to move again. A new Renzo

Piano–designed structure is currently under construction in the Meatpacking District and is scheduled to be completed in 2015.

For food, try the museum's new Danny Meyer comfort eatery in the basement, Untitled. In addition to a variety of snacks and sandwiches, they serve breakfast all day (pancakes $10).

Neue Galerie
Museum

Map p210 (212-628-6200; www.neuegalerie. org; 1048 Fifth Ave cnr E 86th St; admission $20, 6-8pm 1st Fri of every month free, children under 12 not admitted; 11am-6pm Thu-Mon; 4/5/6 to 86th St) This restored Carrère and Hastings mansion from 1914 is a resplendent showcase for German and Austrian art, featuring works by Paul Klee, Ernst Ludwig Kirchner and Egon Schiele. In pride of place on the second floor is Gustav Klimt's golden 1907 portrait of Adele Bloch-Bauer – which was acquired for the museum by cosmetics magnate Ronald Lauder for a whopping $135 million.

This is a small but beautiful place with winding staircases and wrought-iron banisters. It also boasts the lovely, street-level eatery, Café Sabarsky. Avoid weekends if you don't want to deal with gallery-clogging crowds.

Cooper-Hewitt National Design Museum
Museum

Map p210 (212-849-8400; www.cooperhewitt. org; 2 E 91st St at Fifth Ave; adult/child $15/free; 4/5/6 to 86th St) Part of the Smithsonian Institution in Washington, DC, this house of culture is the only museum in the country that's dedicated to both historic and contemporary design. The collection is housed in the 64-room mansion built by billionaire Andrew Carnegie in 1901. The museum closed in 2011 for a two-year renovation and expansion. Check the website for updates.

Jewish Museum
Museum

Map p210 (212-423-3200; www.jewishmu seum.org; 1109 Fifth Ave at 92nd St; adult/ child $12/free, 11am-5:45pm Sat free; 11am-5:45pm Thu-Tue, to 4pm Fri; ; 6 to 96th St) This New York City gem is tucked into a French-Gothic mansion from 1908, which houses 30,000 items of Judaica, as well as sculpture, painting and decorative arts. It is well regarded for its thoughtful temporary exhibits, featuring retrospectives on

Exterior of Guggenheim Museum (p206), designed by Frank Lloyd Wright

0   500 m
0   0.25 miles

The Loch
Conservatory Garden
🏛6
103rd St
E 104th St
E 103rd St
E 102nd St
Ward's Island

To Museum for
African Art (0.25mi)
E 101st St
E 101st St
E 100th St
North Meadow
East Meadow
Park Ave
E 100th St
E 99th St
East River

Second Ave
E 98th St
✕15
E 97th St
96th St
E 96th St
Mill Rock Light Park

Madison Ave
Fifth Ave
E 95th St
E 94th St
E 93rd St
Mill Rock Island

🏛5
✕22
E 92nd St
E 91st St
28
Carl Schurz Park

Jacqueline Kennedy Onassis Reservoir
🏛2
🏛7
E 90th St
E 89th St
Third Ave
UPPER EAST SIDE
4🏛

Guggenheim Museum
11
E 88th St
E 87th St

13
86th St
E 86th St
🍴25
York Ave

Central Park
✕🏛8
E 85th St
E 84th St
YORKVILLE

Great Lawn
E 83rd St

Metropolitan Museum of Art
21✕
Park Ave
E 82nd St
🍴29
First Ave
East End Ave

31🔒
E 81st St
17✕✕18
27🍴

Turtle Pond
🍴23
🍴32
E 80th St
E 79th St
FDR Dr

The Ramble
✕19
E 78th St
E 77th St
John Jay Park

Loeb Boathouse
🍴24
77th St
E 76th St
🍴26
East End Ave

✕12
🍴34
E 75th St
E 74th St
✕14
16
East River

The Lake
Conservatory Water
🏛10
20✕
E 73rd St
E 72nd St

Bethesda Terrace
E 71st St

Rumsey Playfield
Naumburg Bandshell
🏛3
🏛1
E 70th St
E 69th St
Rockefeller University

Sheep Meadow
The Mall
Hunter College
🔒33
E 68th St
68th St-Hunter College
E 67th St

Literary Walk
Lexington Ave
Fifth Ave
E 66th St
E 65th St

Park Ave

The Dairy
Center Dr
E 64th St
Lexington Ave-63rd St
E 63rd St
E 62nd St

Wollman Rink
✕9
30
E 61st St
Lexington Ave-59th St
Roosevelt Island Tramway Station
Roosevelt Island

The Pond
5th Ave-59th St
Central Park South
E 60th St
59th St
E 59th St
59th St
Queensboro-59th St Bridge

Central Park

East Dr

210

Upper East Side

influential figures such as Chaim Soutine and sprawling examinations of socially conscious photography in New York.

There are frequent lectures and events, as well as an array of activities for children. Every January, the museum collaborates with the Film Society of Lincoln Center to present the New York Jewish Film Festival.

Museum of the City of New York   Museum

Map p210 (☎212-534-1672; www.mcny.org; 1220 Fifth Ave btwn 103rd & 104th Sts; suggested donation $20; ⏰10am-6pm; S6 to 103rd St) Situated in a colonial Georgian-style mansion, this local museum focuses solely on New York City's past, present and future. You'll find internet-based historical resources, lots of vintage photographs and a scale model of New Amsterdam shortly after the Dutch arrival. The second-floor gallery includes entire rooms from demolished homes of New York grandees.

One of the museum's star attractions is the 12-room mansion dollhouse fabricated by Carrie Stettheimer over 25 years at the turn of the 20th century – replete with tiny art works (including miniatures of pieces by Marcel Duchamp and Gaston Lachaise).

National Academy Museum   Museum

Map p210 (☎212-369-4880; www.nationalacad emy.org; 1083 Fifth Ave at 89th St; adult/child $12/free; ⏰noon-5pm Wed & Thu, 11am-6pm Fri-Sun; S4/5/6 to 86th St) Co-founded by painter/inventor Samuel Morse in 1825, the National Academy Museum is comprised of an incredible permanent collection of paintings by figures such as Wil Barnet, Thomas Hart Benton and George Bellows. It is housed in a beaux arts structure designed by Ogden Codman and featuring a marble foyer and spiral staircase.

ARCAID IMAGES/ALAMY ©

Don't Miss Frick Collection

This spectacular art collection sits in a mansion built by prickly steel magnate Henry Clay Frick, one of the many such residences that made up Millionaires' Row. The museum has 12 splendid rooms that display masterpieces by Titian, Vermeer, Gilbert Stuart, El Greco and Goya. The Oval Room is graced by Jean-Antoine Houdon's stunning figure 'Diana the Huntress.'

This museum is a treat for a number of reasons. One, it resides in a lovely, rambling beaux arts structure built in 1913–14 by Carrère and Hastings. Two, it is generally not crowded. And, three, it feels refreshingly intimate, with a trickling indoor courtyard fountain and gardens that can be explored on warmer days. A demure new Portico Gallery, opened in 2011, displays decorative works and sculpture.

A worthwhile audio tour (available in several languages) is included in the price of admission. Classical music fans will enjoy the frequent piano and violin concerts that take place on Sundays.

NEED TO KNOW

Map p210; ☎212-288-0700; www.frick.org; 1 E 70th St at Fifth Ave; admission $18, by donation 11am-1pm Sun, children under 10 not admitted; 🕑10am-6pm Tue-Sat, 11am-5pm Sun; [S]6 to 68th St-Hunter College

[FREE] **Temple Emanu-El** Synagogue
Map p210 (☎212-744-1400; www.emanuelnyc.org; 1 E 65th St cnr Fifth Ave; 🕑10am-5pm Mon-Thu; [S]6 to 68th St-Hunter College) Founded in 1845 as the first Reform synagogue in New York, this temple, completed in 1929, is now one of the largest Jewish houses of worship in the world. An imposing Romanesque structure, it is more than 175ft long and a 100ft tall, with a brilliant,

hand-painted ceiling that contains details in gold.

The structure also boasts 60 stained-glass windows and a massive rose window whose dozen panels represent the 12 tribes of Israel.

The temple is home to the small Herbert & Eileen Bernard Museum of Judaica, with more than 650 pieces that date back to the 14th century.

Asia Society & Museum   Museum
Map p210 (212 288 6400; www.asiasociety.org; 725 Park Ave at 70th St; admission $10, 6pm-9pm Fri mid-Sept–Jun free; 11am-6pm Tue-Sun, to 9pm Fri mid-Sept–Jun; S 6 to 68th St-Hunter College) Founded in 1956 by John D Rockefeller, this cultural center is meant to strengthen Western understanding of Asia and the relationships between that region and the US. There are events and lectures, but the biggest draw is the museum, which shows rotating contemporary exhibits, as well as treasures – such as Jain sculptures and Nepalese Buddhist paintings.

Gracie Mansion   Historic Building
Map p210 (212-570-4773, tour reservations 311 or 212-NEW-YORK; www.nyc.gov/gracie; East End Ave at E 88th St; admission $7; tours 10am, 11am, 1pm & 2pm Wed; S 4/5/6 to 86th St) This Federal-style home served as the country residence of merchant Archibald Gracie in 1799. Since 1942, it has been where New York's mayors have lived – with the exception of megabillionaire Mayor Michael Bloomberg, who prefers his own plush, Upper East Side digs. The house has been added to and renovated over the years. Reservations required.

The home is bordered by the pleasant, riverside Carl Schurz Park.

Eating

Earl's Beer & Cheese   American $
Map p210 (www.earlsny.com; 1259 Park Ave btwn 97th & 98th Sts; grilled cheese $6-8, mains $8-17; 4pm-midnight Tue-Fri, 11am-midnight Sat & Sun; S 6 to 96th St) Chef Corey Cova's comfort food outpost channels a hipster hunting vibe, complete with buck's head

Top Tip

The Upper East Side is the place to be for all things luxurious, especially the area that covers the blocks from 60th to 86th Sts between Park and Fifth Aves. As a general rule, if you're looking for eating and drinking spots that are easier on the wallet, head east of Lexington Ave. First, Second and Third Aves are lined with less pricey neighborhood spots.

on the wall. Rest assured that these aren't warmed-over American classics. Basic grilled cheese is a paradigm shifter, served with pork belly, fried egg and Kimchi. There is also mac 'n' cheese and waffles (with foie gras), none of it like anything you've ever eaten.

Earl's is tiny and fills up fast, so order at the bar and grab a seat at the communal picnic table. There is a good selection of craft beers.

Café Sabarsky   Austrian $$
Map p210 (www.wallse.com; 1048 Fifth Ave at E 86th St; mains $12-20; breakfast, lunch & dinner; ; S 4/5/6 to 86th St) The lines get long at this popular cafe, which evokes opulent turn-of-the-20th-century Vienna. Expect crepes with smoked trout, goulash soup and creamed *spätzle* (a type of German noodle). And save room for dessert: there is a long list of specialty sweets, including a divine *sachertorte* (dark chocolate cake laced with apricot preserves).

Café Boulud   French $$$
Map p210 (212-772-2600; www.danielnyc.com/cafebouludny.html; 20 E 76th St at Madison Ave; mains $24-44; breakfast, lunch & dinner; ; S 6 to 77th St) Now steered by Gavin Kaysen, this Michelin-starred bistro – part of Daniel Boulud's gastronomic empire – attracts a staid crowd with its globe-trotting French cuisine. Foodies on a budget will

be interested in the two-course, $37 prix fixe lunch.

Gents should consider wearing a jacket in the evenings. Reservations recommended.

Sandro's
Italian **$$$**

Map p210 (☎212-288-7374; www.sandrosnyc.com; 306 E 81st St near Second Ave; mains $20-35; ⏰4:30pm-11pm Mon-Sat, to 10pm Sun; [S]6 to 77th St) This neighborhood trattoria serves up fresh Roman dishes and homemade pastas by chef Sandro Fioriti. Specialties include crisp fried artichokes and sea urchin ravioli. From 4:30pm to 6:30pm on weekdays, all pasta dishes are priced according to the closing average of the Dow Jones Index. (If the Dow closes at 11,000, your pasta will be $11.)

Sant Ambroeus
Cafe **$$**

Map p210 (☎212-570-2211; www.santambroeus.com; 1000 Madison Ave btwn 77th & 78th St; tea sandwiches $8, pastries $10, mains $22-48; ⏰8am-11pm; ✎; [S]6 to 77th St) Behind a demure facade lies this dressy Milanese bistro and cafe that oozes old-world charm. Up front, a long granite counter dispenses inky espressos, pastries and tea sandwiches (think vegetable frittata and parma ham), while the elegant dining room in the back dishes up northern Italian specialties such as octopus salad and saffron risotto.

Luke's
Seafood **$$**

Map p210 (www.lukeslobster.com; 242 E 81st St near Second Ave; lobster roll $15; ⏰11am-10pm Sun-Thu, to 11pm Fri & Sat; [S]6 to 77th St) This place delivers one hell of a succulent lobster roll: a buttered, toasted, split-top bun stuffed with chilled lobster salad that is dabbed with a swipe of mayonnaise and a sprinkle of lemon butter.

William Greenberg Desserts
Bakery **$**

Map p210 (www.wmgreenbergdesserts.com; 1100 Madison Ave btwn 82nd & 83rd; baked goods from $1.50; ⏰8am-6:30pm Mon-Fri, to 6pm Sat, 10am-4pm Sun; 👪; [S]4/5/6 to 86th St) This pristine bakery serves up a delectable array of traditional Jewish treats including *hamantaschen* (a triangular, jam-filled cookie), cupcakes, brownies and what has to be New York City's finest black-and-white cookie, a soft vanilla disc dipped in white sugar and dark chocolate glazes.

Via Quadronno
Cafe **$$**

Map p210 (☎212-650-9880; www.viaquadronno.com; 25 E 73rd St btwn Madison & Fifth Aves; sandwiches $7-17, mains $20-26; ⏰8am-11pm Mon-Fri, 9am-11pm Sat, 10am-9pm Sun; ✎; [S]6 to 77th St) A little slice of Italy that looks like it's been airlifted into New York, this cozy cafe-bistro has exquisite coffee (rich, not bitter), as well as a mind-boggling selection of sandwiches – one of which is stuffed with venison prosciutto and Camembert. There

Café Boulud (p213)
OWEN FRANKEN/CORBIS ©

Roosevelt: The Island Off the Island of Manhattan

Not exactly part of the Upper East Side but floating in the East River between Manhattan's eastern edge and Queens, New York's anomalous, planned neighborhood sits on a tiny island no wider than a football field. It was once known as Blackwell's Island after the farming family who lived here; the city bought the island in 1828 and constructed several public hospitals and a mental hospital. In the 1970s, New York State built housing for 10,000 people along Roosevelt Island's Main St (the only street on the island). The planned area along the cobblestone roadway resembles an Olympic village or, as some observe more cynically, cookie-cutter college housing.

Zipping across the river via the four-minute aerial tram is a trip in itself and worth it for the stunning view of the East Side of Manhattan framed by the 59th St Bridge. Instead of heading straight back like most do, however, bring a picnic or a bike, as this quiet island is conducive to lounging and cycling. Trams leave from the Roosevelt Island tramway station every 15 minutes on the quarter-hour from 6am to 2am Sunday to Thursday, and until 3:30am Friday and Saturday; the one-way fare is $2. Roosevelt Island also has a subway station.

are soups, pastas and a very popular daily lasagna.

If you're pressed for time, belly up to the granite counter for a quick macchiato and a cookie snack.

Candle Cafe   Vegan $$
Map p210 (212-472-0970; www.candlecafe. com; 1307 Third Ave btwn 74th & 75th Sts; mains $15-20; 11:30am-10:30pm Mon-Sat, to 9:30pm Sun; ; 6 to 77th St) The moneyed, yoga set piles into this attractive vegan cafe serving a long list of sandwiches, salads, comfort food and market-driven specials. The specialty here is the house-made seitan. (Try it crusted with porcini and served with mashed potatoes and gravy – the perfect cold-day dish.)

JG Melon   Pub $
Map p210 (212-744-0585; 1291 Third Ave at 74th St; burgers $10; 11:30am-4am; 6 to 77th St) JG's is a loud, old-school, melon-themed pub that has been serving basic burgers on tea plates since 1972. It's a local favorite for both eating and drinking (the Bloody Marys are excellent) and it gets crowded in the after-work hours.

Yura on Madison   Deli $
Map p210 (www.yuraonmadison.com; 1292 Madison Ave cnr E 92nd St; sandwiches $6-9, box lunches $7-10; 6:30am-7pm Mon-Fri, 7am-4pm Sat & Sun; ; 6 to 96th St) A crisp, white emporium of yuppiedom sells fresh sandwiches, premade salads and excellent scones. Everything here is designed for quick eating or take-out. The ready-made box lunches are ideal for Central Park picnics.

Drinking & Nightlife

Metropolitan Museum Roof Garden Café & Martini Bar   Cocktail Bar
Map p210 (www.metmuseum.org; 1000 Fifth Ave at 82nd St; 10am-4:30pm Sun & Tue-Thu, to 8pm Fri & Sat, Martini Bar 5:30pm-8pm Fri & Sat May-Oct; 4/5/6 to 86th St) The sort of setting you can't get enough of (even if you are a jaded local). The roof garden's bar sits right above Central Park's tree canopy, allowing for splendid views of the park and the city skyline all around. Sun-

MICHAEL HEIMAN/GETTY IMAGES ©

set is when you'll find fools in love – then again it could all be those martinis.

Bemelmans Bar   Lounge
Map p210 (www.thecarlyle.com/dining/bemel mans_bar; Carlyle Hotel, 35 E 76th St at Madison Ave; ⏰noon-2am Mon-Sat, to 12:30am Sun; Ⓢ6 to 77th St) Sink into a chocolate leather banquette and take in the glorious 1940s elegance of this fabled bar – the sort of place where the waiters wear white jackets, a baby grand is always tinkling and the ceiling is 24-carat gold leaf. Show up before 9:30pm if you don't want to pay a cover (per person $15 to $30).

Heidelberg   Beer Garden
Map p210 (www.heidelbergrestaurant.com; 1648 Second Ave btwn 85th & 86th Sts; ⏰11:30am-10pm Sun-Thu, to 11pm Fri & Sat; Ⓢ4/5/6 to 86th St) Beer, schnapps and schnitzel. This old-school German beer garden supplies the trifecta of Teutonic pleasure – as well as servers decked out in Bavarian costume. Feeling thirsty? You can order your Spaten in a 2L Stiefel (glass boot). Hokey-good fun. *Ein Prosit!*

Iggy's   Karaoke
Map p210 (www.iggysnewyork.com; 1452 Second Ave; ⏰noon-4am; Ⓢ6 to 77th St) How much you love this skinny Irish-lite pub with its 100ft long bar depends on how badly you need to misbehave in the Upper East Side. The karaoke mic certainly helps the raucous regulars, who bring on a bit of a frat-house atmosphere some nights.

Luke's Bar & Grill   Pub
Map p210 (www.lukesbarandgrill.com; 1394 Third Ave btwn 79th & 80th St; ⏰11:30am-1am Mon-Fri, to 2am Sat; Ⓢ6 to 77th St) This laid-back local hangout offers a respite from Red Bull and ridiculous drink prices, with an inexpensive selection of beers and solid pub grub. Cash only.

⭐ Entertainment

Feinstein's at the Regency   Cabaret
Map p210 (www.feinsteinsattheregency.com; 540 Park Ave at 61st St; tickets $40-280; Ⓢ F to Lexington Ave-63rd St, N/Q/R to Lexington Ave-59th St) You'll be puttin' on the ritz at this old-

school cabaret spot from crooner Michael Feinstein. The storied stage has hosted everyone from Rosemary Clooney to Vikki Carr to Tony Danza. (Yes, Tony Danza.) It's a small room, so buy tickets in advance for big-name Broadway acts.

Café Carlyle
Map p210 (www.thecarlyle.com/dining/cafe_carlyle; 35 E 76th St at Madison Ave; cover $90-175; S 6 to 77th St) This swanky spot at the Carlyle Hotel draws top-shelf talent, from Bettye Lavette to Woody Allen, who plays his clarinet here with the Eddy Davis New Orleans Jazz Band on Mondays at 8:45pm (September through May). Bring bucks: the cover doesn't include food or drinks.

Frick Collection   Classical Music
Map p210 (www.frick.org; 1 E 70th St at Fifth Ave; S 6 to 68th St Hunter College) This opulent mansion-museum also hosts Sunday concerts that bring world-renowned performers such as cellist Yehuda Hanani and violinist Thomas Zehetmair. This is a lovely, intimate space and a very special type of concert experience.

92nd St Y   Cultural Center
Map p210 (www.92y.org; 1395 Lexington Ave at 92nd St; ⛎; S 6 to 96th St) In addition to its wide spectrum of wonderful readings, this nonprofit cultural center hosts an excellent lecture and conversation series. Past presenters have included playwright Edward Albee, cellist Yo-Yo Ma, crooner Lou Reed and novelist Gary Shteyngart.

Comic Strip Live   Comedy
Map p210 (📞212-861-9386; www.comicstriplive.com; 1568 Second Ave btwn 81st & 82nd Sts; cover charge $22-28 plus 2-drink min; ⏰ shows 8:30pm Sun-Thu, 8:30pm, 10:30pm & 12:30pm Fri, 8pm, 10:30pm & 12:30am Sat; S 4/5/6 to

86th St) Adam Sandler, Jerry Seinfeld and Eddie Murphy have all performed at this club. Not recently, but you're sure to find somebody stealing their acts here most nights. Reservations required.

 # Shopping

Michael's   Consignment Store
Map p210 (www.michaelsconsignment.com; 2nd fl, 1041 Madison Ave btwn 79th & 80th Sts; ⏰9:30am-6pm Mon-Sat, to 8pm Thu; S 6 to 77th St) In operation since the 1950s, this is a vaunted Upper East Side resale shop that is strong on high-end labels, including Chanel, Gucci and Prada. Almost everything on display is less than two years old. It's pricey, but cheaper than shopping the flagship boutiques on Madison Ave.

Crawford Doyle Booksellers   Books
Map p210 (1082 Madison Ave btwn 81st & 82nd Sts; ⏰10am-6pm Mon-Sat, noon-5pm Sun; S 6 to 77th St) This genteel Upper East Side book shop invites browsing, with stacks devoted to art, literature and the history of New York – not to mention plenty of first editions. A wonderful place to while away a chilly afternoon.

Zitomer   Beauty
Map p210 (www.zitomer.com; 969 Madison Ave btwn 75th & 76th Sts; ⏰9am-8pm Mon-Fri, to 7pm Sat, 10am-6pm Sun; S 6 to 77th St) This three-story retro pharmacy carries all things European, including products that aren't exactly (ahem) FDA approved. We're not talking illicit drugs, just high-powered sunscreens and skin-care creams that are usually only available across the pond.

Upper West Side & Central Park

A sprawling park and high culture define this neighborhood's unique ecosystem. Home to aging liberals, wealthy young families and an eclectic mix of actors and musicians, the Upper West Side stretches up along the western side of Central Park to Riverside Park, which runs along the Hudson River. Quaint residential blocks and bustling sections of Broadway have been hyperdeveloped into strips of high-rise condos, drugstore chains and banks. Much of the area is still an architectural wonderland, though, with everything from opulent apartment buildings to the redesigned Lincoln Center.

Designed as a leisure space for all New Yorkers, the vast and majestic Central Park is an oasis from the urban insanity. The lush lawns, cool forests, flowering gardens, glassy bodies of water, and meandering, wooded paths provide the dose of serene nature that New Yorkers crave.

Central Park (p224), the Upper West Side and George Washington Bridge
ANGUS OBORN/LONELY PLANET IMAGES ©

Upper West Side & Central Park Highlights

American Museum of Natural History (p234)

Kids of all ages will find something intriguing at the American Museum of Natural History, whether it's the stuffed Alaskan brown bear, the Star of India sapphire in the Hall of Minerals and Gems, the IMAX film on jungle life, or the skullcap of a pachycephalosaurus. Step inside the Rose Center for Earth & Space, a high-tech planetarium that traces the origins of the planets. Allosaurus skeleton, Roosevelt Rotunda

Lincoln Center (p237)

This stark arrangement of gleaming Modernist temples contains some of Manhattan's most important performance spaces: Avery Fisher Hall, David H Koch Theater, and the iconic Metropolitan Opera House, whose interior walls are dressed with bright murals by painter Marc Chagall. Various other venues are tucked around the 16-acre campus, including the renowned Juilliard School.

Avery Fisher Hall, designed by Max Abramovitz

Riverside Park (p230)

Riverside Park stretches for 4 miles between W 72nd St and W 158th St along the Hudson River, and is a great place for strolling, running, cycling or simply gazing at the sun as it sets over the Hudson River. There are well-placed benches, a dog run and various works of public art, including a statue of Eleanor Roosevelt at the 72nd St entrance.

3

4

5

Broadway (p233)

While it's a far cry from the bad ol' days of the 1970s and even '80s – when there was an unsavory feel in the air – today's stretch of Broadway on the Upper West Side has been colonized by banks, pharmacies and retail chains. However, it's still the spine of the neighborhood, lined with prewar apartments, used-book dealers and traditional diners.

Loeb Boathouse (p236)

Perched on the shores of the Lake in the heart of Central Park, the historic Loeb Boathouse is one of the city's best settings for an idyllic meal and an escape from the urban madness. It is also an oft-filmed setting. There's no better romantic gesture or first date than renting a rowboat and powering your way around the nooks and crannies of the lake until you find a little corner all your own.

Upper West Side & Central Park Walk

While Broadway is carpeted with charmless chains, the Upper West Side is still an architectural bonanza. Stroll through the the city's premier high arts center, walk among the large dinosaurs, and escape the city's frantic madness in Central Park.

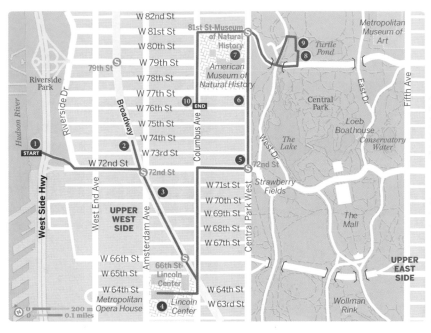

WALK FACTS

- **Start** Riverside Park
- **Finish** Columbus Ave
- **Distance** 2.3 miles
- **Duration** One to two hours

1 Riverside Park

Begin your walk in **Riverside Park** (p230) – a lovely stretch of green on the western edge of the neighborhood. Be sure to visit the wonderful bronze statue of native New Yorker Eleanor Roosevelt, by sculptor Penelope Jencks, added to the park at 72nd St with some pomp and circumstance in 1996.

2 Ansonia

Walk east on 72nd St and turn left on Broadway, heading uptown to the grand and sophisticated **Ansonia** building between 73rd 74th Sts.

3 Dorilton

Turn back south on Broadway to 71st St to gaze at the **Dorilton** building, with an enormous arched entryway and beaux arts magnificence.

4 Lincoln Center

Continue south on Broadway, heading downtown to 64th St and the grand entrance of the **Lincoln Center's** (p237) vast campus of performance spaces. Take a gander at the large and lovely Chagall paintings in the windows of the Metropolitan Opera House.

Dakota

Head up Columbus Ave to 72nd St and turn right, continuing until you hit Central Park. On your left you'll see the **Dakota** building, the exterior of which was used for the film *Rosemary's Baby*. It's also where John Lennon lived, and the site of his 1980 murder. Across the street, just inside Central Park, is **Strawberry Fields**, a touching shrine to the late star.

6 New-York Historical Society

Continue up along Central Park West to 77th St for a fascinating collection of city ephemera from both the distant and more recent pasts at the **New-York Historical Society** (p230).

7 American Museum of Natural History

The **American Museum of Natural History** (p234) is one block north and filled with wildlife, geological and astronomical exhibits. Gaze at the ethereal Rose Center for Earth & Space, on the 79th St side.

8 Belvedere Castle

Enter back into the park at 81st St and cross West Dr until you see the lovely 19th-century **Belvedere Castle**, which rises up out of Vista Rock and provides breezy, beautiful views of the parkland; a great perch for a photo.

9 Delacorte Theater

Just on the other side of Turtle Pond is the **Delacorte Theater**, home to summertime Shakespeare in the Park productions.

10 Columbus Ave

Head west out of the park to **Columbus Ave**, where you can stroll the bustling stretch of shops and eateries in this family-filled 'hood. There's no shortage of tempting cafes. If you're up for some vintage shopping, comb through the **Greenflea** (between 76th and 77th Sts), one of the first open-air city markets, offering goods from clothing to furniture.

✦ The Best...

PLACES TO EAT

Fatty Crab Creative Malaysian-inspired dishes served in a stylish setting. (p235)

Dovetail For foodies watching their dollars, the tasting menu is a bargain. (p233)

Barney Greengrass It doesn't get more Upper West Side than lox, herring and sturgeon at this local institution. (p235)

Gray's Papaya Nothing is more New York than soaking up the evening's liquor damage with a midnight hot dog from here. (p235)

PLACES TO DRINK

Ding Dong Lounge Popular with Columbia students and guests from nearby hostels for its beer-and-a-shot combo. (p238)

Barcibo Enoteca Near Lincoln Center, great for a pre-show glass of expertly curated Italian wine. (p236)

PLACES FOR LIVE PERFORMANCE

Metropolitan Opera House Top stars and mind-boggling costumes and sets. (p238)

Delacorte Theater Magical summer evening performances of Shakespeare in Central Park. (p226)

Beacon Theatre Like a mini Radio City Music Hall, this renovated concert hall skews to classic rock. (p239)

Dovetail (p233)

Don't Miss
Central Park

Comprised of more than 800 acres of picturesque meadows, ponds and woods, it might be tempting to think that Central Park represents Manhattan in its raw state. It does not. Designed by Frederick Law Olmsted and Calvert Vaux, the park is the result of serious engineering: thousands of workers shifted 10 million cartloads of soil to transform swamp and rocky outcroppings into the 'people's park' of today.

Map p231

www.centralpark
nyc.org

59th & 110th Sts
btwn Central Park
West & Fifth Ave

⊘6am-1am

Strawberry Fields

This tear-shaped **garden** serves as a memorial to former Beatle John Lennon. The garden is composed of a grove of stately elms and a tiled mosaic that reads, simply, 'Imagine.' Find it at the level of 72nd St on the west side of the park.

Bethesda Terrace & the Mall

The arched walkways of **Bethesda Terrace**, crowned by the magnificent **Bethesda Fountain** (at the level of 72nd St), have long been a gathering area for New Yorkers of all flavors. To the south is the Mall (featured in countless movies), a promenade shrouded in mature North American elms. The southern stretch, known as **Literary Walk**, is flanked by statues of famous authors.

Central Park Zoo

Officially known as the Central Park Wildlife Center (no one calls it that), this small **zoo** is home to penguins, polar bears, snow leopards and red pandas. Feeding times in the sea lion and penguin tanks make for a rowdy spectacle. (Check the website for times.)

The attached **Tisch Children's Zoo**, a petting zoo, has alpacas and mini-Nubian goats and is perfect for small children.

Conservatory Water & Around

North of the zoo at the level of 74th St is the Conservatory Water, where model sailboats drift lazily and kids scramble about on a toadstool-studded statue of Alice in Wonderland. There are Saturday story hours at the Hans Christian Andersen statue to the west of the water (at 11am from June to September).

Great Lawn & the Ramble

The **Great Lawn** is a massive emerald carpet at the center of the park – between 79th and 86th Sts – and is surrounded by ball fields and London plane trees. (This is where Simon & Garfunkel played their famous 1981 concert.)

Don't Miss List

BY 'WILDMAN' STEVE BRILL,
AUTHOR, NATURALIST, EDUCATOR
AND TOUR GUIDE

1 THE PARK'S IMPORTANCE

This was the first park designed to mimic nature rather than overly landscaped to resemble a formal garden – the centerpiece of this is the wooded area called the Ramble. Of course, it's since been much imitated. The hills and gradients of some parts of the park, which make it difficult to see very far, were conscious efforts to make the area seem more vast than it is.

2 ANIMALS & PLANTS

The animal life and abundance of intrinsically valuable plants are often overlooked by visitors. There are around 160 edible plants, almost as many with medicinal properties and 40 or so choice gourmet species of mushrooms including hen of the woods and chicken mushrooms.

3 FAVORITES

The red bud trees, one of the first flowering springtime plants found all over the park, are especially beautiful, as are the black locust plants whose white flowers smell like vanilla. There used to be a wild Kentucky coffee tree found just north of the boat house, but sadly it was destroyed in a recent thunderstorm. The roasted seeds taste like coffee, or you can mix them with a concoction of cocoa powder, dark chocolate etc to make delicious chocolate truffles.

4 JAZZ & CHESS

I love the jazz musicians who play near the Delacorte Theater on weekends. I head over there on lunch breaks and jam with them on my 'brillophone' – I cup my hands in front of my mouth and blow. Chess players should check out the area mid-park around 64th St. Of course, I enjoy the zoo, boating and of the simple feeling of peacefulness. And a big improvement is that smoking is no longer allowed.

UPPER WEST SIDE & CENTRAL PARK   CENTRAL PARK

STEVEN GREAVES/LONELY PLANET IMAGES ©

ISTOCK ©

Immediately to the southeast is the **Delacorte Theater**, home to an annual Shakespeare in the Park festival, as well as **Belvedere Castle**, a lookout.

Further south, between 72nd and 79th Sts, is the leafy **Ramble**, a popular birding destination (and legendary gay pick-up spot). On the southeastern end is the Loeb Boathouse (p236), home to a waterside restaurant that offers rowboat and bicycle rentals.

Jacqueline Kennedy Onassis Reservoir

The **reservoir** takes up almost the entire width of the park at the level of 90th street and serves as a gorgeous reflecting pool for the city skyline. It is surrounded by a 1.58-mile track that draws legions of joggers in the warmer months. Nearby, at Fifth Ave and 90th St, is a statue of New York City Marathon founder Fred Lebow, peering at his watch.

Conservatory Garden

If you want a little peace and quiet (as in, no runners, cyclists or boom boxes), the 6-acre Conservatory Garden serves as one of the park's official quiet zones. And it's beautiful, to boot: bursting with crab apple trees, meandering boxwood and, in the spring, lots of flowers. It's located at 105th St off of Fifth Ave. Otherwise, you can catch maximum calm (and maximum bird life) in all areas of the park just after dawn.

Public Art in the Park

Scattered among the many natural sculptures otherwise known as trees is a host of wonderful, freestanding, crafted works of art. If you enter the park at the **Merchants' Gate**, you'll see the mighty Maine Monument, a tribute to the sailors killed in the mysterious explosion in Havana Harbor in 1898 that sparked the Spanish-American War. Further east, toward the Seventh Ave entrance, there are statues of Latin America's greatest liberators, including José Martí, 'The

Apostle of Cuban Independence' (history buffs will find Martí's proximity to the Maine Monument ironic, to say the least). Further east still, at the **Scholars' Gate**, there is a small plaza dedicated to Doris Chanin Freedman, the founder of the Public Art Fund, where you can see a new sculpture every six months or so.

At the **Conservatory Water**, model sailboats drift lazily by and kids crawl over the giant toadstools of the **Alice in Wonderland statue**. Replete with Alice of flowing hair and dress, a dapper Mad Hatter and mischievous Cheshire Cat, this is a Central Park treasure and a favorite with kids of all ages. Nearby is the Hans Christian Andersen statue, where Saturday story hour (11am from June to September) is an entertaining draw.

The obelisk Cleopatra's Needle, a gift from Egypt to the US in 1877 for helping to build the Suez Canal, is located on the hillock above 82nd St and East Dr, near the Metropolitan Museum of Art (p204). Drop down to East Dr and look up to see the crouching cat sculpture, poised to pounce on unsuspecting inline skaters.

At the northeastern edge of the park is the soaring **Duke Ellington statue**, depicting the man and his piano. An oft-overlooked site because of its northern location at 110th St and Fifth Ave, this stunning tribute to the jazz master, featuring a 25ft bronze tableau, was unveiled in 1997 after being conceived and funded by the late jazz-pianist Bobby Short.

Free and custom walking tours are available via the **Central Park Conservancy**, the nonprofit organization that supports park maintenance.

Central Park

The Lungs of New York

The rectangular patch of green that occupies Manhattan's heart began life in the mid-19th century as a swampy piece of land that was carefully bulldozed into the idyllic natures-cape you see today. Since officially becoming Central Park, it has brought New Yorkers of all stripes together in interesting and unexpected ways. The park has served as a place for the rich to show off their fancy carriages (1860s),

for the poor to enjoy free Sunday concerts (1880s) and for activists to hold be-ins against the Vietnam War (1960s).

Since then, legions of locals – not to mention travelers from all kinds of faraway places – have poured in to stroll, picnic, sunbathe, play ball and catch free concerts and performances of works by Shakespeare.

The park's varied terrain offers a wonderland of experiences. There are quiet, woodsy knolls

Loeb Boathouse
Perched on the shores of the Lake, the historic Loeb Boathouse is one of the city's best settings for an idyllic meal. You can also rent rowboats and bicycles and ride on a Venetian gondola.

Duke Ellington Circle

Harlem Meer

The Blockhouse

North Woods

97th St Transverse

Fifth Ave

86th St Transverse

The Gre Lawn

Conservatory Garden
The only formal garden in Central Park is perhaps the most tranquil. On the northern end, chrysan-themums bloom in late October. To the south, the park's largest crab apple tree grows by the Burnett Fountain.

Central Pa West

Jacqueline Kennedy Onassis Reservoir
This 106-acre body of water covers roughly an eighth of the park's territory. Its original purpose was to provide clean water for the city. Now it's a good spot to catch a glimpse of waterbirds.

Belvedere Castle
A so-called 'Victorian folly,' this Gothic-Romanesque castle serves no other purpose than to be a very dramatic lookout point. It was built by Central Park co-designer Calvert Vaux in 1869.

in the north. To the south is the reservoir, crowded with joggers. There are European gardens, a zoo and various bodies of water. For maximum flamboyance, hit the Sheep Meadow on a sunny day, when all of New York shows up to lounge.

Central Park is more than just a green space. It is New York City's backyard.

Conservatory Water
This pond is popular in the warmer months, when children sail their model boats across its surface. Conservatory Water was inspired by 19th-century Parisian model-boat ponds and figured prominently in EB White's classic book, *Stuart Little*.

Bethesda Fountain
This neoclassical fountain is one of New York's largest. It's capped by the *Angel of the Waters*, who is supported by four cherubim. The fountain was created by bohemian-feminist sculptor Emma Stebbins in 1868.

Metropolitan Museum of Art

Alice in Wonderland Statue

79th St Transverse

The Ramble

Delacorte Theater

The Lake

Fifth Ave

Central Park Zoo

65th St Transverse

Sheep Meadow

Strawberry Fields
A simple mosaic memorial pays tribute to musician John Lennon, who was killed across the street outside the Dakota Building. Funded by Yoko Ono, its name is inspired by the Beatles song 'Strawberry Fields Forever.'

The Mall/ Literary Walk
A Parisian-style promenade – the only straight line in the park – is flanked by statues of literati on the southern end, including Robert Burns and Shakespeare. It is lined with rare North American elms.

Columbus Center

Discover Upper West Side & Central Park

Getting There & Away

• **Subway** On the Upper West Side, the 1/2/3 subway lines are good for destinations along Broadway and points west, while the B and C trains are best for points of interest and access to Central Park. The park can be accessed from all sides, making every subway that travels north/south through Manhattan convenient. The A/C, B/D and 1 all stop at Columbus Circle at Central Park's southwestern edge, while the N/R/Q will leave you at the southeast corner. The 2/3 will deposit you at the northern gate in Harlem.

• **Bus** The M104 bus runs north to south along Broadway, and the M10 plies the scenic ride along the western edge of the park. Crosstown buses at 66th, 72nd, 79th, 86th and 96th Sts take you through the park to the Upper East Side.

◉ Sights

Upper West Side

Riverside Park — Outdoors

Map p231 (☏212-870-3070; www.riverside parkfund.org; Riverside Dr btwn 68th & 155th Sts; ⏰6am-1am; 🚼; Ⓢ1/2/3 to any stop btwn 66th & 157th Sts) A classic beauty designed by Central Park creators Frederick Law Olmsted and Calvert Vaux, this waterside spot, running north on the Upper West Side and banked by the Hudson River from 59th to 158th Sts, is lusciously leafy. Plenty of bike paths and playgrounds make it a family favorite.

From late March through October (weather permitting), a rowdy waterside restaurant, the West 79th Street Boat Basin Café, serves a light menu at the level of 79th St.

New-York Historical Society — Museum

Map p231 (www.nyhistory.org; 2 W 77th St at Central Park West; adult/child $15/5, by donation 6pm-8pm, library free; ⏰10am-6pm Tue-Thu & Sat, to 8pm Fri, 11am-5pm Sun; Ⓢ B, C to 81st St-Museum of Natural History) As the antiquated hyphenated name implies, the Historical Society is the city's oldest museum, founded in 1804 to preserve the city's historical and cultural artifacts. Its collection of more than 60,000 objects is quirky and fascinating and includes everything from George Washington's inauguration chair to a 19th-century Tiffany ice-cream dish (gilded, of course). Other treasures include a leg brace worn by President Franklin D Roosevelt, a 19th-century mechanical bank in which a political figure slips coins into his pocket and photographer Jack Stewart's

Central Park (p224)

Upper West Side & Central Park

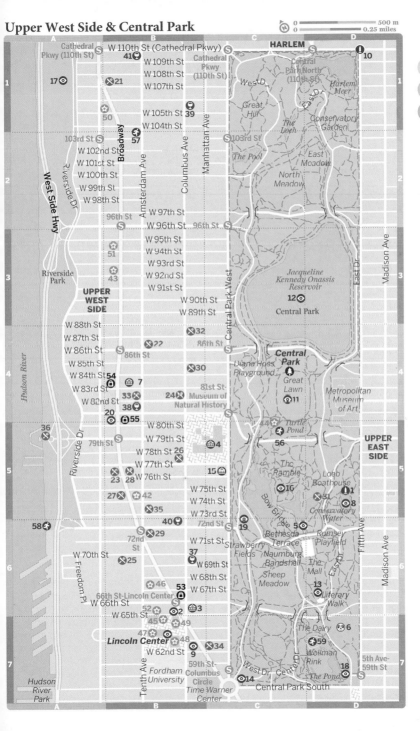

0 — 500 m
0 — 0.25 miles

HARLEM

W 110th St (Cathedral Pkwy)
Cathedral Pkwy (110th St)
41
W 109th St
W 108th St
W 107th St
Cathedral Pkwy (110th St)
21
17
50
W 105th St
W 104th St
39
57
103rd St
Broadway
W 102nd St
W 101st St
W 100th St
W 99th St
W 98th St
Amsterdam Ave
Columbus Ave
Manhattan Ave
W 97th St
96th St
W 96th St
96th St
West Side Hwy
Riverside Dr
Riverside Park
51
W 95th St
W 94th St
W 93rd St
W 92nd St
W 91st St
43
UPPER WEST SIDE
W 90th St
W 89th St
Central Park West
Jacqueline Kennedy Onassis Reservoir
12
Central Park
Madison Ave
Hudson River
W 88th St
W 87th St
W 86th St
W 85th St
W 84th St
W 83rd St
W 82nd St
32
22
86th St
30
54
7
33
24
38
20
55
81st St-Museum of Natural History
Central Park
Diana Ross Playground
Great Lawn
11
Metropolitan Museum of Art
36
79th St
W 80th St
W 79th St
W 78th St
W 77th St
W 76th St
4
26
15
Turtle Pond
56
UPPER EAST SIDE
The Ramble
Loeb Boathouse
1
8
23 28
27
42
35
40
29
25
W 75th St
W 74th St
W 73rd St
72nd St
W 71st St
72nd St
37
W 69th St
19
Bow Bridge
16
51
Conservatory Water
5
Bethesda Terrace
Strawberry Fields
Naumburg Bandshell
The Mall
Rumsey Playfield
Fifth Ave
Madison Ave
58
W 70th St
46
53
52
2
3
45 49
47
48
9
34
66th St-Lincoln Center
W 68th St
W 67th St
W 66th St
W 65th St
Lincoln Center
Freedom Pl
W 62nd St
Fordham University
59th St-Columbus Circle
Time Warner Center
Sheep Meadow
13
Literary Walk
The Dairy
6
59
Wollman Rink
18
The Pond
5th Ave-59th St
Tenth Ave
14
West Dr
Central
Central Park South
Hudson River Park
10

DISCOVER UPPER WEST SIDE & CENTRAL PARK SIGHTS

231

Upper West Side & Central Park

graffiti-covered door from the 1970s (featuring tags by known graffiti writers such as Tracy 168). In the lobby, be sure to look up: the ceiling mural from Keith Haring's 1986 'Pop Shop' hangs above the admissions desk.

Zabar's   Market
Map p231 (www.zabars.com; 2245 Broadway at 80th St; ☺8am-7:30pm Mon-Fri, to 8pm Sat, 9am-6pm Sun; S 1 to 79th St) A bastion of

gourmet-Kosher foodie-ism, this sprawling local market has been a neighborhood fixture since the 1930s. And what a fixture it is: featuring a heavenly array of cheeses, meats, olives, caviar, smoked fish, pickles, dried fruits, nuts and baked goods, including pillowy fresh-out-of-the-oven knishes (Eastern European-style potato dumplings wrapped in dough).

FREE American Folk Art Museum
Museum

Map p231 (www.folkartmuseum.org; 2 Lincoln Sq, Columbus Ave at 66th St; ☉noon-7:30pm Tue-Sat, to 6pm Sun; S 1 to 66th St-Lincoln Center) This tiny institution contains a couple of centuries worth of folk and outsider art treasures, including pieces by Henry Darger (known for his girl-filled battle-scapes) and Martín Ramírez (producer of hallucinatory *caballeros* on horseback). There is also an array of wood carvings, paintings, hand-tinted photographs and decorative objects. On Wednesdays there are guitar concerts, and free music on Fridays.

Children's Museum of Manhattan
Museum

Map p231 (www.cmom.org; 212 W 83rd St btwn Amsterdam Ave & Broadway; admission $11; ☉10am-5pm Tue-Sun; ; S B, C to 81st St-Museum of Natural History; 1 to 86th St) This small museum features interactive exhibits scaled down for the little people. This includes toddler discovery programs and exhibits that stimulate play, like operating a giant heart with a pedal or tumbling around a set with *Dora the*

Explorer elements. It's not very exciting, but it can be a rainy-day saver if you're traveling with antsy toddlers.

Central Park

Central Park
Park

See p224.

🍴 Eating

Upper West Side

Dovetail
Modern American $$$

Map p231 (www.dovetailnyc.com; 103 W 77th St cnr Columbus Ave; tasting menu/Monday vegetarian menu $85/46, mains $34-55; ☉dinner daily, brunch Sun; ; S A/C, B to 81st St-Museum of Natural History, 1 to 79th St) Everything about this Michelin-starred restaurant is simple, from the decor (exposed brick, bare tables) to the uncomplicated seasonal menus focused on bracingly fresh produce and quality meats (think: pistachio crusted duck with sunchokes, dates and spinach). On Mondays, chef John Fraser has a three-course vegetarian tasting

Children's Museum of Manhattan

COREY WISE/LONELY PLANET IMAGES ©

Don't Miss

American Museum of Natural History

Founded in 1869, this classic museum contains a veritable wonderland of more than 30 million artifacts, including lots of menacing dinosaur skeletons. From October through May, the museum is home to the Butterfly Conservatory, a glass house featuring 500-plus butterflies from all over the world. On the natural history side, the museum is perhaps best known for its Fossil Halls, containing nearly 600 specimens, including the skeletons of a massive mammoth and a fearsome Tyrannosaurus Rex.

There are also plentiful animal exhibits, galleries devoted to gems, and an IMAX theater that plays films on natural phenomena. The Milstein Hall of Ocean Life contains dioramas devoted to ecologies, weather and conservation, as well as a beloved 94ft replica of a blue whale. Visitors are greeted to the 77th St Lobby Gallery by a 63ft canoe carved in the 19th century by the Haida people of British Columbia.

For the space set, it's the Rose Center for Earth & Space – with its mesmerizing glass box facade, space-show theaters and planetarium – that is the star. Every half hour between 10:30am and 4:30pm, you can see *Journey to the Stars*, which charts the life and death of astral bodies using telescopic images and hallucinatory visualizations – the sort of thing that will have you exclaiming, 'Whoaaaaaa.'

Needless to say, the museum is a hit with kids, and as a result, it's swamped on weekends. Early on a weekday is the best time to go. Hall of Biodiversity

NEED TO KNOW

Map p231; ☎212-769-5100; www.amnh.org; Central Park West at 79th St; adult/child $16/9, interactive exhibits $14-24; 🕒10am-5:45pm, Rose Center to 8:45pm Fri, Butterfly Conservancy Oct-May; 👪; [S] B, C to 81st St-Museum of Natural History, 1 to 79th St

menu that is winning over carnivores with dishes like crisp cauliflower in jerk spice.

Fatty Crab — Malaysian $$

Map p231 (www.fattycrab.com; 2170 Broadway btwn 76th & 77th Sts; Fatty Dog $12, mains $16-29; ⌚noon-11pm Mon-Wed, to midnight Thu-Sat, to 10pm Sun; 👪; [S]1 to 79th St) A brick-lined, industrial chic spot steered by chef Zakary Pelaccio serves winning Malaysian influenced specialties. Start with sweet and sticky Julan Alor chicken wings, follow-up with shrimp and pork wontons and then dig into the Dungeness crab with chili sauce.

Try the 'Fatty Dog,' a plump sausage laced with chili sauce, fresh cilantro and pickled radish on a toasty bun.

Gray's Papaya — Hot Dogs $

Map p231 (☎212-799-0243; 2090 Broadway at 72nd St; hot dog $2; ⌚24hr; [S]A/B/C, 1/2/3 to 72nd St) The lights are bright, the color palette is 1970s and the hot dogs are unpretentiously good.

Granted the papaya drink is more 'drink' than papaya, but you can't go wrong with Gray's famous 'Recession Special' – $4.95 for two grilled dogs and a beverage. Deal.

Barney Greengrass — Deli $$

Map p231 (www.barneygreengrass.com; 541 Amsterdam Ave at 86th St; mains $9-18, bagel with cream cheese $5; ⌚8:30am-4pm Tues-Fri, to 5pm Sat & Sun; 👪; [S]1 to 86th St) The self-proclaimed 'King of Sturgeon' Barney Greengrass serves up the same heaping dishes of eggs and salty lox, luxuriant caviar, and melt-in-your mouth chocolate babkas that first made it famous when it opened a century ago. Pop in to fuel up in the morning or for a quick lunch; there are rickety tables set amid the crowded produce aisles.

Café Luxembourg — French $$$

Map p231 (www.cafeluxembourg.com; 200 W 70th St btwn Broadway & West End Ave; lunch mains $16-34, dinner mains $25-34; ⌚breakfast, lunch & dinner daily, brunch Sun; [S]1/2/3 to 72nd St) This quintessential French bistro is generally crowded with locals – and it's no mystery why: the setting is elegant, the staff is friendly, and there's an outstanding menu to boot. The classics – salmon tartare, cassoulet and steak frites – are all deftly executed, and its proximity to Lincoln Center makes it a perfect pre-performance destination. There is a lighter lunch menu and eggy dishes at brunch.

Big Nick's — Burgers $

Map p231 (www.bignicksnyc.com; 2175 Broadway btwn 76th & 77th Sts; burgers $7-13; ⌚24hr; [S]1 to 79th St) This grimy dive is an institution – not for its food, but for its overwhelming 27-page menu and cluttered walls. (There isn't a surface that doesn't have a framed something on it.) They serve everything from pizza to baked clams, but do yourself a favor and stick to the burgers, a good way of countering a night of boozing.

Momofuku Milk Bar — Asian $

Map p231 (www.momofuku.com; 561 Columbus Ave btwn 87th & 88th Sts; pork buns $8; ⌚8am-10pm; [S]A/C, B to 86th St) Two words: pork buns. And not just any pork buns, but David Chang's slow-braised-pork-on-a-puffy-steamed-bun-concoction, which will make you wish that pork was a major food group. There are also plenty of diabetes-inducing baked goods, including chewy-delicious cornflake-marshmallow cookies that seem to be designed to rip out your fillings.

Shake Shack — Burgers $

Map p231 (www.shakeshacknyc.com; 366 Columbus Ave, btwn 77th & 78th Sts; burgers $4-9, shakes $5-7; ⌚10:45am-11pm; 👪; [S]B, C, 1/2/3 to 72nd St) Part of chef Danny Meyer gourmet burger chainlet, Shake Shack whips up hyper-fresh burgers, crinkle-cut fries and a rotating line-up of frozen custards. Veg-heads can dip into the crisp Portobello burger. Lines are long, but worth it.

Kefi — Greek $$

Map p231 (www.kefirestaurant.com; 505 Columbus Ave btwn 84th & 85th Sts; lunch mains $9-18, dinner mains $11-18; ⌚lunch & dinner daily, brunch Sat & Sun; 👪; [S]B, C to 86th St) A homey, whitewashed eatery run by chef

Michael Psilakis channels a sleek taverna vibe while dispensing excellent rustic Greek dishes. Expect favorites like spicy lamb sausage, sheep-milk dumplings and grilled octopus. The platter featuring four types of spreads is delicious, as is the flat pasta with braised rabbit. The wine list features a comprehensive selection of Greek vintages (from $22 per bottle).

Peacefood Cafe — Vegan $$

Map p231 (☎212-362-2266; www.peacefoodcafe. com; 460 Amsterdam Ave at 82nd St; paninis $13, mains $10-17; ⏰lunch & dinner; �🌿; ⎣S⎦1 to 79th St) This bright and airy vegan haven run by Eric Yu dishes up a popular fried seitan panini (served on homemade focaccia and topped with cashew, arugula, tomatoes and pesto), as well as an excellent quinoa salad. There are daily raw specials, organic coffees and delectable bakery selections.

Salumeria Rosi Parmacotto — Italian $$

Map p231 (☎212-877-4800; www.salumeriarosi. com; 284 Amsterdam Ave at 73rd St; mains $11-14; ⏰11am-11pm; ⎣S⎦1/2/3 to 72nd St) This is an intimate little meat-loving nook, where you can dip into tasting plates that feature cheeses, salumi, slow-roasted pork loin, sausages, cured hams and every other piece of the pig you care to imagine. There are other tasty Tuscan-inspired offerings too, including homemade lasagna, savory leek tart, escarole-anchovy salad and hand-rolled sweet potato gnocchi.

PJ Clarke's — Pub $$

Map p231 (☎212-957-9700; www.pjclarkes. com/lincoln-square-location.php; 44 W 63rd St cnr Broadway; burgers $10-14, mains $18-40; ⏰11:30am-1am; ⎣S⎦1 to 66th St-Lincoln Center) Right across the street from Lincoln Center, this red-checker-tablecloth spot has a buttoned down crowd, friendly bartenders and solid eats. If you're in a rush, belly up to the bar for a Black Angus burger and a Brooklyn Lager. A raw bar offers fresh Long Island Little Neck and Cherry Stone clams, as well as jumbo shrimp cocktails.

Fairway — Self-Catering $

Map p231 (www.fairwaymarket.com/store-upper -west-side; 2127 Broadway at 75th St; ⏰6am-1am; ⎣S⎦1/2/3 to 72nd St) Like a museum of good eats, this incredible grocery spills its lovely mounds of produce into its sidewalk bins, seducing you inside with international goodies, fine cooking oils, nuts, cheeses, prepared foods and, upstairs, an organic market and cafe.

Absolute Bagels — Bakery $

Map p231 (☎212-932-2052; 2788 Broadway btwn 107th & 108th Sts; bagel $1; ⏰6am-9pm Mon-Sat, to 8pm Sun; ☀🚻; ⎣S⎦1 to Cathedral Parkway-110th St) This popular neighborhood bagel joint has 16 varieties of hot, chewy, hand-rolled bagels – and myriad cream cheeses to top them with (including the tofu variety).

Central Park

Loeb Boathouse — American $$$

Map p231 (☎212-517-2233; www.thecentralpark boathouse.com; Central Park Lake, Central Park at 74th St; mains $22-44; ⏰lunch daily & brunch Sat & Sun year-round, dinner daily Apr-Nov; ⎣S⎦A/C, B to 72nd St, 6 to 77th St) Perched on the northeastern tip of the Central Park Lake, the Loeb Boathouse, with its views of the Midtown skyline in the distance, provides one of New York's most idyllic spots for a meal. That said, what you're paying for is the setting. While the food is generally good (the crab cakes are the standout), the service is often indifferent.

If you want to experience the location without having to lay out the bucks, a better bet is to hit the adjacent Bar & Grill, which offers a limited bar menu (plates $16), where you can still get crabcakes and excellent views.

🍷 Drinking & Nightlife

Barcibo Enoteca — Wine Bar

Map p231 (www.barciboenoteca.com; 2020 Broadway cnr 69th St; ⏰4:30pm-2am; ⎣S⎦1/2/3 to 72nd St) Just north of Lincoln Center, this casual chic marble-table spot is ideal

WDSTOCK/ISTOCK ©

Don't Miss
Lincoln Center

Built in the 1960s, this imposing campus replaced a group of tenements called San Juan Hill, a predominantly African American neighborhood where the exterior shots for the movie West Side Story were filmed. In addition to being a controversial urban planning move, Lincoln Center wasn't exactly well-received at an architectural level – it was relentlessly criticized for its conservative design, fortress-like aspect and poor acoustics. For the center's 50th anniversary (2009–10), Diller Scofidio + Renfro and other architects gave the complex a much-needed and critically acclaimed freshening up.

Of the refurbished structures, there are a number that are worth examining, including Alice Tully Hall, now displaying a very contemporary translucent, angled facade, and the David Rubenstein Atrium, a public space offering a lounge area (free wi-fi), a cafe, an information desk and a ticket vendor plying day-of discount tickets to Lincoln Center performances. Free events are held here on Thursday evenings.

On any given night, there are at least 10 performances happening throughout Lincoln Center – and even more in summer, when Lincoln Center Out of Doors (a series of dance and music concerts) and Midsummer Night Swing (ballroom dancing under the stars) lure those who love parks and culture.

Daily tours of the complex explore the Metropolitan Opera House, Revson Fountain and Alice Tully Hall and are a great way to get acquainted with the complex.

NEED TO KNOW

Map p231; ☎ 212-875-5456, tours 212-875-5350; www.lincolncenter.org; Columbus Ave btwn 62nd & 66th Sts; public plazas free, tours adults/child $15/8; ☺ performance hours vary, tours 10:30am & 4:30pm; ♿; S 1 to 66th St-Lincoln Center

for sipping, with a long list of vintages from all over Italy, including 40 different varieties sold by the glass. There is a short menu of small plates and light meals. The staff is knowledgeable; ask for recommendations.

Ding Dong Lounge
Bar

Map p231 (www.dingdonglounge.com; 929 Columbus Ave btwn 105th & 106th Sts; $\boxed{S}$B, C, 1 to 103rd St) It's hard to be too bad-ass in the Upper West, but this former crack den turned punk bar makes a wholesome attempt by supplying graffiti-covered bathrooms to go with its exposed-brick walls. It also, interestingly, features an array of cuckoo clocks. It's popular with Columbia students and guests from nearby hostels for its beer-and-a-shot combo (only $6).

Dead Poet
Bar

Map p231 (www.thedeadpoet.com; 450 Amsterdam Ave btwn 81st & 82nd Sts; ⏰9am-4am Mon-Sat, noon-4am Sun; $\boxed{S}$1 to 79th St) A skinny, mahogany-paneled pub has been a neighborhood favorite for over a decade, with a mix of locals and students nursing pints of Guinness. There are cocktails named after dead poets, including a Jack Kerouac margarita ($12) and a Pablo Neruda spiced rum sangria ($9).

Sip
Cocktail Bar

Map p231 (www.sipbar.com; 998 Amsterdam Ave btwn 109th & 110th Sts; ⏰10:30am-4am; $\boxed{S}$1 to Cathedral Parkway-110 St) This quirky storefront decked out in bright tiles and red leather serves as coffee house by day and friendly little cocktail lounge by night. The mixologists here produce various signature drinks including, appropriately enough, a cappuccino martini. There are tapas, too, including small plates of chorizo and cheeses.

Malachy's
Pub

Map p231 (www.malachys.com; 103 W 72nd St btwn Amsterdam & Columbus Aves; ⏰noon-4am; $\boxed{S}$B/C, 1/2/3 to 72nd St) Giving new meaning to the word 'dive,' this crusty local holdout has a long bar, a line-up of regulars and a bartender with a sense of humor. In other words: the perfect place

for day-time drinking. There's a cheap menu if you're feeling lucky.

 # Entertainment

Lincoln Center

This vast cultural complex is a mecca for high art in Manhattan. In addition to the venues and companies listed here, the Vivian Beaumont Theater and the Mitzi E Newhouse Theater showcase works of drama and musical theater. Both of these have programming information listed on Lincoln Center's main website at www.new.lincolncenter.org.

Metropolitan Opera House
Opera

Map p231 (www.metopera.org; Lincoln Center, 64th St at Columbus Ave; $\boxed{S}$1 to 66th St-Lincoln Center) New York's premier opera company, the Metropolitan Opera is the place to see classics such as *Carmen*, *Madame Butterfly* and *Macbeth*, not to mention Wagner's *Ring Cycle*. The Opera also hosts premieres and revivals of more contemporary works, such as Peter Sellars' *Nixon in China,* which played here in 2011. The season runs from September to April.

Ticket prices start at $30 and can get close to $500. Note that the box seats can be a bargain, but unless you're in boxes right over the stage, the views are dreadful. Seeing the stage requires sitting with your head cocked over a handrail – a literal pain in the neck.

For last-minute ticket-buyers there are other deals. You can get bargain-priced standing-room tickets ($17 to $22) starting at 10am on the day of the performance. (You won't see much, but you'll hear everything.) Two hours before shows on Mondays through Thursdays, 200 rush tickets are put on sale for the starving artist types – just $20 for an orchestra seat (excluding galas and opening nights)! Line up early.

Film Society of Lincoln Center
Map p231 (☎212-875-5456; www.filmlinc.com; Lincoln Center, Columbus Ave btwn 62nd & 66th

Summer Happenings in Central Park

During the warm months, the park is home to countless cultural events, many of which are free. The two most popular are: **Shakespeare in the Park** (www.shakespeareinthepark.org), which is managed by the Public Theater, and **SummerStage** (www.summerstage.org), a series of free concerts.

Shakespeare tickets are given out at 1pm on the day of the performance, but if you want to lay your hands on a seat, get there by 8am and make sure you have something to sit on and your entire group with you. Tickets are free and one per person; no latecomers allowed in line.

SummerStage concert venues are generally opened to the public 90 minutes prior to the start of the show. But if it's a popular act, start queuing up early or you're not getting in.

Sts; **S**1 to 66th St-Lincoln Center) The Film Society is one of New York's cinematic gems, providing an invaluable platform for a wide gamut of documentary, feature, independent, foreign and avant-garde art pictures. Films screen in one of two facilities at Lincoln Center: the new **Elinor Bunin Munroe Film Center** (Map p231; 212-875-5601, film schedule 212-875-5600; www.filmlinc.com; Lincoln Center, 144 W 65th St; **S**1 to 66 St-Lincoln Center), a more intimate, experimental venue, or the **Walter Reade Theater** (Map p231; 212-875-5600; www.filmlinc.com; Lincoln Center, 165 W 65th St; **S**1 to 66th St-Lincoln Center), with wonderfully-wide, screening room-style seats.

Every September, both venues host the New York Film Festival, featuring plenty of New York and world premieres. In the spring, you'll find the New Directors/New Films series on view.

New York Philharmonic
Classical Music

Map p231 (www.nyphil.org; Avery Fisher Hall, Lincoln Center, cnr Columbus Ave & 65th St; ; **S**1 to 66 St-Lincoln Center) The oldest professional orchestra in the US (dating back to 1842), holds its season every year at Avery Fisher Hall. Directed by Alan Gilbert, the son of two Philharmonic musicians, the orchestra plays a mix of classics (Tchaikovsky, Mahler, Haydn), some contemporary works, as well as concerts geared at children.

Tickets run in the $33 to $83 range. If you're on a budget, check out their open rehearsals on Thursdays during the day (at the discretion of the conductor) for only $18. In addition, students with a valid school ID can pick up rush tickets for $12.50 up to 10 days before an event.

New York City Ballet
Dance

Map p231 (212-870-5656, student rush tickets 212-870-7766; www.nycballet.com; David H Koch Theater, Lincoln Center, Columbus Ave at 62nd St; ; **S**1 to 66th St-Lincoln Center) This prestigious company was first directed by renowned Russian-born choreographer George Balanchine back in the 1940s. Today, the company has 90 dancers and is the largest ballet organization in the US, performing 23 weeks a year at Lincoln Center's David H Koch Theater. During the holidays the troop is best known for its annual production of *The Nutcracker*.

Depending on the ballet, ticket prices can range from $29 to $250. Student rush tickets (valid high school or university ID required) are posted on Mondays and cost $15. Fourth ring seats are often a deal, but the views can be lousy.

Upper West Side

Beacon Theatre
Live Music

Map p231 (www.beacontheatre.com; 2124 Broadway btwn 74th & 75th Sts; **S**1/2/3 to 72nd St) This historic theater from 1929 is a perfect in-between-size venue, with 2600 seats (not a terrible one in the house) and a constant flow of popular acts, from The Cure to Paul Simon to Adele. A $15 million restoration in 2009 has left the gilded interiors – a mix of Greek, Roman, Renaissance and Rococo design elements – totally sparkling.

Cleopatra's Needle   Club

Map p231 (www.cleopatrasneedleny.com; 2485 Broadway btwn 92nd & 93rd Sts; ☺4pm-late; **S**1/2/3 to 96th St) Named after an Egyptian obelisk that resides in Central Park, this venue is small and narrow like its namesake. There's no cover, but there's a $10 minimum spend. Come early and you can enjoy happy hour, when martinis are half price. But be prepared to stay late: Cleopatra's is famous for all-night jam sessions that hit their peak around 4am.

Smoke   Jazz

Map p231 (www.smokejazz.com; 2751 Broadway btwn 105th & 106th Sts; ☺5pm-4am; **S**1 to 103rd St) This swank but laid-back lounge – with good stage views from plush sofas –

brings out old-timers and local faves, like George Coleman and Wynton Marsalis. Most nights there's a $10 cover, plus a $20 to $30 food and drink minimum. Smoke is smoke-free but then again so is the rest of NYC.

Merkin Concert
Hall   Classical Music

Map p231 (www.kaufman-center.org/mch; 129 W 67th St btwn Amsterdam Ave & Broadway; admission varies; **S**1 to 66th St-Lincoln Center) Just north of Lincoln Center, this 450-seat hall, part of the Kaufman Center, is one of the city's more intimate venues for classical music, as well as jazz, world music and pop. The hall hosts Tuesday matinees (a deal at $17) that highlight emerging classical solo artists.

Symphony Space   Live Music

Map p231 (☎212-864-5400; www.symphonyspace.org; 2537 Broadway btwn 94th & 95th Sts; ♿; **S**1/2/3 to 96th St) Home to National Public Radio's renowned literary readings, Symphony Space is a multidisciplinary gem supported by the local community. It often hosts three-day series that are dedicated to one musician, and has an affinity for world music, theater, film and dance.

🔒 Shopping

Westsider Books   Books

Map p231 (www.westsiderbooks.com; 2246 Broadway btwn 80th & 81st Sts; ☺10am-late; **S**1 to 79th St) A great little shop packed to the gills with rare and used books, including a good selection of fiction and illustrated tomes. There are first editions and a smattering of vintage vinyl. There is a sister shop, Westsider Records, that dispenses vinyl, too.

Century 21
RICHARD LEVINE/ALAMY ©

Century 21 Department Store

Map p231 (www.c21stores.com; 1972 Broadway btwn 66th & 67th Sts; 🕐9am-10pm Mon-Sat, 11am-8pm Sun; [S]1 to 66th St-Lincoln Center) Exceedingly popular with fashionable locals and foreign travelers, the Century 21 chain is a bounty of season-old brand name and designer brands sold at steeply discounted prices. Featuring everything from Missoni to Marc Jacobs, prices may sometimes seem high, but compared to retail, they're a steal.

Harry's Shoes Shoes

Map p231 (www.harrys-shoes.com; 2299 Broadway at 83rd St; 🕐10am-6:45pm Tue, Wed, Fri & Sat, to 7:45pm Mon & Thu, 11am-6pm Sun; [S]1 to 86th St) Around since the 1930s, Harry's is a classic. It's staffed by gentlemen who measure your foot in an old-school metal contraption and then wait on you patiently, making sure the shoe fits. If your feet are killing you from all the walking, you'll find sturdy, comfortable brands (Merrel, Dansko, Birkenstock) as well as Earth, a vegan brand.

Sports & Activities

Loeb Boathouse Cycling

Map p231 (☎212-517-2233; www.thecentralparkboathouse.com; Central Park btwn 74th & 75th Sts; boating per hr $12, bike rentals per hr $9-15; 🕐10am-dusk Apr-Nov; 👪; [S]B, C to 72nd St, 6 to 77th St) Central Park's boathouse has a fleet of 100 rowboats plus three kayaks available for rent from April to November. In the summer, there is also a Venetian-style gondola that seats up to six (per 30 minutes $30). Bicycles are also available from April to November. Rentals require an ID and credit card and are weather permitting.

Bike & Roll Cycling

Map p231 (www.bikeandroll.com/newyork; Columbus Circle at Central Park West; from per hr/day $12/39; 🕐9am-7pm Mar-May, 8am-8pm Jun-Aug, 9am-5pm Sep-Nov; 👪; [S]A/C, B/D, 1/2 to 59th St-Columbus Circle) At the southwestern entrance to the park, a small, pop-up kiosk dispenses beach cruisers and 10-speeds for rides around Central Park. They also have child seats and tandem bikes.

Champion Bicycles Inc Cycling

Map p231 (www.championbicycles.com; 896 Amsterdam Ave at 104th St; rentals per 24hr $40; 🕐10am-7pm Mon-Fri, to 6pm Sat & Sun; [S]1 to 103rd St) This place stocks a variety of bikes for rent and has free copies of the helpful **NYC Cycling Map** (www.nyc.gov/bikes), which details more than 50 miles of bike lanes around New York City.

Wollman Skating Rink Ice Skating

Map p231 (☎212-439-6900; www.wollmanskatingrink.com; Central Park btwn 62nd & 63rd Sts; adult Mon-Thu/Fri-Sun $11/16, child $6, skate rentals $7, lock rental $5, spectator fee $5; 🕐Nov-Mar; 👪; [S]F to 57 St, N/Q/R to 5th Ave-59th St) Larger than Rockefeller Center skating rink, and allowing all-day skating, this rink is at the southeastern edge of Central Park and offers nice views. It's open mid-October through April. Cash only.

Upper Manhattan & the Outer Boroughs

Upper Manhattan (p244)

The top half of Manhattan covers a lot of territory including an extravagant museum, a soaring cathedral and a vibrant neighborhood, still a bastion of African American culture.

Brooklyn (p247)

Historic 'hoods, hopping nightlife, gorgeous riverside parks and world-class museums, Brooklyn has everything the sophisticated and hip urbanite needs. Manhattan? Who needs it?

Queens (p253)

Throughout Queen's mighty ethnic and cultural sprawl are several top-flight museums. On the streets you'll find a cross section of humanity chattering in a million different languages. It's unmistakably New York.

Coney Island (p248)
VICKI SMITH/ALAMY ©

Upper Manhattan

Harlem, a neighborhood soaked in history, remains one of the country's most fabled centers of African American life – where Cab Calloway crooned, where Ralph Ellison penned *Invisible Man* and where Romare Bearden pieced together his first collages. Like everywhere else in New York, however, it's changing. National chains now blanket 125th St and of-the-moment eateries, luxury condos and young professionals (of all creeds and races) are moving in.

Just above the Upper West Side is Morningside Heights – a neighborhood covering the area between 110th and 125th Sts on the far west side, and a bedroom community for Columbia University. Nearby is the glorious Gothic-style Cathedral Church of St John the Divine, the largest place of worship in the US.

Inwood, at Manhattan's northern tip (from about 175th St), is a chilled-out residential zone with lovely parks and an extravagant must-see museum.

Getting There & Away

Subway Harlem's main drag – 125th St – is just one subway stop from the 59th St–Columbus Circle Station in Midtown on the A and D trains. Other areas of Harlem and northern Manhattan can be reached on the A/C, B/D, 1/2/3 and 4/5/6 trains.

Bus Dozens of buses ply the north–south route between upper and lower Manhattan along all the major avenues. The M10 bus provides a scenic trip along the west side of Central Park into Harlem. The M100 and the M101 run east to west along 125th St.

Taxi If yellow cabs are in short supply, look for livery cabs (big town cars bearing a company name and number); negotiate a price before you get in.

◉ Sights

Cloisters Museum & Gardens
Museum

(www.metmuseum.org/cloisters; Fort Tryon Park; suggested donation adult/child $25/free; ⏱9:30am-4:45pm Tue-Sun Nov-Feb, to 5:15pm Mar-Oct; S A to 190th St) On a hilltop overlooking the Hudson River, the Cloisters is a mesmerizing mish-mash of various European monasteries. Built in the 1930s to house the Metropolitan Museum's medieval treasures, it also contains the beguiling 16th-century tapestry *The Hunt of the Unicorn*.

The frescoes, tapestries and paintings are set in galleries that sit around an airy courtyard, connected by grand archways and topped with Moorish terra-cotta roofs. Among the many rare treasures you'll get to gaze at are a 9th-century gold plaque of St John the Evangelist and an English-made ivory sculpture of the Virgin and Child from 1290, not to mention the stunning 12th-century Saint-Guilhem Cloister, made of French limestone standing 30ft high.

Apollo Theater
Historic Building

(🕿212-531-5305, tours 212-531-5337; www.apollotheater.org; 253 W 125th St at Frederick Douglass Blvd, Harlem; admission weeknights/weekends $16/18; S A/C, B/D to 125th St) The Apollo has been Harlem's leading space for concerts and political rallies since 1914 and, with its gleaming marquee, is one of the neighborhood's most visible icons. Virtually every major black artist in the 1930s and '40s performed here, including Duke Ellington and Billie Holiday. And to this day it hosts regular concerts by high-profile entertainers. Everyone from Tony Bennett to Usher has played here.

The theatre is most famous, however, for its long-running Amateur Night – 'where stars are born and legends are made' – which takes place every Wednesday night.

Upper Manhattan & the Outer Boroughs

N 0 ———————— 5 km
    0 ———————— 2.5 miles

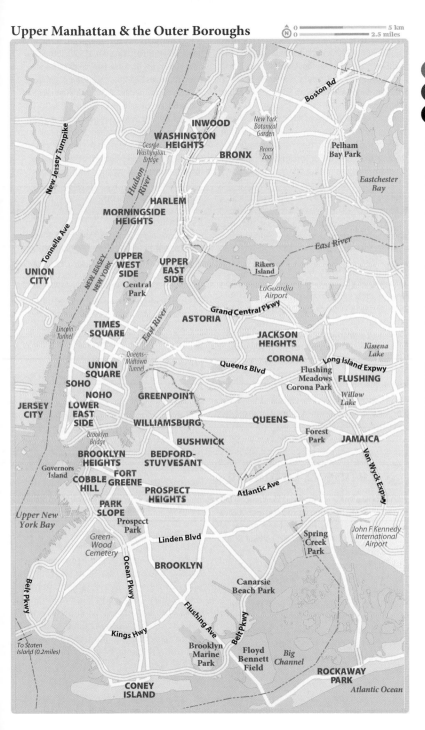

INWOOD
WASHINGTON HEIGHTS
George Washington Bridge
New York Botanical Garden
BRONX
Bronx Zoo
Pelham Bay Park
Eastchester Bay
Hudson River
HARLEM
MORNINGSIDE HEIGHTS
New Jersey Turnpike
Tonnelle Ave
NEW JERSEY / NEW YORK
UNION CITY
UPPER WEST SIDE
UPPER EAST SIDE
Central Park
Rikers Island
East River
LaGuardia Airport
Lincoln Tunnel
TIMES SQUARE
Grand Central Pkwy
ASTORIA
JACKSON HEIGHTS
Kissena Lake
CORONA
Long Island Expwy
UNION SQUARE
Queens-Midtown Tunnel
Queens Blvd
Flushing Meadows Corona Park
FLUSHING
Willow Lake
SOHO
NOHO
LOWER EAST SIDE
JERSEY CITY
GREENPOINT
WILLIAMSBURG
QUEENS
Brooklyn Bridge
BUSHWICK
Forest Park
JAMAICA
Van Wyck Expwy
BROOKLYN HEIGHTS
BEDFORD-STUYVESANT
Governors Island
COBBLE HILL
FORT GREENE
PROSPECT HEIGHTS
Atlantic Ave
Upper New York Bay
PARK SLOPE
Prospect Park
Green-Wood Cemetery
Linden Blvd
Spring Creek Park
John F Kennedy International Airport
Ocean Pkwy
BROOKLYN
Canarsie Beach Park
Belt Pkwy
Kings Hwy
Flushing Ave
Belt Pkwy
Brooklyn Marine Park
Floyd Bennett Field
Big Channel
ROCKAWAY PARK
To Staten Island (0.2miles)
CONEY ISLAND
Atlantic Ocean

UPPER MANHATTAN & THE OUTER BOROUGHS UPPER MANHATTAN

245

Studio Museum
in Harlem   Museum
(212-864-4500; www.studiomuseum.org; 144 W 125th St at Adam Clayton Powell Jr Blvd, Harlem; suggested donation $7; noon-9pm Thu & Fri, 10am-6pm Sat, noon-6pm Sun; ; 2/3 to 125th St) This small, cultural gem has been exhibiting the works of African American artists for more than four decades. While it contains a notable permanent collection, and its exhibition program is always challenging, the museum is not just another art display center. It is an important point of connection for Harlem cultural figures of all stripes, who arrive to check out a rotating selection of shows, attend film screenings or sign up for gallery talks.

FREE Columbia
University   University
(www.columbia.edu; Broadway at 116th St, Morningside Heights; 1 to 116th St-Columbia University) Founded in 1754 as King's College downtown, the oldest university in New York is now one of the premiere research institutions in the world. It moved to its current location (the site of a former insane asylum) in 1897, where its gated campus now channels a staid, New England vibe and offers plenty in the way of cultural happenings.

 Eating & Drinking

Red Rooster   Modern American $$
(www.redroosterharlem.com; 310 Malcolm X Blvd btwn 125th & 126th Sts, Harlem; dinner mains $16-35; lunch & dinner daily, brunch Sat & Sun; 2/3 to 125th St) This hot spot is run by Ethiopian-Swedish chef Marcus Samuelsson, who laces upscale comfort food with a world of flavors. Best of all are the Swedish meatballs, served with potatoes and lingonberries.

Tip: the menu is largely the same and significantly cheaper at lunch and on Sundays when they host a popular gospel brunch.

Amy Ruth's
Restaurant   Southern Cooking $$
(www.amyruthsharlem.com; 113 W 116th St near Malcolm X Blvd, Harlem; chicken & waffles $10, mains $12-20; 11:30am-11pm Mon, 8:30am-11pm Tue-Thu, 8:30am-5:30pm Fri-Sat, 7:30am-11pm Sun; B, C, 2/3 to 116th St) This perennially crowded restaurant is *the* place to go for classic soul food, serving up delicious fried catfish, mac 'n' cheese and fluffy biscuits. But it's their waffles (served at all hours) that are most famous – dished up 13 different ways, including with shrimp.

Lenox Lounge   Lounge
(www.lenoxlounge.com; 288 Malcolm X Blvd btwn W 124th & W 125th Sts, Harlem; noon-4am; 2/3 to 125th St) A classic art deco spot in the heart of Harlem – once the haunt of big-time jazz cats Miles Davis and John Coltrane – is now a lovely place to imbibe. Don't miss the luxe Zebra Room in the back. The bar is home to semi-regular jazz and other musical performances.

New Leaf
Cafe   Modern American $$$
(212-568-5323; www.newleafrestaurant.com; 1 Margaret Corbin Dr, Inwood; lunch mains $14-20, dinner mains $26-34; lunch & dinner; A to 190th St) Nestled into Fort Tryon Park, a short jaunt from the Cloisters Museum & Gardens, this 1930s stone edifice has idyllic views and a lofty, wood-ceiling dining room that feels like a stylish country tavern. The seasonal menu is an international mix of pasta, seafood and salads.

Paris Blues   Bar
(2012 Adam Clayton Powell Jr Blvd cnr 121st St, Harlem; noon-2am Sun-Wed, noon-4am Thu-Sat; A/C, B to 116th St, 2/3 to 125th St) This down-home dive is named after the 1961 Sidney Poitier and Paul Newman flick about two expats living and loving in Paris. It's a little worn in places and the booze selection is limited, but it makes up for it with plenty of charm and jazz performances on Wednesdays and Thursdays from about 8pm.

Brooklyn

If Brooklyn were its own city, it'd be the fourth largest in the US. It is home to more than 2.5 million people and is a rambling 71 sq miles (easily three times larger than Manhattan); one set of subway lines services the north end of the borough, and another set travels to points south. So if you think you can see it all in a day, as the locals say: 'Fuhgedaboudit!'

For day-trip purposes, it is best to pick a neighborhood and stick to it. South Brooklyn, especially brownstone-studded Brooklyn Heights, offers lots of history and great Manhattan views. Fans of vintage amusement parks should head to Coney Island. For the night owls, the trendy enclave of Williamsburg lies just a single subway stop from Manhattan and is loaded with bars and restaurants.

Getting There & Away

Subway Sixteen subway lines travel between Manhattan and Brooklyn, with an additional line (the G) connecting the Park Slope area of Brooklyn to Williamsburg and Queens. For southern Brooklyn, you'll want the A/C line that stops in Brooklyn Heights, downtown and Bed-Stuy. Park Slope and Coney Island are serviced by the D/F and the N/Q. Brooklyn Heights, downtown and Prospect Heights can be accessed by the 2/3 and the 4/5. In north Brooklyn, Bushwick and Williamsburg are reached primarily on the L.

Need to Know

- **Area code** ☎718
- **Location** Across the East River from Manhattan.
- **Tourist office** (☎718-802-3846; www.visitbrooklyn.org; 209 Joralemon St btwn Court St & Brooklyn Bridge Blvd; ⏰10am-6pm Mon-Fri; [S]2/3, 4/5 to Borough Hall)

Detour: Yankee Stadium

The house that Babe Ruth built, **Yankee Stadium (☎718-293-6000, tickets 877-469-9849; www.yankees.com; E 161st St at River Ave; tours $20, tickets $5-375; 👪; [S]B/D, 4 to 161st St-Yankee Stadium)**, is known for its very expensive team, its very expensive stadium ($1.5 billion; opened in 2009), and its 27 World Series wins. The 52,000-seat stadium channels the intimacy of the '23 original, so if you're into baseball – or *béisbol* or *beysbol* or *baseboll* – consider this a must. The stadium is located in the Bronx, which lies just north of Manhattan between the Hudson, Harlem and East Rivers and Long Island Sound.

Sights

Brooklyn Bridge Park

[FREE] Brooklyn Bridge Park Park

(☎718-222-9939; www.brooklynbridgeparknyc.org; East River Waterfront btwn Atlantic Ave & Adams St; ⏰6am-1am; 👪; [S]A/C to High St, 2/3 to Clark St, F to York St) This 85-acre park is one of Brooklyn's most talked-about new sights. Wrapping around a bend on the East River, it runs for 1.3 miles from Jay St in Dumbo to the west end of Atlantic Ave in Cobble Hill. It has revitalized a once-barren stretch of shoreline, turning a series of abandoned piers into public park land. Two of these are now open (Piers 1 and 6); others are scheduled to open in 2012 and 2013.

Empire Fulton Ferry State Park Outdoors

(☎718-858-4708; www.nysparks.state.ny.us; 26 New Dock St; ⏰8am-dusk; [S]A/C to High

St, F to York St) On the water, set snugly between the bridges and backed by Civil War–era warehouses, the 9-acre Empire-Fulton Ferry State Park has a cozy lawn on the East River.

Jane's Carousel
Historic Site
(www.janescarousel.com; Brooklyn Bridge Park, Empire Fulton Ferry, Dumbo; tickets $2; ⏰11am-7pm Wed-Mon, to 6pm Nov-April; 🚻; S̄ F to York St) Behold the star attraction of Empire Fulton Ferry State Park: a vintage carousel built by the Philadelphia Toboggan Company back in 1922.

It is the first carousel to be placed on the National Register of Historic Places. Housing this treasure is an acrylic glass pavilion designed by Pritzker Prize–winning architect Jean Nouvel. Do not miss.

Brooklyn Heights Promenade
Lookout
(btwn Orange & Remsen Sts; ⏰24hr; 🚻; S̄ 2/3 to Clark St) All of the neighborhood's east–west lanes (such as Clark and Pineapple Sts) lead to the neighborhood's number-one attraction: a narrow park with breathtaking views of Lower Manhattan and New York Harbor. Though it hangs over the busy Brooklyn–Queens Expressway (BQE), this little slice of urban perfection is a great spot for a sunset walk.

Brooklyn Museum of Art
Museum
(📞718-638-5000; www.brooklynmuseum.org; 200 Eastern Parkway at Washington Ave; suggested donation $12; ⏰11am-6pm Wed & Fri-Sun, to 10pm Thu, to 5-11pm first Sat of the month (except Sept); 🚻; S̄ 2/3 to Eastern Parkway-Brooklyn Museum) This encyclopedic museum is housed in a five-story, 560,000-sq-ft beaux arts building designed by McKim, Mead & White. Today, the building houses more than 1.5 million objects, including ancient artifacts, 19th-century period rooms, and sculptures and painting from across several centuries.

Brooklyn Botanic Garden
Gardens
(www.bbg.org; 1000 Washington Ave at Crown St; adult/child $10/free, Tue & 10am-noon Sat free; ⏰8am-6pm Tue-Fri, 10am-6pm Sat

& Sun mid-March–Oct, 8am-4:30pm Tue-Fri, 10am-4:30pm Sat & Sun Nov–Mar; 🚻; S̄ 2/3 to Eastern Pkwy-Brooklyn Museum) One of Brooklyn's most picturesque attractions, this 52-acre garden is home to thousands of plants and trees, as well as a Japanese garden where river turtles swim alongside a Shinto shrine.

A network of trails connect the Japanese garden to other popular sections devoted to native flora, bonsai trees, a wood covered in bluebells and a rose garden.

Coney Island & Brighton Beach

Located about an hour by subway from Lower Manhattan, these two beachside neighborhoods sit side by side, facing the Atlantic. Brighton Beach, to the east, is quieter, with coffee shops and grocery stands that display signs in Cyrillic, catering to the largely Ukrainian and Russian population. Coney Island, a mile to the west, is brassier with carnival rides and boardwalk bars and a surreal parade of humanity.

The two communities are connected by a boardwalk that runs along the beach, the best see-and-be-seen spot in Brooklyn during the steamy summer months.

Luna Park
Amusement Park
(Cyclone roller coaster; www.lunaparknyc.com; Surf Ave & 10th St; ⏰late Mar-Oct; 🚻; S̄ D/F, N/Q to Coney Island-Stillwell Ave) Luna Park is one of Coney Island's most popular amusement parks and contains one of its most legendary rides: the Cyclone ($8), a wooden roller coaster that reaches speeds of 60mph and makes near-vertical drops. (Way scarier than anything at Universal Studios.) It is now listed on the National Register of Historic Places. There are also newer rides, including the Soarin' Eagle ($7), a roller coaster in which riders fly around on their bellies.

Coney Island USA
Amusement Park
(📞718-372-5159; www.coneyisland.com; 1208 Surf Ave at 12th St; Sideshows by the Seashore adult/child $7.50/5, Burlesque at the Beach

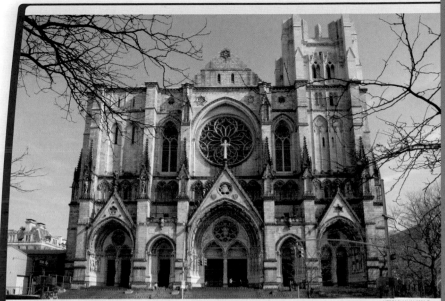

VESPASIAN/ALAMY ©

 Don't Miss
Cathedral Church of St John the Divine

The largest place of worship in the United States has yet to be completed – and probably won't be any time soon. But this storied Episcopal cathedral nonetheless commands attention with its ornate Byzantine-style facade, booming vintage organ and extravagantly scaled nave – twice as wide as Westminster Abbey in London.

If it is ever completed, the 601ft-long cathedral will rank as the third-largest church in the world, after St Peter's Basilica in Rome and Basilica of Our Lady of Peace at Yamoussoukro in Côte d'Ivoire. Just don't count on this happening any time soon.

Tours are offered at 11am and 1pm Saturdays and at 1pm Sundays. Vertical tours, which take you on a steep climb to the top of the cathedral (bring your own flashlight), are at noon and 2pm Saturdays. Regular prayer services are held four times daily (see the website for the schedule).

The cathedral has a storied institutional history. It was involved in civil rights issues back in the early 1950s and has regularly worked with members of the community on issues of inequity. It is also a long-running cultural outpost, hosting holiday concerts, lectures and exhibits. And it has been the site of memorial services for many famous New Yorkers, including choreographer George Balanchine, jazz trumpeter Louis Armstrong and artist Keith Haring.

NEED TO KNOW

📞 tours 212-932-7347; www.stjohndivine.org; 1047 Amsterdam Ave at W 112th St, Morningside Heights; admission by donation, tours $6, vertical tours $15; 🕐 7am-6pm Mon-Sat, to 7pm Sun; ♿; Ⓢ B, C, 1 to 110th St-Cathedral Pkwy

Full Pews: Gospel Church Services in Harlem

What started as an occasional pilgrimage has turned into a tourist-industry spectacle: entire busloads of travelers now make their way to Harlem every Sunday to attend a gospel service. The number of visitors is so high that some churches turn away people due to space constraints. In some cases, tourists have been known to outnumber congregants.

Naturally, this has led to friction. Many locals are upset by visitors who chat during sermons, leave in the middle of services or show up in skimpy attire. Plus, there's the uncomfortable sense that black spirituality is something to be consumed like a Broadway show.

The churches, to their credit, remain welcoming spaces. But if you do decide to attend, be respectful: dress modestly (Sunday best!), do not take pictures, and remain present for the duration of the service.

Sunday services generally start at 11am and can last for two or more hours. Below are just a few of the roughly five dozen participating churches.

○ **Abyssinian Baptist Church** (www.abyssinian.org; 132 W 138th St btwn Adam Clayton Powell Jr & Malcolm X Blvds; 🚹; S 2/3 to 135th St) This famed congregation, now more than a century old, is the number one spot for foreign travelers (hence the separate tourist seating section). It's so popular, in fact, that you may not get in.

○ **Canaan Baptist Church** (www.cbccnyc.org; 132 W 116th St btwn Adam Clayton Powell Jr & Malcolm X Blvds; 🚹; S 2/3 to 116th St) A neighborhood church, founded in 1932.

○ **Convent Avenue Baptist Church** (📞 212-234-6767; www.conventchurch.org; 420 W 145th St btwn St Nicholas Pl & Convent Ave; 🚹; S A/C, B/D or 1 to 145th St) Traditional baptist services since the 1940s.

○ **Greater Hood Memorial AME Zion Church** (www.greaterhood.org; 160 W 146th St btwn Adam Clayton Powell Jr & Malcolm X Blvds; 🚹; S 3 to 145th) Also hosts hip-hop services on Thursdays at 7pm.

○ **St Paul Baptist Church** (249 W 132nd St btwn Frederick Douglass & Adam Clayton Powell Jr Blvds; 🚹; S B, C to 135th St) A neighborhood-focused church.

admission $15, Coney Island Museum admission $5, Saturday night film series ticket incl free popcorn $5; ◷ May-Sep; S D/F, N/Q to Coney Island-Stillwell Ave) This complex is home to various activities. The best of the bunch is the **Sideshows by the Seashore**, where you can see a face-tattooed fire-eater and a Mormon sword-swallower. Upstairs, the small **Coney Island Museum** showcases local memorabilia. Most attractions operate in the afternoon from Wednesday to Sunday in summer.

Williamsburg

Williamsburg is essentially a college town without a college – it's New York's of-the-moment Bohemian magnet, drawing slouchy, baby-faced artists, musicians, writers and graphic designers. Once a bastion of Latino working-class life, it's become a prominent dining and nightlife center – and, as a result, has attracted plenty of young urban professionals (and their attendant condo towers). It may not be full of major museums and picturesque architecture, but Williamsburg nonetheless offers plenty to do.

Most of the neighborhood is located along the East River waterfront, to the north of the Williamsburg Bridge. Bedford Ave serves as the main drag, with clusters of side-by-side cafes, boutiques and restaurants tucked into the area between N 10th St and Metropolitan Ave.

Eating & Drinking

Brooklyn Bridge Park

Grimaldi's
Pizza **$$**

(718-858-4300; www.grimaldisbrooklyn.com; 1 Front St cnr of Old Fulton St, Brooklyn Heights; pizzas $12-16; lunch & dinner; A/C to High St) Legendary lines and pizzas are still dished up daily at this touristy pizza mecca. Thankfully, they live up to the hype: thin-crust pies are dabbed with San Marzano tomato sauce and topped with fresh mozzarella, and delivered bub bling to your table. They also make gooey calzones that could make a pacemaker skip a beat. Be prepared for long lines; whole pies only.

Superfine
American **$$**

(718-243-9005; 126 Front St cnr Pearl Pl, Dumbo; mains $14-22; lunch & dinner Tue-Fri & Sun, dinner Sat; F to York St) This casual hangout is known for its Sunday brunches where Dumbonians sip Bloody Marys while catching bluegrass shows onstage. Windows line two sides, and the rumble of the subway on the Manhattan Bridge overhead puts a bumpy thrill into the meal. The menu covers Mediterranean, Mexican and American dishes. Try the grilled chicken sandwich with pancetta at lunch.

Brooklyn Museum

Cheryl's Global Soul
Cafe **$$**

(www.cherylsglobalsoul.com; 236 Underhill Ave btwn Eastern Pkwy & St Johns Pl, Prospect Heights; sandwiches $8-13, mains $13-24; 8am-4pm Mon, to 10pm Tue-Thu, to 11pm Fri & Sat; ; 2/3 to Eastern Pkwy-Brooklyn Museum) Around the corner from the Brooklyn Museum and the Brooklyn Botanic Garden, this homey brick-and-wood favorite serves up fresh, unpretentious cooking that draws on a world of influences. Expect everything from roasted tamarind chicken to exceptional homemade quiche to a long list of tasty sandwiches. There are veggie options, as well as kid-friendly peanut butter and jelly.

Tom's Restaurant
Diner **$**

(718-636-9738; 782 Washington Ave at Sterling Pl, Prospect Heights; breakfast & lunch Mon-Sat; 2/3 to Eastern Pkwy-Brooklyn Museum) Open since 1936, this diner looks like grandma's cluttered living room and delivers good, greasy-spoon cooking just three blocks from the Brooklyn Museum. Breakfast is served all day and it's a deal: two eggs, toast and coffee with home fries or grits comes to $4. If you want to go old school, order an egg cream (milk, soda with chocolate syrup).

Coney Island & Brighton Beach

Nathan's Famous
Hot Dogs **$**

(1310 Surf Ave cnr Stillwell Ave, Coney Island; hot dog $4; breakfast, lunch & dinner till late; D/F to Coney Island-Stillwell Ave) The hot dog was invented in Coney Island in 1867 – which means that eating a frankfurter is practically obligatory when you're here. The best place to do it is at Nathan's Famous, which has been around since 1916. The hot dogs are the real deal and the clam bar is tops in summer.

The restaurant's annual 4th of July hot-dog-eating contest is the stuff of legends.

Café Glechik
Russian **$$**

(718-616-0766; 3159 Coney Island Ave, Brighton Beach; cabbage rolls $11, kebabs $11-15, dumplings $7-9; breakfast, lunch & dinner; B, Q to Brighton Beach) The dishes to get here are the dumplings: *pelmeni* (Siberian meat dumplings) and *vareniki* (Ukrainian ravioli) with a wide assortment of stuffings. (Sour-cherry *vareniki* are the jam!) You'll also find classics like borscht, kebabs and hyper-sweet compote drinks. Cash only.

Totonno's Pizzeria $$
(☎718-372-8606; 1524 Neptune Ave cnr 16th St, Coney Island; large pizza $16-18; 🕒noon-8pm Wed-Sun; 🚭; [S]D/F, N/Q to Coney Island-Stillwell Ave) This old-school pizza parlor is open daily – as long as there's fresh dough. The toppings menu is slim (check the board above the open kitchen), but this is the kind of pie that doesn't need lots of overwrought decoration: coal-fired dough is topped with mozzarella first, followed by tomato sauce, so your crust never gets soggy.

Williamsburg

Peter Luger Steakhouse Steakhouse $$$
(☎718-387-7400; www.peterluger.com; 178 Broadway near Driggs Ave, Williamsburg; porterhouse for two $88; 🕒lunch & dinner; [S]J/M/Z to Marcy Ave) New York's most storied steakhouse (in operation since 1887) serves up one hell of a tender porterhouse cut. The creamed spinach and the tomato salad are good, but skip the greasy German potatoes and sugary steak sauce. Walk it off on the nearby Williamsburg Bridge. Reservations recommended; cash only.

Dressler Modern American $$$
(☎718-384-6343; www.dresslernyc.com; 149 Broadway btwn Bedford & Driggs Aves, Williamsburg; mains $26-35, bar menu $14-16; 🕒dinner Mon-Fri, lunch & dinner Sat & Sun; [S]J/M/Z to Marcy Ave) One of Williamsburg's top gastronomic destinations, the Michelin-starred Dressler serves a creative market-fresh mix of New American fare like crisp baby artichokes, bacon-wrapped monkfish and its famous oxtail ragout with herbed ricotta. The dining room is no less a work of art, with elaborately sculpted chandeliers, mosaic floors, a zinc bar and light box screens, all created by Brooklyn artisans.

Fette Sau Barbecue $$
(☎718-963-3404; www.fettesaubbq.com; 354 Metropolitan Ave btwn Havenmeyer & Roebling Sts, Williamsburg; pork ribs or brisket per pound $20; 🕒5pm-11pm Mon-Fri, noon-11pm Sat & Sun; [S]L to Bedford Ave) Dry-rubbed, BBQ-craving Brooklynites descend en masse to the 'Fat Pig,' a cement-floored, wood-beamed space (formerly an auto body repair shop) that dishes up ribs, brisket and pastrami. Everything is smoked in-house and there is a range of accompaniments, but don't miss the burnt-end baked beans ($6), which are peppery, not-too-sweet and chock full of meaty bits.

Commodore Bar
(366 Metropolitan Ave cnr Havenmeyer St, Williamsburg; 🕒4pm-midnight Sun-Thu, to 1am Fri & Sat; [S]L to Lorimer St) This corner bar is a faux '70s recreation room with plenty of wood paneling and a few big booths to spread out in. The cocktails are good and the atmosphere uncomplicated. Don't leave without sampling the food: they make the best damn barroom burger in Williamsburg.

Spuyten Duyvil Bar
(www.spuytenduyvilnyc.com; 359 Metropolitan Ave btwn Havemayer & Roebling, Williamsburg; 🕒5pm-closing Mon-Fri, 1pm-closing Sat & Sun; [S]L to Lorimer St, G to Metropolitan Ave) This low-key Williamsburg bar looks like it was pieced together from a rummage sale. The ceilings are painted red, there are vintage maps on the walls and the furniture consists of tattered armchairs. But the beer selection is excellent, the locals from various eras are chatty and there's a decent sized patio with leafy trees that is open in good weather.

★ Entertainment

Brooklyn Academy of Music Dance
(BAM; www.bam.org; 30 Lafayette Ave at Ashland Pl, Fort Greene; [S]D, N/R to Pacific St, B, Q, 2/3, 4/5 to Atlantic Ave) Founded in 1861, BAM is the country's oldest performing arts center and supplies New York City with its edgier works of modern dance, music and theater. The complex contains a 2109-seat opera house, an 874-seat theater and the four-screen Rose Cinemas. Its stage has showcased Mercer Cunningham retrospectives, contemporary

African dance and avant-garde interpretations of Shakespeare.

Music Hall of Williamsburg
Live Music

(www.musichallofwilliamsburg.com; 66 N 6th St btwn Wythe & Kent Aves, Williamsburg; **S** L to Bedford Ave) This popular Williamsburg music venue is *the* place to see indie bands in Brooklyn. (For many groups traveling through New York, this is their one and only spot.) It is intimate and the programming is solid.

Warsaw
Live Music

(www.warsawconcerts.com; Polish National Home, 261 Driggs Ave at Eckford St, Greenpoint; **S** L to Bedford Ave, G to Nassau Ave) A burgeoning New York classic, this stage is in the Polish National Home, with good views in the old ballroom, for bands ranging from indie darlings (The Dead Milkmen) to legends (George Clinton). Polish ladies serve $5 *pierogis* (dumplings) and $4 beers under the disco balls.

Bargemusic
Classical Music

(www.bargemusic.org; Fulton Ferry Landing, Brooklyn Heights; tickets $35; **♦**; **S** A/C to High St) The chamber-music concerts held on this 125-seat converted coffee barge (built c 1899) are a unique, intimate affair. For over 35 years, it has been a beloved venue, with beautiful views of the East River and Manhattan. Performances of classical favorites are hosted four days a week throughout the year. Enjoy Beethoven as you gently float and bob on the river. There are free children's concerts on some Saturdays.

Zebulon
Live Music

(www.zebuloncafeconcert.com; 258 Wythe Ave, Williamsburg; **S** L to Bedford Ave) Ever arty and experimental, the Zeb is an unlikely tight space for reliably engaging shows of voodoo funk, dub, jazz and poetry – even Super Bowl parties come with a DJ spinning things you don't recognize.

Barbes
Live Music

(**✆** 347-422-0248; www.barbesbrooklyn.com; 376 9th St at Sixth Ave; suggested donation for live music $10; **◷** 5pm-2am Mon-Thu, noon-4am Fri & Sat, noon-2am Sun; **S** F to 7th Ave) This bar and performance space, owned by two French musicians and longtime Brooklyn residents, has a world music vibe, offering eclectic music, ranging from Lebanese diva Asmahan to Mexican *bandas*, Venezuelan *joropos* and Romanian brass bands. There are readings and film screenings, too.

Queens

Of the city's five boroughs, Queens is top dog in size and runner-up in head count. Anywhere else, it would be a major city in its own right. So where to begin?

Assuming it's not Tuesday or Wednesday (when most of the galleries are closed), start your explorations in Long Island City (LIC). A quick subway ride from Midtown, it's packed with contemporary art musts like MoMA PS1 and the lesser-known Fisher Landau Center for Art.

Spend some time in neighboring Astoria, taste-testing its ethnic delis and nosh spots, downing Czech beers at the Bohemian Hall & Beer Garden, and spending a few happy hours at the impressive Museum of the Moving Image.

Further out, Flushing (home to NYC's biggest Chinatown) merits a half-day at least. If you're short on time, spend the morning exploring the area around Main St and Roosevelt Ave, chow down freshly made dumplings, then spend the afternoon in neighboring Corona, dropping your jaw over the giant scale model of NYC at Queens Museum of Art.

Getting There & Away

Subway Twelve lines service Queens. Useful lines from Manhattan include the N/Q/R and M to Astoria, the 7 to Long Island City, Jackson Heights, Sunnyside, Woodside, Corona and Flushing, and the A to Rockaway Beach. The E and J/Z lines reach Jamaica, while the G directly connects Long Island City to Brooklyn (including Williamsburg).

Train Long Island Rail Road (LIRR) has a useful connection from Manhattan's Penn Station to Flushing.

Bus Useful routes include the M60, which runs from La Guardia Airport to Harlem and Columbia University in Manhattan, via Astoria.

Need to Know

○ **Area code** ☎718

○ **Location** Across the East River from Manhattan

○ **Tourist office** (www.discoverqueens.info; Queens Center Mall, 90-15 Queens Blvd; ⏰10am-6pm Mon-Fri, 11am-7pm Sat & Sun; **S**M, R to Woodhaven Blvd)

◎ Sights

MoMA PS1 Gallery

(www.momaps1.org; 22-25 Jackson Ave at 46th Ave, Long Island City; suggested donation $10, admission for MoMA ticket holders free, Warm Up party admission $15; ⏰noon-6pm Thu-Mon, Warm Up parties 2pm-9pm Sat Jul & Aug; **S**E,M

to 23rd St-Ely Ave; G to 21st; 7 to 45th Rd-Court House Sq) This smaller, hipper relative of Manhattan's Museum of Modern Art is a master at hunting down fresh, bold contemporary art and serving it up in a Berlin-esque, ex-school locale. Expect more than 50 exhibitions a year, exploring anything from Middle Eastern video art to giant mounds of thread. Best of all, admission is free with your MoMA ticket – so hold on tight!

FREE Fisher Landau Center for Art Museum

(www.flcart.org; 38-27 30th St, Long Island City; ⏰noon-5pm Thu-Mon; **S**N/Q to 39th Ave) Surprisingly under the radar, this private art museum is a must for fans of modern and contemporary art. On any given visit you can expect to catch important works from some of the most iconic artists of the 20th and 21st centuries.

Museum of the Moving Image Museum

(www.movingimage.us; 35th Ave at 36th St, Astoria; adult/child $12/6, admission 4-8pm Fri free; ⏰10.30am-5pm Tue-Thu, to 8pm Fri, to 7pm Sat & Sun; 🎧; **S**M, R to Steinway St) Fresh from a $65-million upgrade, this super-cool complex is now one of the world's top film, television and video museums. State-of-the-art galleries show off the museum's collection of 130,000-plus TV and movie artifacts, including Robert De Niro's wig from *Taxi Driver*, Robin Williams' space suit from *Mork & Mindy* and the creepy stunt doll used in *The Exorcist*.

Queens Museum of Art Museum

(QMA; www.queensmuseum.org; Flushing Meadows Corona Park, Queens; suggested donation adult/child $5/free; ⏰noon-6pm Wed-Sun, to 8pm Fri Jul & Aug; 🎧; **S**7 to 111th St) Undergoing a massive

MoMA PS1 (architect: Frederick Fisher)
/LONELY PLANET IMAGES ©

expansion at the time of research, the QMA's most famous drawcard is the *Panorama of the City of New York*, a gob-smacking 9335-sq-ft miniature New York City, with all buildings accounted for and a 15-minute dusk-to-dawn light simulation of a New York day. The museum also hosts top-notch exhibitions of modern art, from contemporary photography to site-specific installations.

Flushing Meadows Corona Park
Outdoors

(www.nycgovparks.org/parks/fmcp; Grand Central Pkwy; S 7 to Mets-Willets Point) The area's biggest attraction is this 1225-acre park, built for the 1939 World's Fair and dominated by Queens' most famous landmark, the stainless steel **Unisphere** (the world's biggest globe, 120ft high and weighing 380 tons). Facing it is the former New York City Building, now home to the highly underrated Queens Museum of Art.

Also nearby is the **Arthur Ashe Stadium**, and the rest of the **USTA Billie Jean King National Tennis Center** (718-760-6200; www.usta.com; Flushing Meadows Corona Park, Queens; S 7 to Mets-Willets Pt). Head west on the pedestrian bridge over the Grand Central Pkwy to find a few more attractions, including the **New York Hall of Science** (718-699-0005; www.nyhallsci.org; 47-01 111th St; adult/ child $11/8, 2pm-5pm Fri Sep-Jun free; daily Apr-Aug, closed Mon Sep-Mar; 7 to 111th St).

Eating & Drinking

Golden Shopping Mall
Chinese $

(41-28 Main St, Flushing; meals from $2.50; S 7 to Flushing-Main St) You're not in Kowloon, though you'd be forgiven for thinking so. A heaving, chaotic jumble of airborne noodles, hanging ducks and greasy Laminex tables, Golden Mall's basement food court serves up some of the city's

best Asian hawker-style grub. Indeed, this headily scented warren – entered directly from the street – gives new meaning to the term 'cheap thrill.'

Two musts are the lamb dumplings from Xie Family Dishes (stall 38) – best dipped in a little black vinegar, soy sauce and chili oil – and the spicy cumin lamb burger at Xi'an Famous Foods next door.

Taverna Kyclades
Greek $$

(718-545-8666; www.tavernakyclades.com; 33-07 Ditmars Ave at 33rd St, Astoria; mains $12-26; S N/Q to Astoria-Ditmars Blvd) Kyclades is hands down our favorite spot for a decent Hellenic feed. Fresh seafood is its forte, shining through in simple classics like succulent grilled octopus and fried calamari. The grilled fish dishes are testament to the adage that 'less is more,' while the *saganaki* (pan-fried cheese) is sinfully good.

El Ay Si
American $$

(www.elaysi.com; 47-38 Vernon Blvd btwn 47th Rd & 48th Ave, Long Island City; mains $9-19; dinner Wed-Sun, brunch Sat & Sun; S 7 to Vernon Blvd-Jackson Ave) Good-lovin' comfort grub, camaraderie and Gen-X anthems lurk behind the velvet drapes at this feel-good, bar-style nosh spot. Squeeze in at the bar or score yourself a booth for fresh, lip-licking numbers like jalapeño sweet corn fritters, tequila-lime fire-grilled shrimps and one seriously good wild boar shepherd's pie.

Bohemian Hall & Beer Garden
Beer Hall

(www.bohemianhall.com; 29-19 24th Ave btwn 29th & 31st Sts, Astoria; S N/Q to Astoria Blvd) Easily one of NYC's great happy-drinking grounds, this outdoor beer garden is especially brilliant when the weather is warm. The mouthwatering list of cold Czech imports on draft are served with Czech accents, as are the potato dumplings and burgers.

New York City
In Focus

The Lake, Central Park (p224)
HUW JONES/LONELY PLANET IMAGES ©

New York City Today

> *New York City continues to fulfill its destiny as a shining beacon of progress*

housing
(% of population)

67.5 Renters

32 Homeowners

0.05 Homeless (documented)

if New York City were 100 people

34 would be Caucasian
28 would be Hispanic/Latino
23 would be African American
13 would be Asian
2 would be Other

population per sq mile

 ≈ 5000 people

Manhattan   New York State

Occupy Wall Street

Inspired by the revolutionary spirit in Tunisia and Egypt, thousands took to the Financial District's Liberty Sq on September 17, 2011, to take a stand against the nation's unfair division of personal wealth, and how the so-called '99%' are at the mercy of the rule-writing wealthiest '1%'. Known as Occupy Wall Street, the movement is largely a byproduct of the Global Economic Crisis that saw the bankruptcy and closure of several heavyweight money movers – most headquartered in New York City. And in true NYC fashion, the protests have since spread like wildfire through the rest of the country (100 cities and counting) and beyond. For more information, see www. occupywallst.org.

Start-Up, Up & Away!

The dot-com days may be long over, but in New York City, America's networking hive, social media is still raking in the chips. A wave of

an additional $200 million in tourist funds fueled by rainbow-flag-toting travelers looking to get hitched.

Freedom Tower

A great day of solemn remembrance occurred on September 11, 2011 – 10 years after the tragic terrorist attacks that caused the felling of the twin towers. Thousands gathered at Ground Zero to honor the dead, surrounded by the foundations of the buildings and monuments that will take the place of the Twin Towers. After years of planning, the centerpiece – the Freedom Tower, as it's commonly known, both a symbol of a hopeful future and a reminder of a painful past – is nearing completion. In 2014, its target opening date, the building will be America's tallest, with an observation deck on the 100th, 101st and 102nd floors.

LEE FOSTER/LONELY PLANET IMAGES ©

New York–based start-ups are giving people a new way of engaging with a variety of consumables from packaged vacations to medical supplies, and everything in between. Exclusive web clubs, 24-hour flash sales, and dynamic cross-media synergy have taken the virtual world by storm, and most of them are based here.

Marriage Is So Gay

Now more than ever, New York City continues to fulfill its destiny as a shining beacon of progress. Long a hub of gay rights in America, the state government granted a major boon to the LGBT community when on June 24, 2011 it legalized marriage between two persons of the same gender in the Marriage Equality Act. It had been a long, arduous fight full of divisive political maneuvers, but the promise of minting gay and lesbian couples has begun in earnest. Economic pundits predict that the state will receive

New Eats, Old Drinks

Gourmet food trucks and pop-up restaurants remain stalwarts of the city's hip eating scene, but so-called 'new American' fare is the true darling of the dinner plate. A gourmet spin on traditional comfort food – or peasant food, if you will – the long-established movement seeks to fuse repast standards with a lofty dedication to market-fresh produce and seasonal ingredients.

Meanwhile, the situation behind the bar is thoroughly old-fashioned. Ironically inspired by the years when public tipples were obsolete, the city's penchant for speakeasy-style digs means entrances through secret doors, barkeeps in period clothing (slacks and suspenders!) and delicious mixed beverages stirred with utmost care.

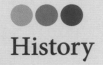

History

Liberty Island (p52)

JULIET COOMBE/LONELY PLANET IMAG[...]

This is the tale of a city that never sleeps, of a kingdom where tycoons and world leaders converge, of a place that's seen the highest of highs and the most devastating lows. Yet through it all, it continues to reach for the sky (both figuratively and literally). And to think it all started with $24 and a pile of beads...

Encounters

About 11,000 years before the first Europeans arrived, the Lenape ('original people') foraged, hunted and fished the regional bounty. European explorers muscled in, touching off decades of raids on Lenape villages. Dutch West India Company employee Henry Hudson arrived in 1609, and in 1624 the company sent 110 settlers to begin a trading post. They settled in Lower Manhattan and called their colony New Amsterdam. In

c AD 1500

About 15,000 Native Americans live in 80 different sites around the island.

1626 the colony's first governor, Peter Minuit, offered to buy Manhattan's 14,000 acres from the Lenape for 60 guilders ($24) and some glass beads. The Lenape agreed, possibly thinking the exchange was about rent and permission to hunt, fish and trade. By the time peg-legged Peter Stuyvesant arrived in 1647, the Lenape population had dwindled to about 700.

Governor Stuyvesant set about remaking the colony into an orderly and prosperous trading port. By the 1650s, warehouses, workshops and gabled houses spread back from the dense establishments at the river's edge on Pearl St.

In 1664 the English arrived in battleships. Stuyvesant avoided bloodshed by surrendering without a shot. King Charles II renamed the colony after his brother the Duke of York. New York was becoming a prosperous British port and the population rose to 11,000 by the mid-1700s; however, colonists were becoming resentful of British taxation.

The Best... Places to Learn About NYC's History

Revolution & the City

By the 18th century the economy was so robust that the locals were improvising ways to avoid sharing the wealth with London; New York became the stage for the fatal confrontation with King George III. Revolutionary battle began in August of 1776, when General George Washington's army lost about a quarter of its men in just a few days. He retreated, and fire encompassed much of the colony. But soon the British left and Washington's army reclaimed their city.

In 1789 the retired general found himself addressing crowds at Federal Hall, gathered to witness his presidential inauguration. Alexander Hamilton began rebuilding New York as Washington's secretary of the treasury, working to establish the New York Stock Exchange. But people distrusted a capitol located adjacent to the financial power of Wall St, and New Yorkers lost the seat of the presidency to Philadelphia.

1625–26
The Dutch West India Company imports slaves from Africa for fur trade and construction work.

1646
The Dutch found the village of Breuckelen on the eastern shore of Long Island.

1784
Alexander Hamilton founds America's first bank, the Bank of New York, with holdings of $500,000.

Population Bust, Infrastructure Boom

There were setbacks at the start of the 19th century: the bloody Draft Riots of 1863, cholera epidemics, tensions among 'old' and new immigrants, and poverty and crime in Five Points, the city's first slum. But the city prospered and found resources for mighty public works. Begun in 1855, Central Park was a vision of green reform and a boon to real estate speculation, and it offered work relief when the Panic of 1857 shattered the nation's finance system. Another vision was realized by German-born engineer John Roebling who designed the Brooklyn Bridge, spanning the East River and connecting lower Manhattan and Brooklyn.

19th-Century Corruption & Immigration

Out of such growth and prosperity came the infamous William 'Boss' Tweed – a powerful, charming politician and leader of the political organization Tammany Hall. He took charge of the city treasury and spent years embezzling funds, putting the city in debt and contributing to citizens' growing poverty.

By the turn of the 20th century, elevated trains carried a million people a day in and out of the city. Rapid transit opened up areas of the Bronx and Upper Manhattan. Tenements were overflowing with immigrants arriving from southern Italy and Eastern Europe, who boosted the metropolis to about three million.

Newly wealthy folks – boosted by an economy jump-started by financier JP Morgan – built splendid mansions on Fifth Ave. Reporter and photographer Jacob Riis illuminated the widening gap between the classes, leading the city to pass much-needed housing reforms.

1898: Boroughs Join Manhattan

After years of governmental chaos caused by the 40 independent municipalities around the area, 1898 saw the ratification of the Charter of New York, which joined the five boroughs of Brooklyn, Staten Island, Queens, the Bronx and Manhattan into the largest city in America.

Factory Conditions, Women's Rights

Wretched factory conditions in the early 20th century were illuminated when the 1911 Triangle Shirtwaist Company fire killed 146 women workers trapped behind locked doors. The event led to sweeping labor reforms. Nurse and midwife Margaret Sanger opened the first birth-control clinic in Brooklyn and suffragists held rallies to obtain the vote for women.

1811

Manhattan's grid plan is developed by Mayor DeWitt Clinton, reshaping of the city.
Grave of DeWitt Clinton (right)

1825

The Erie Canal, an engineering feat, is completed, influencing trade and commerce in New York.

DENNIS JOHNSON/LONELY PLANET IMAGES ©

Beats & Gays

The 1960s ushered in an era of legendary creativity and anti-establishment expression, with many of its creators centered in Greenwich Village. Writers such as Beat poets Allen Ginsberg and Jack Kerouac gathered in coffeehouses to exchange ideas and find inspiration, often in the form of folk music from burgeoning stars, like Bob Dylan. The environment was ripe for rebellion – a task gay revelers took on with gusto, finding their political strength and voice in fighting a police raid at the Stonewall Inn in 1969.

The Jazz Age

James Walker was elected mayor in 1925 – a time when jazz ruled; Babe Ruth reigned at Yankee Stadium; and the Great Migration from the South led to the Harlem Renaissance, when the neighborhood became the center of African American culture and society, producing poetry, music, art and an innovative attitude that continues to influence and inspire. Harlem's nightlife attracted the flappers and gin-soaked revelers that marked the complete failure of Prohibition.

Hard Times

The stock market crashed in 1929 and the city dealt with the Great Depression through grit, endurance, rent parties, militancy and public works projects. Texas-born, Yiddish-speaking Mayor Fiorello LaGuardia worked to bring relief in the form of New Deal–funded projects.

WWII brought troops to the city, ready to party in Times Sq before shipping off to Europe. Converted to war industries, factories hummed, staffed by women and African Americans who had rarely before had access to good, unionized jobs. With few evident controls on business, Midtown bulked up with skyscrapers after the war. The financial center marched north, while banker David Rockefeller and his brother Governor Nelson Rockefeller dreamed up the Twin Towers to revitalize downtown.

Enter Robert Moses

Working with LaGuardia to usher the city into the modern age was Robert Moses, an urban planner who influenced the physical shape of the city more than anyone else in the 20th century. He was the mastermind behind the Triborough and Verrazano-

1853

The State Legislature authorizes the allotment of public lands for what will later become Central Park.

1863

Civil War Draft Riots erupt; order restored by the Federal Army.

1919

The Yankees acquire slugger Babe Ruth from Boston, leading to their first championship.

September 11

On September 11, 2001, terrorists flew two hijacked planes into the World Trade Center's Twin Towers, turning the complex into dust and rubble and killing nearly 2800 people. Downtown Manhattan took months to recover from the fumes wafting from the ruins, as forlorn missing-person posters grew ragged on brick walls. While recovery crews coughed their way through the debris, the city mourned the dead amid constant terrorist alerts and an anthrax scare. Shock and grief drew people together in a determined effort not to succumb to despair.

Narrows Bridges, Jones Beach State Park, the West Side Hwy and the Long Island parkway system – plus endless highways, tunnels and bridges, which shifted this mass-transit area into one largely dependent on the automobile.

'Drop Dead'

By the early 1970s deficits had created a fiscal crisis. President Ford refused to lend federal aid – summed up by the *Daily News* headline 'Ford to City, Drop Dead!' Massive layoffs decimated the working class; untended bridges, roads and parks reeked of hard times.

The traumatic '70s – which reached a low point in 1977 with a citywide blackout and the existence of serial killer Son of Sam – drove down rents, helping to nourish an alternative culture that transformed the former industrial precincts of SoHo and Tribeca into energized nightlife districts.

Out of the Ashes

While the stock market boomed for much of the 1980s, neighborhoods struggled with the spread of crack cocaine; the city reeled from the impact of addiction, crime, and AIDS. Squatters in the East Village fought back when police tried to clear a big home-less encampment, leading to the Tompkins Square Park riots of 1988. In South Bronx, a wave of arson reduced blocks of apartments to cinders. But amid the smoke, an influential hip-hop culture was born there and in Brooklyn.

Still convalescing from the real estate crash of the late 1980s, the city faced crumbling infrastructure, jobs leaking south and Fortune 500 companies leaving for suburbia. Then the dot-com market roared in, turning the New York Stock Exchange

1931
The Empire State Building becomes the world's tallest skyscraper. Empire State Building (p184; right)

1961
Nineteen-year-old folk singer Bob Dylan arrives in NYC.

into a speculator's fun park and the city launched a frenzy of building and partying unparalleled since the 1920s.

With pro-business, law-and-order Rudy Giuliani as mayor, the dingy and destitute were swept from Manhattan's yuppified streets to the outer boroughs, leaving room for Generation X to live the high life. Giuliani grabbed headlines with his campaign to stamp out crime, even kicking the sex shops off notoriously seedy 42nd St.

Real estate prices sizzled, setting off a construction spree of high-rises. Though no new housing for ordinary people was built, the city's population grew, as ambitious graduates flocked to the financial center.

The Naughts in New York

The 10 years after 9/11 were a period of rebuilding – both physically and emotionally. In 2002 Mayor Michael Bloomberg began the unenviable task of picking up the pieces of a shattered city; he found his critics during his four-year campaign to build a huge sports arena atop the West Side Hwy, in order to bring the Jets back from Jersey and score a bid for the 2012 Olympic Games. All three failed, but Bloomberg didn't take a dent in the 2005 elections, comfortably topping the Bronx Democrat Fernando Ferrer.

Much to Bloomberg's pleasure, however, New York did see a ton of renovation and reconstruction, especially after the city hit its stride with spiking tourist numbers in 2005. By the latter part of Bloomberg's second term as mayor, the entire city seemed to be under construction, with luxury high-rise condos sprouting up in every neighborhood.

Soon the economy buckled under its own weight in what has largely become known as the Global Financial Crisis. The city was paralyzed as the cornerstones of the business world were forced to close shop. Although much less hit than many pockets of the country, NYC still saw a significant dip in real estate prices and many cranes turned to frozen monuments of a broken economy. Bloomberg amended the local constitution to allow for a third term, which he won in 2009 – but not by a landslide.

In 2011 the city celebrated the 10th anniversary of the 9/11 attacks with the opening of a remembrance center and a half-built Freedom Tower – a new corporate behemoth – looming overhead.

1977

A 24-hour blackout leads to rioting around the city.

1988

Crowds of squatters riot when cops attempt to forcibly remove them from East Village's Tompkins Square Park.

2001

On September 11, terrorist hijackers fly two planes into the Twin Towers, killing nearly 2800 people.

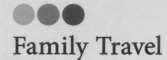

Family Travel

Hans Christian Andersen, Central Park (p225), sculpted by Georg John Lober

KARSTEN BIDSTRUP/LONELY PLANET IMAGES

Contrary to popular belief, New York can be a child-friendly city – it just takes a bit of guidance to find all the little creature comforts that you're accustomed to having back home. Visiting during warm weather tends to make things easier, as you can always resort to the many parks, playgrounds and zoos to let your kids expel some pent-up energy.

Accommodations

When seeking accommodations, steer clear of the supertrendy boutique hotels that tend to have tiny rooms and single-person party-monster vibes (and, often, no-children policies); there are plenty of other options that welcome kids with open arms. At the Crosby Street Hotel, kids are welcomed with robes and slippers, and parents can depend on babysitting services and planned kids' activities run by staff. The Four Seasons offers free cribs, high chairs and strollers. As a rule, the larger hotel chains – Sheraton, Hilton, Doubletree – are kid friendly, offering babysitting services and other amenities.

For more child-friendly accommodations options, visit www.gocitykids.com.

Sights & Activities

Museums, especially those geared toward kids such as the Children's Museum of Manhattan and the American Museum of Natural History, are always great places, as are children's theaters, movie theaters, book and toy stores and aquariums. The city is dotted with vintage carousels; rides cost from $2 to $3.

The boat ride to the Statue of Liberty offers the opportunity to chug around New York Harbor and get to know an icon that most kids only know from textbooks.

The city has a number of zoos. The best, by far, is the Bronx Zoo; otherwise, if you're pressed for time, the Central Park Zoo will keep the tots entertained.

Hot dogs. Vintage coasters. An open stretch of beach. Coney Island is just what the doctor ordered if the family is in need of some fun in the sun.

Transportation

The biggest pitfalls tend to revolve around public transportation, as a startling lack of subway-station elevators will have you lugging strollers up and down flights of stairs (though you can avoid the turnstile by getting buzzed through an easy access gate); visit www.mta.info/mta/ada to find a guide to subway stations with elevators and escalators.

Not for Parents

For an insight into New York City aimed directly at kids, pick up a copy of Lonely Planet's *Not for Parents: New York*. Perfect for children aged eight and up, it opens up a world of intriguing stories and fascinating facts about New York's people, places, history and culture.

Babysitting

While most major hotels (and a handful of boutique-style places) offer on-site babysitting services – or can at least provide you with referrals – you could also turn to a local childcare organization. **Baby Sitters' Guild** (☎212-682-0227; www.babysittersguild.com), established in 1940 specifically to serve travelers staying in hotels with children, has a stable of sitters who speak a range of 16 languages. All are carefully screened, most are CPR-certified and many have nursing backgrounds; they'll come to your hotel room and even bring games and arts-and-crafts projects. Another good option is **Pinch Sitters** (☎212-260-6005). Both will set you back about $20 per hour.

Need to Know

- **Change facilities** Not common in restaurants.
- **Online resource Time Out New York Kids** (www.timeoutnewyorkkids.com) has helpful tips.
- **Strollers** Not allowed on buses unless folded up.
- **Transport** Subway stairs can be challenging with strollers; taxis are exempt from car seat laws.

Food

ROGER GAESS/LONELY PLANET IMAGES

Chowing down in New York City is not your standard affair. That's no surprise in a far-from-typical city but, still, lining up for an hour to consume a bowl of homemade soba noodles or a sugary cupcake? Forking out more than $20 for a Kobe-beef burger? Trolling the greenmarkets for local organic gooseberries and artisanal tofu? Getting exactly what you want in your belly is what the foodie scene is all about.

Specialties

Unlike California, the South or the Southwest, New York is never really referred to as having one defining cuisine. Try asking for some 'New York food,' for example, and you could wind up getting anything from a hot dog, a South Indian feast or a $500 Japanese prix fixe at the Time Warner Center's Masa. Cuisine in this multicultural town is global by definition, and constantly evolving by its very nature.

That said, it's the food items with the longest histories that folks usually have in mind when they refer to New York City specialties. Those at the top of the list – bagels and slices of pizza – were introduced by Eastern European Jews and Italians, because those groups were among the earliest wave of immigrants. But egg creams, cheesecake and hot dogs (just to name a few) are also uncontested staples of a New York feed.

Going Global

The range of global cuisine you'll find in NYC is staggering. Get ready to dive your chopsticks into some authentic Cantonese or Korean; sop up Ethiopian with a spongy shred of *injera* bread; pull apart a fresh lobster with your bare hands; chase Turkish mezes, Spanish tapas or Mexican torta sandwiches with a glass of raki, sherry or *mezcal*, respectively.

Keep in mind that while plenty of tourists descend on Manhattan's Little Italy and Curry Row, you can truly find authenticity in the outer boroughs, where the latest waves of immigrants have settled and continue to arrive.

The Best...
Brunch

1 Cafe Orlin (p106)

2 Café Luxembourg (p235)

3 Marseille (p186)

4 Balthazar (p86)

IN FOCUS FOOD

Trends
Fine Dining

Dining trends in New York City come and go, but there's one thing that will forever remain certain: fine dining never goes out of style. Sure, the culture of haute eats has changed over the years, but locals and visitors alike will never tire of dressing up to chow down. These days the scene very much revolves around fresh, locally sourced, modern American cuisine and high-end comfort food (hello gourmet burgers!).

Need to Know

○ **Price ranges** The following price symbols indicate the average cost of a main dish, exclusive of tax and tip:

$ less than $12

$$ $12–$25

$$$ more than $25

○ **Tipping** New Yorkers tip between 15% and 20% of the final price of the meal. You needn't tip for takeaway, though it's polite to drop a dollar in a tip jar at the register.

○ **Reservations** Popular restaurants abide by one of two rules: either they take reservations and you need to plan in advance (even weeks or months early for the real treasures) or they only seat patrons on a first-come basis, in which case you should eat early or late to avoid the impossibly long lines.

○ **Online resources** Find reliable blog-style reviews on **Grub Street** (www.newyork.grubstreet.com); **Open Table** (www.opentable.com) provides a click-and-book reservation service for a wide spread of restaurants around town; and sign up for handy news blasts about the latest and greatest at **Tasting Table** (www.tastingtable.com).

Celebrity Chefs

The era of reality TV shows continues the trend of celebrity chefdom in NYC; a city where restaurateurs are just as famous as their fare (if not more). It's not just buzz though – these taste masters really know their trade.

To Market, to Market

Don't let the concrete streets and buildings fool you – New York City has a thriving greens scene that comes in many shapes and sizes. Also quite popular are the high-end market-cum-grocers with fresh produce and ready-made fare.

Food Trucks & Carts

The hot tin carts along the sides of busy intersections that dish out steaming halal snacks or plump bagels have long been a New York City staple. But these days, there's a new crew in town that has classed up the meals-on-wheels culture with high-end treats and unique fusion fare. The trucks ply various routes, stopping in designated parking zones throughout the city – namely around Union Square, Midtown and the Financial District.

Vegetarians & Vegans

Thanks in part to the local-food movement, which has hit NYC like a ton of potatoes, as well as a slow but steady trickle of new eateries with big doses of cool ambience, herbivore oases now dot the entire landscape. While many come and go, a few delicious stalwarts include Counter, Pure Food & Wine, Blossom, Soy Luck Club, as well as the unique vegan frozen-dessert parlor, Lula's Sweet Apothecary. Uptown standouts include Candle Cafe and the new Peacefood Cafe.

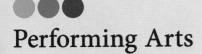

Performing Arts

American Ballet Theater and New York City Ballet in Christopher Wheeldon's Morphoses ballet, *Commedia*

JULIE LEMBERGER/CORBIS ©

The sheer number of performance venues and companies is testament to how in love with culture this city's residents and tourists are. You could pick your favorite medium – classical music, jazz or ballet, for example – and then try to see all of the options, or you could skim through and see a little of everything: a poetry reading one night, followed by an indie film matinee and a night at the opera, with an off-off-Broadway show thrown in for good measure.

Music

This is the city where jazz players like Ornette Coleman, Miles Davis and John Coltrane pushed the limits of improvisation in the '50s. It's where various Latin sounds – from cha-cha-cha to rumba to mambo – came together to form the hybrid we now call *salsa;* where folk singers like Bob Dylan and Joan Baez crooned protest songs in coffee houses; and where bands like the New York Dolls and the Ramones tore up the stage in Manhattan's gritty downtown. It was the capital of disco. And it was the cultural crucible where hip-hop was nurtured and grew – then exploded.

The city remains a magnet to musicians to this day. The local indie rock scene is especially vibrant: groups like the Yeah Yeah Yeahs and Animal Collective all emerged out of New York; Williamsburg is at the heart of the scene.

Theater

Big, splashy Broadway shows are probably what are most associated with NYC's entertainment scene. But Broadway shows refer strictly to productions staged in the 40 official Broadway theaters – lavish early-20th-century jewels surrounding Times Sq.

Off-Broadway (more adventurous, less costly theater played to smaller houses) and off-off-Broadway (even edgier, more affordable performances housed in theaters for crowds of less than 100) are both big businesses here.

Experimental theater fans should watch for the Fringe Festival, held in various downtown venues every August. Also in summer is the acclaimed Shakespeare in the Park festival.

Comedy & Cabaret

The comedy scene is divided between the big-name, big-ticket clubs and the more experimental and obscure places. Check out the Upright Citizens Brigade Theatre, the Magnet Theater (www.magnettheater.com) and the PIT (People's Improv Theater; www.thepit-nyc.com).

When it comes to cabaret, styles differ depending on the pricing and on whether the venue is considered 'classic,' such as Feinstein's and Café Carlyle. Though most cabaret has a gay bent by its very nature, the queer feel is more evident at places like the Duplex.

Classical Music & Opera

Lincoln Center houses the main halls of Alice Tully, Avery Fisher and the Metropolitan Opera House. The smaller Carnegie Hall is just as beloved a venue, offering piano concerts as well as eclectic alt-folk and world music. At the Brooklyn Academy of Music (BAM), the country's oldest academy for the performing arts, you'll find opera seasons and concerts from its resident Brooklyn Philharmonic.

Dance

For nearly 100 years, the city has been at the center of American dance. It is here that the American Ballet Theatre (ABT) – led by the fabled George Balanchine – was founded in 1949; the company continues to perform in New York and around the world.

But the city is perhaps best known for nurturing a generation of modern dance choreographers – figures like Martha Graham and Merce Cunningham, who disassociated dance from music. Today's companies are pushing dance to its physical and gymnastic limits.

The Best... Alternative Performance Spaces

1 Performance Space 122 (p116)

2 Amore Opera (p117)

3 Joyce Theater (p144)

4 Don't Tell Mama (p194)

Literature & the Arts

Neue Galerie (p209)

MICHELLE BENNETT/LONELY PLANET IMAGES ©

For more than a century, New York City has been the capital of cultural production in the United States. And while gentrification has pushed many artists out to the city's fringes and beyond, the city nonetheless remains a vital center for literature and the visual arts. The history is rich – and for the visitor, it provides an endless stream of things to see and do.

Literature

The city that is home to the country's biggest publishing houses has also been home to some of its best-known writers. In the 19th century, Herman Melville (*Moby Dick*), Edith Wharton (*The House of Mirth*) and Walt Whitman (*Leaves of Grass*) all congregated here. There were the liquor-fueled literary salons of poet-communist John Reed in the 1910s, the acerbic wisecracks of the Algonquin Round Table in the 1920s, and the thinly-veiled novels of Dawn Powell in the 1940s.

The 1950s and '60s saw the rise of writers who began to question the status quo, be it literary or political. Poet Langston Hughes examined the condition of African Americans in Harlem, and Beat poets like Allen Ginsberg rejected traditional rhyme in favor of free-flowing musings. The last few decades of the 20th century offered myriad styles, including chronicler of the greed- and coke-fueled '80s (Jay McInerney) to new voices from underrepresented corners of the city (Piri Thomas, Audre Lorde).

These days, New York writers continue to cover a vast array of realities in their work – from zombies (Colson Whitehead), to postmodern narrative techniques (Jennifer Egan), to the crazy impossibility that is New York (Michael Chabon).

Painting & Visual Arts

Today, the arts scene is mixed and wide-ranging. The major institutions – the Metropolitan Museum of Art, the Museum of Modern Art, the Whitney Museum, the Guggenheim Museum and the Brooklyn Museum – show major retrospectives covering everything from Renaissance portraiture to contemporary installation. The New Museum, on the Lower East Side, is more daring. And countless smaller institutions focus on narrower pieces of art history.

The gallery scene is equally diffuse, with more than 800 galleries showcasing all kinds of art all over the city. The blue chip dealers can be found clustered in Chelsea and the Upper East Side. Spaces that showcase emerging and mid-career artists have settled into the Lower East Side. The most experimental happenings generally take place in Bushwick, in old warehouses and basements.

The Best... Lesser-Known NYC Art Spaces

1 New Museum of Contemporary Art (p104)

2 Frick Collection (p212)

3 International Center of Photography (p181)

4 Neue Galerie (p209)

Film & Television

New York City has a long and storied life on screen. It was on these streets that a bumbling Woody Allen fell for Diane Keaton in *Annie Hall*, that Meg Ryan faked her orgasm in *When Harry Met Sally*, and that Sarah Jessica Parker philosophized about the finer points of dating and Jimmy Choos in *Sex and the City*. To fans of American film and television, traversing the city can feel like one big déjà vu of memorable scenes, characters and one-liners.

Numerous film and TV studios are based in the city, including the 15-acre Steiner Studios in the Brooklyn Navy Yard, the largest studio complex outside Hollywood. Rockefeller Center is home to the NBC TV network, its long-running variety show *Saturday Night Live* the real inspiration behind Tina Fey's *30 Rock*. Other media networks are dotted across Manhattan.

Beyond the studios and headquarters are some of the top film schools – New York University's (NYU) Tisch Film School, the New York Film Academy, the School of Visual Arts, Columbia University and the New School.

But you don't have to be a student to appreciate the Paley Center for Media in Midtown Manhattan and the Museum of the Moving Image in Astoria, Queens, both showcases for screenings and seminars.

Gay & Lesbian New York City

ROGER GAESS/LONELYPLANETIMAGES/LONELY PLANET IMAGES ©

The future has arrived in NYC: men seek out other men using apps with geolocators, drag queens are so 'out' that they're practically 'in,' bouncers thumb through guest lists on their iPads, and gay marriage is – at long last – legal. Although New York City has a smattering of neighborhoods that are infamous for their gay hangouts, the city's LGBT scene is hardly segregated, let alone ghettoized.

Drinking & Nightlife

This is one category that is unapologetically separated from the straight version – probably because gay bars hold such an important place in gay history, as they used to be the only places where being out was free and easy. You'll find endless options here and watering holes that appeal to all sorts of sub-cultures, from pierced and tattooed baby dykes to aging circuit boys. Note that places come and go very quickly – especially nightclubs – only to reopen a few weeks later under a new moniker; some parties are only one-night affairs. Visit the websites of some of the community's favorite roving weekly or monthly bashes to see what's next or try one of the following online resources:

○ **Next Magazine** (www.nextmagazine.com) Online version of the ubiquitous print guide to all things gay in NYC.

o **Gayletter** (www.gayletter.com) An e-newsletter about what to do in NYC.

o **La Daily Musto** (http://blogs.villagevoice.com/dailymusto) Michael Musto's queer-themed blog/column for the Village Voice.

Gay Pride

Gay Pride is a month-long celebration in June of the city's long-standing and diverse queer communities, and an apt description of New York's gay and lesbian lifestyle: unabashedly out and empowered in a city noted for its overachievers. For more details on Gay Pride, check out www.nycpride.org.

Gay & Lesbian by Neighborhood

o **East Village & Lower East Side** Slightly grittier, sweatier, grungier versions of the west side haunts.

o **Greenwich Village, Chelsea & the Meatpacking District** The original flavor of gay New York still shines as a rainbow beacon.

o **Union Square, Flatiron District & Gramercy** Hosts a spillover of gay venues from the East Village, West Village and Chelsea.

o **Midtown** Midtown West's Hell's Kitchen neighborhood is the 'new Chelsea' (read: 'Hellsea'), with an ever-expanding booty of gay and gay-friendly shops, bars, nosh spots and clubs.

o **Brooklyn** Multineighborhood borough with gays of every ilk, and diverse watering holes peppered throughout.

Further Information

The magazines *HX* and *Next* are available at restaurants and bars, or pick up *LGNY* and *NY Blade* from street-corner boxes. The lifestyle magazine *Metrosource* is available at shops and the LGBT Community Center. *Time Out New York* features a good events section.

The Best... Classic NYC Gay

1 Julius Bar (p140)

2 Stonewall Inn (p140)

3 Marie's Crisis (p139)

4 Rawhide (p143)

5 Cock (p114)

Shopping

Catherine Malandrino, Hudson St, Meatpacking District

DAN HERRICK/LONELY PLANET IMAGES ©

Shopping here isn't just about collecting pretty, fanciful things. It's also about experiencing the city in all its variety and connecting to New York's many subcultures. There are shops for lovers of chess, street art, artist monographs, Danish things, handmade jewelry, Ukrainian handicrafts, old-fashioned toys, vintage boots and New York State wine. This is just the beginning and there really is no end.

Fashion & Couture

The 'Gold Coast' along Madison Ave is a 40-block stretch of big-name designers: Armani, Kors, Ferragamo, Bulgari, Prada and many more. The few thrift shops that populate this area, as you can imagine, have waiting lists to inspect the merchandise: these stores get last year's cast-offs from the well-heeled, and the working-class girls line up waiting to buy.

In the Meatpacking District, the aura is a little less rarefied, but the focus is still on high-end fashion. Edgier, more youthful names like Malandrino, Miele and McQueen are all the rage.

Downtown in Tribeca is where almost-but-not-quite-discovered young models like to browse; the flashy boutiques are more willing to take a chance on the latest European and Asian imports.

Bargain & Souvenir Seeking

Chinatown and Times Sq are famous for T-shirts. Shops around here are generally open from 10am to 8pm daily, with stores owned by Orthodox Jews closing Fridays and reopening Sunday mornings.

For real finds, dig through Chelsea's Antiques Garage Flea Market, the affiliated Hell's Kitchen Flea Market, the Chelsea Outdoor Market or the 17th Street Market: all of them are open weekends and are full of gently used hand-me-downs.

Tribeca, SoHo and Lower Manhattan are great for window shopping and browsing. Mainstream department store offshoots like SoHo Bloomingdale's abound, but you'll also find quirkier options around Nolita, the Lower East Side, and Greenwich and East Villages.

While clothing sales happen year-round, sample sales are held frequently, mostly in the huge warehouses in the Fashion District of Midtown or in SoHo.

The Best... Stores

1 Century 21 (p241)

2 Zabar's (p232)

3 Strand Book Store (p144)

4 J&R Music & Computer World (p69)

5 Barneys (p194)

6 FAO Schwarz (p196)

Best Shopping Strips

○ **West Broadway** between Houston and Grand Sts in SoHo is one big shopping mall, with high-end fashion well represented.

○ **Mott St** between Houston and Broome Sts in Nolita has lovely little clothing, shoe and accessory shops carrying up-and-coming designers.

○ **Orchard St** between Houston and Grand Sts has edgy fashions and urban style.

○ **E 9th St** between Second Ave and Ave A is a good intro to the vintage stores and curio shops of the East Village.

○ **Christopher St** between Greenwich and W 4th Sts, proudly flying the rainbow colors, has its fair share of leather and sex shops, with some friendly bars and cafes along the way.

○ **Bleecker St** between Bank and W 10th Sts, running south from Abingdon Sq, is sprinkled with eye-catching storefronts and boutiques selling trendy apparel.

○ **Fifth Ave** between Central Park and Rockefeller Center, this commercial strip is the El Dorado of shopping. Stepping into Tiffany's, Bergdorf Goodman and Takashimaya is just the beginning.

○ **Madison Ave** and 72nd, gateway to the bejeweled storefronts of the Upper East Side.

○ **Bedford Ave** between N 4th and N 10th Sts has alternative fashions, record stores and lots of flashy-trashy stuff.

Survival
Guide

Central Park (p224)

JEAN-PIERRE LESCOURRET/LONELY PLANET IMAGES ©

Sleeping

Accommodation Types

Classic Hotels
Typified by old-fashioned, small-scale European grandeur; these usually cost the same as boutiques and aren't always any larger.

Boutique Hotels
Usually have tiny rooms decked out with fantastic amenities and at least one celebrity-filled basement bar, rooftop bar or hip, flashy eatery on site.

European-Style Travelers' Hotels
Have creaky floors and small but cheap and clean (if chintzily decorated) rooms, often with a shared bathroom.

B&Bs & Family-Style Guesthouses
Offer mix-and-match furnishings and some serious savings (if you don't mind some Victorian styles or eating breakfast with strangers).

Hostels
Functional dorms (bunk beds and bare walls) that are nonetheless communal and friendly. Many have a backyard garden, kitchen and

a pretty lounge that make up for the soulless rooms.

Private Apartments
We can all thank little Plaza-dweller Eloise for conjuring up fanciful dreams of hanging one's hat in a luxury New York City hotel room, but these days, finding a place to sleep in the city that never does is hardy restricted to the traditional spectrum of lodging.

Websites like **Airbnb** (www.airbnb.com) are providing a truly unique – and not to mention economical – alternative to the wallet-busting glitz and glam. Selling 'unique spaces' to tourists looking for their home away from home, sites like Airbnb offer locals the opportunity to rent out their apartments while they're out of town, or lease a space (be it a bedroom or pull-out couch) in their home. Airbnb is an undeniable hit in NYC, where space comes at a premium and obscenely high real estate prices act as quite the incentive for locals to supplement their housing income.

Costs
The average room is $340 a night, with some seasonal fluctuations (lowest in January and February, highest in September and October), and plenty of options both below and above (especially above) this rate. When you get your bill, the hotel will also tack on a 14.75% room tax and a $3.50 per night occupancy tax.

If you're looking to find the best room rates, then flexibility is key – weekdays

Need to Know

PRICE GUIDE
Prices in the guide represent the standard range in rates at each establishment, regardless of the time of year.

- $ less than $150
- $$$ 150–350
- $$$ more than $350

BREAKFAST
Breakfast is not included in the price of the room unless specified in the review. Many hotels do, however, include breakfast.

RESERVATIONS
Reservations are essential – walk-ins are practically impossible and rack rates are almost always unfavorable relative to online deals. Reserve your room as early as possible.

TIPPING
Always tip your maid – leave $3 to $5 per night in an obvious location with a note. Porters should receive a dollar or two, and service staff bringing items to your room should be tipped accordingly as well.

are often cheaper. If you are visiting over a weekend, try for a business hotel in the Financial District, which tends to empty out when the workweek ends.

It's also worth checking out the slew of members-only websites, like Jetsetter (www.jetsetter.com) that offer discounted rates and 'flash sales' (limited time only sales akin to Groupon) for their devotees. Flash sales are a great way to scoop up discounted beds when planning a holiday at the last minute.

Useful Websites

Lonely Planet (www.lonelyplanet.com) Lots of accommodation reviews; it's also possible to book your room online here.

Playbill (www.playbill.com) Members get select rates on a variety of Manhattan hotels.

Kayak (www.kayak.com) Simple all-purpose search engine.

Where to Stay

NEIGHBORHOOD	FOR	AGAINST
LOWER MANHATTAN & THE FINANCIAL DISTRICT	Convenient to Tribeca's night scene and ferries. Cheap weekend rates at business hotels.	The area can feel impersonal, corporate and even a bit desolate after business hours.
SOHO & CHINATOWN	Shop to your heart's content right on your doorstep.	Crowds (mostly tourists) swarm the commercial streets of SoHo almost all day.
EAST VILLAGE & LOWER EAST SIDE	Funky and fun, the area feels the most quintessentially 'New York' to visitors and Manhattanites alike.	Not tons to choose from when it comes to hotel sleeps.
GREENWICH VILLAGE, CHELSEA & THE MEATPACKING DISTRICT	Brilliantly close to everything in a thriving, picturesque part of town that almost has a European feel.	Space is at a premium, so penny-pinchers need not apply. Rooms can sometimes be on the small side, even for NYC.
UNION SQUARE, FLATIRON DISTRICT & GRAMERCY	Convenient subway access to anywhere in the city. You're also steps away from the Village and Midtown in either direction.	Prices are high and there's not much in the way of neighborhood flavor.
MIDTOWN	In the heart of the postcard's version of NYC: skyscrapers, museums, shopping and Broadway shows.	One of the most expensive areas in the city – and expect small rooms. Midtown can often feel touristy and impersonal.
UPPER EAST SIDE	You're a stone's throw from top-notch museums and the rolling hills of Central Park.	Wallet-busting prices are not uncommon; and you're not particularly central.
UPPER WEST SIDE & CENTRAL PARK	Convenient access to Central Park and the Museum of Natural History.	Tends to swing a bit too far in the familial direction if you're looking for a livelier scene.

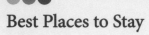

Best Places to Stay

NAME		REVIEW
GREENWICH HOTEL $$$	Lower Manhattan & the Financial District	From the drawing room to the individually designed rooms, nothing about Robert De Niro's hotel is generic.
ANDAZ WALL ST $$$	Lower Manhattan & the Financial District	The new favorite of hipper downtown business types, sleek and handsome with a relaxed, new-school vibe.
CROSBY STREET HOTEL $$$	SoHo & Chinatown	A fun and upbeat lobby and unique rooms – some as pretty and flowery as an English garden.
NOLITAN HOTEL $	SoHo & Chinatown	Situated between SoHo and the Village, rooms look like they're ready to be photographed for the next CB2 catalog.
BOWERY HOTEL $$$	East Village & Lower East Side	A symbol of the new downtown, combining old-fashioned elements with modern elegance; includes a happening bar and Italian eatery.
STANDARD COOPER SQUARE $$	East Village & Lower East Side	Monochromatic rooms that elegantly incorporate subtle wooden elements; brilliant skyline views, and complimentary bicycle use comes standard.
HOTEL ON RIVINGTON $$	East Village & Lower East Side	This 20-floor hotel looks like a shimmering new-Shanghai building with glass-walled rooms and enviable views over the East River.
EAST VILLAGE BED & COFFEE $	East Village & Lower East Side	A quirky, arty, offbeat B&B with colorful, themed private rooms and great amenities; each floor has shared common and kitchen space.
HÔTEL AMERICANO $$	Greenwich Village, Chelsea & the Meatpacking District	Perfectly polished rooms with a carefully curated selection of minimalist and muted furniture.
STANDARD $$$	Greenwich Village, Chelsea & the Meatpacking District	A wide, boxy, glass tower that straddles the High Line with floor-to-ceiling windows, glossy, wood-framed beds and marbled bathrooms.
CHELSEA PINES INN $$	Greenwich Village, Chelsea & the Meatpacking District	With its five walk-up floors coded to the rainbow flag, the Chelsea Pines welcomes guests of all stripes.
MARITIME HOTEL $$$	Greenwich Village, Chelsea & the Meatpacking District	This white tower dotted with portholes has been transformed into a marine-themed luxury inn by a hip team of architects.

PRACTICALITIES	BEST FOR
☎ 212-941-8900; www.greenwichhotelny.com; 377 Greenwich St btwn N Moore & Franklin Sts; r from $495; ⊖ ❄ 🛜 🏊; S 1 to Franklin St, A/C/E to Canal St	Rustic glamour.
☎ 212-590-1234; http://andaz.hyatt.com; 75 Wall St at Water St; 🛜; S 2/3 to Wall St	Unpretentious jetsetters.
☎ 212-226-6400; www.firmdalehotels.com; 79 Crosby St near Spring St; r from $500; S 6 to Lafayette St, R/W to Prince St	Impeccable whimsy.
☎ 212-925-2555; www.nolitanhotel.com; 30 Kenmare St btwn Elizabeth & Mott Sts; r from $143; S J to Bowery, 4/6 to Spring St, B/D to Grand St	Good value style.
☎ 212-505-9100; www.theboweryhotel.com; 335 Bowery btwn 2nd & 3rd Sts; r from $325; 🛜; S F/V to Lower East Side-2nd Ave; 6 to Bleecker St	The well-heeled hip.
☎ 212-475-5700; www.standardhotels.com/eastvillageny; 25 Cooper Sq btwn the Bowery & 4th St; r from $245; 🛜; S N/R to 8th St-NYU; 4/6 to Bleecker St; 4/6 to Astor Pl	Happening location.
THOR; ☎ 212-475-2600; www.hotelonrivington.com; 107 Rivington St btwn Essex & Ludlow Sts; r from $160; 🛜; S F to Delancey St; J/M/Z to Essex St; F to 2nd Ave	Downtown panoramas.
☎ 212-533-4175; www.bedandcoffee.com; 110 Ave C btwn 7th & 8th Sts; r with shared bath from $115; ❄ 🛜; S F/V to Lower East Side-2nd Ave	Homey, personal charm.
☎ 212-216-0000; www.hotel-americano.com; 518 W 27th St btwn Tenth & Eleventh Aves; r from $255 ; S A/C/E to 23 St	Design geeks.
☎ 877-550-4646, 212-645-4646; www.standardhotels.com; 848 Washington St at 13th St; r from $325; S A/C/E to 14th St; L to 8th Ave	Wannabe exhibitionists.
☎ 888-546-2700, 212-929-1023; www.chelseapinesinn.com; 317 W 14th St btwn Eighth & Ninth Aves; r from $159; S A/C/E to 14th St; L to 8th Ave	Gay-and-lesbian central.
☎ 212-242-4300; www.themaritimehotel.com; 363 W 16th St btwn Eighth & Ninth Aves; r $229-725; S A/C/E to 14th St; L to 8th Ave	Staying in a luxury Love Boat.

NAME		REVIEW
CHELSEA LODGE $$	Greenwich Village, Chelsea & the Meatpacking District	Housed in a landmark brownstone in Chelsea's lovely historic district, this European-style lodge is a super deal, with well-kept rooms.
GRAMERCY PARK HOTEL $$$	Union Square, Flatiron District & Gramercy	Dark-wood paneling and sumptuous furnishings in the rooms, celebrity-studded bars, and a guest-only rooftop terrace.
INN AT IRVING PLACE $$$	Union Square, Flatiron District & Gramercy	Richly Victorian, this intimate and exquisite 11-room red-brick townhouse has spacious rooms with massive four-poster beds.
ANDAZ FIFTH AVENUE $$$	Midtown	Youthful and hip, the Andaz has sleek rooms with NYC-inspired details, a 'secret' basement bar, locavore restaurant, and talks by guest artists.
PIERRE $$$	Midtown	The opulent and historic Pierre looks like a Gilded Age period piece with sweeping views of Central Park.
ACE HOTEL NEW YORK CITY $$	Midtown	A hit with cool creatives, rooms are best described as upscale bachelor pads and the hipster-packed lobby is fun.
CHATWAL NEW YORK $$$	Midtown	A restored art deco jewel in the heart of the Theater District, the Chatwal is as atmospheric as it is historic.
YOTEL $$	Midtown	This uber-cool 669-room futuristic-looking option bases its rooms on airplane classes; all cabins feature floor-to-ceiling windows with killer views.
IVY TERRACE $$	Midtown	A seriously charming B&B with spacious, Victorian-inspired rooms.
NIGHT $$	Midtown	In the glare of Times Sq's neon, Night is dark and decadent, from the rocker-glam entrance, to the sleek-and-sexy black and white rooms.
BUBBA & BEAN LODGES $$	Upper East Side	A charming Manhattan townhouse with five simply furnished guest rooms; one suite is ideal for families.
1871 HOUSE $$$	Upper East Side	Named for the year it was built, this historic home has five light-filled mini-apartments with kitchenettes and working fireplaces.
COUNTRY INN THE CITY $$	Upper West Side & Central Park	A landmark 1891 townhouse on a picturesque tree-lined block with four roomy, self-contained apartments with wood floors and four-poster beds.
HOTEL BEACON $$	Upper West Side & Central Park	Adjacent to the Beacon Theatre, this hotel offers a winning mix of attentive service, comfortable rooms and good location.
HOTEL BELLECLAIRE $$	Upper West Side & Central Park	A landmark beaux arts building (plenty of literary lore) with contemporary rooms in a variety of sizes and configurations.

PRACTICALITIES	BEST FOR
☏ 212-243-4499; www.chelsealodge.com; 318 W 20th St btwn Eighth & Ninth Aves; s/d $134/144; S A/C/E to 14th St; 1 to 18th St	Homey value.
☏ 212-475-4320; www.gramercyparkhotel.com; 2 Lexington Ave at 21st St; r from $350; S 6 to 23rd St	Living like a Spanish grandee.
☏ 800 685 1447, 212 533 4600; www.innatirving.com; 56 Irving Pl btwn 17th & 18th Sts; r $379; S L, N/Q/R/W, 4/5/6 to 14th St-Union Sq	Old-fashioned atmosphere.
☏ 212-601-1234; http://andaz.hyatt.com; 485 Fifth Ave at 41st St; d $355-595; 🛜; S S, 4/5/6 to Grand Central-42nd St, 7 to Fifth Ave	Uber-chic.
☏ 212-838-8000; www.tajhotels.com; 2 E 61st St at Fifth Ave; r from $595; 🛜; S N/Q/R to 5th Ave-59th St	Well-heeled romantics.
☏ 212-679-2222; www.acehotel.com/newyork; 20 W 29th St btwn Broadway & Fifth Ave; r from $99-369; 🛜; S N/R to 28th St	Social media types.
☏ 212-764-6200; www.thechatwalny.com; 130 W 44th St btwn Sixth Ave & Broadway; r $450-795; 🛜 ≋; S N/Q/R, S, 1/2/3, 7 to Times Sq-42nd St	Luxury-loving architectural buffs.
☏ 646-449-7700; www.yotel.com; 570 Tenth Ave at 41st St; r from $150; 🛜; S A/C/E to 42nd St-Port Authority Bus Terminal; 1/2/3, N/Q/R, S, 7 to Times Sq-42nd St	Jetsons fanatics.
☏ 516-662-6862; www.ivyterrace.com; 230 E 58th St btwn Second & Third Aves; r $269-325; 🛜; S 4/5/6 to 59th St; N/Q/R to Lexington Ave-59th St	Couples.
☏ 212-835-9600; www.nighthotelny.com; 132 W 45th St btwn Sixth & Seventh Aves; r from $329; 🛜; S B/D/F, M to 47th-50th Sts-Rockefeller Center	Sleeping in an Anne Rice novel.
☏ 917-345-7914; www.bblodges.com; 1598 Lexington Ave btwn 101st & 102nd Sts; r from $180; 🛜; S 6 to 103rd St	A home away from home.
☏ 212-756-8823; www.1871house.com; 130 E 62nd St btwn Park & Lexington Aves; r $265-445; 🛜; S N/R/W to Lexington Ave-59th St	Living like a New Yorker.
☏ 212-580-4183; www.countryinnthecity.com; 270 W 77th St btwn Broadway & West End Aves; apt $220-350; 🛜; S 1 to 79th St	Taste of 19th-century city living.
☏ 212-787-1100, reservations 800-572-4969; www.beaconhotel.com; 2130 Broadway btwn 74th & 75th St; d $230-300, ste $300-450; 🛜 ♟; S 1/2/3 to 72nd St	Families and convenience.
☏ 212-362-7700; www.hotelbelleclaire.com; 250 W 77th St at Broadway; d $129-359, Broadway King $220-480, ste $310-600; 🛜; S 1 to 79th St	Good value for location.

Transport

●●●

Getting to New York City

With its three bustling airports, two train stations and a monolithic bus terminal, New York City rolls out the welcome mat for the more than 50 million visitors who come to take a bite out of the Big Apple each year.

Direct flights are possible from most major American and international cities. Figure six hours from Los Angeles, seven hours from London and Amsterdam, and 14 hours from Tokyo. Consider getting here by train instead of car or plane to enjoy a mix of bucolic and urban scenery en route, without unnecessary traffic hassles, security checks and excess carbon emissions.

Flights, tours and rail tickets can be booked online at lonelyplanet.com/bookings.

John F Kennedy International Airport

John F Kennedy International Airport (JFK; ☎ 718-244-4444; www.panynj.

gov), 15 miles from Midtown in southeastern Queens, has eight terminals, serves 45 million passengers annually and hosts flights coming and going from all corners of the globe.

Taxi

A yellow taxi from Manhattan to the airport will use the meter; prices (often about $55) depend on traffic – it can take 45 to 60 minutes. From JFK, taxis charge a flat rate of $45 to any destination in Manhattan (not including tolls or tip); it can take 45 to 60 minutes for most destinations in Manhattan.

Car Service

Car services have set fares from $45. Note that the Williamsburg, Manhattan, Brooklyn and Queensboro-59th St Bridges have no toll either way, while the Queens-Midtown Tunnel and the Brooklyn-Battery Tunnel cost $6.50 going into Manhattan.

Private Vehicle

If you're driving from the airport, either go around Brooklyn's south tip via the Belt Parkway to US 278 (the Brooklyn-Queens Expressway, or BQE), or via US 678 (Van Wyck Expressway) to US 495 (Long Island Expressway; LIE), which heads into Manhattan via the Queens-Midtown Tunnel (all tunnels are free leaving Manhattan). Often the Manhattan or Williamsburg Bridges are just as easy to use – and free.

Express Bus

The New York Airport Service Express Bus costs $15.50.

Subway

Take either the A line (bound for Rockaway Beach) to

Howard Beach–JFK Airport station, or the E, J or Z line or the Long Island Rail Road to Sutphin Blvd–Archer Ave (Jamaica Station), where you can catch the AirTrain to JFK. The overpriced AirTrain finishes the tail end of a long trip for $5 one way; you can use a MetroCard to swipe yourself in. Expect it to take at least 90 minutes from Midtown.

LaGuardia Airport

Used mainly for domestic flights, **LaGuardia** (LGA; ☎ 718-533-3400; www.panynj.gov) is smaller than JFK but only eight miles from midtown Manhattan; it sees about 26 million passengers per year.

Taxi

A taxi to/from Manhattan costs about $40 for the approximately half-hour ride.

Car Service

A car service to LaGuardia costs $35 (off hours/rush hour).

Express Bus

The New York Airport Service Express Bus costs $10 to $13.

Private Vehicle

The most common driving route from the airport is along Grand Central Expressway to the BQE (US 278), then to the Queens-Midtown Tunnel via the LIE (US 495); downtown-bound drivers can stay on the BQE and cross (free) via the Williamsburg Bridge.

Subway/Bus

It's less convenient to get to LaGuardia by public transportation than the other airports. The best subway link is the 74th St–Broadway station (7 line, or the E, F, G, R, V lines at the connecting Jackson Hts–Roosevelt Ave station) in Queens, where you can pick up the Q33, Q47 or Q48 Bus to the airport (about 30 minutes by bus alone); you can also take the 4/5/6 line to connect to the M60 bus, which runs east along Harlem's 125th St and often takes more than an hour in traffic.

Newark Liberty International Airport

About the same distance from Midtown as JFK (16 miles), **Newark's airport (EWR; off Map p69;** 973-961-6000; **www.panynj.gov)** brings many New Yorkers out for flights (there's some 36 million passengers annually).

Car Service

A car service runs about $45 to $60 for the 45-minute ride from Midtown – a taxi is roughly the same. You'll have to pay $12 to get into NYC through the Lincoln (at 42nd St) and Holland (at Canal St) Tunnels and, further north, the George Washington Bridge, though there's no charge going back through to New Jersey. There are a couple of cheap tolls on New Jersey highways, too, unless you ask your driver to take Highway 1 or 9.

Subway/Train

NJ Transit runs rail service (with an AirTrain connection) between Newark airport (EWR) and New York's Penn Station for a shocking $12.50 each way (hardly worth it if you're traveling with a couple of others). The trip uses a commuter train, takes 25 minutes and runs every 20 or 30 minutes from 4:20am to about 1:40am. Hold onto your ticket, which you must show upon exiting at the airport. A clumsier, 'stick-it-to-the-man' alternative is riding NJ Transit from New York's Penn Station to Newark's Penn Station ($4 one way), then catching bus 62 (every 10 or 20 minutes) for the 20-minute ride to the airport ($1.35).

Express Bus

The Newark Liberty Airport Express has a bus service between the airport and Port Authority Bus Terminal, Bryant Park and Grand Central Terminal in Midtown ($15 one way). The 45-minute ride goes every 15 minutes from 6:45am to 11:15pm (and every half hour from 4:45am to 6:45am and 11:15pm to 1:15am).

Port Authority Bus Terminal

For long-distance bus trips, you'll leave and depart from the world's busiest bus station, the **Port Authority Bus Terminal** (212-564-8484; www.pan ynj.gov; 41st St at Eighth Ave), which sees nearly 60 million passengers pass through each year. Bus companies leaving from here include the following:

Greyhound (800-231-2222; www.greyhound.com) Connects New York with major cities across the country.

New Jersey Transit (800-772-2287; www. njtransit.com) Serves New Jersey; its 319 bus goes 10 or 12 times daily to Atlantic City (round trip $39).

Peter Pan Trailways (800-343-9999; www. peterpanbus.com) Daily express service to Boston (one way/round trip $14/28), Washington, DC ($17/34) and Philadelphia ($9/18).

ShortLine Bus (201-529-3666, 800-631-8405; www.shortlinebus. com) Goes to northern New Jersey and upstate New York (Rhinebeck for $25.30, Woodbury Common for $21).

Climate Change & Travel

Every form of transport that relies on carbon-based fuel generates CO_2, the main cause of human-induced climate change. Modern travel is dependent on airplanes, which might use less fuel per kilometer per person than most cars but travel much greater distances. The altitude at which aircraft emit gases (including CO_2) and particles also contributes to their climate change impact. Many websites offer 'carbon calculators' that allow people to estimate the carbon emissions generated by their journey and, for those who wish to do so, to offset the impact of the greenhouse gases emitted with contributions to portfolios of climate-friendly initiatives throughout the world. Lonely Planet offsets the carbon footprint of all staff and author travel.

Penn Station

Train

Penn Station (33rd St, btwn Seventh & Eighth Aves) is the departure point for all Amtrak trains, including the Metroliner and Acela Express services to Princeton, NJ, and Washington, DC (note that both these express services will cost twice as much as a normal fare). All fares vary, based on the day of the week and the time you want to travel. There is no baggage-storage facility at Penn Station.

Long Island Rail Road (LIRR; www.mta.nyc.ny.us/lirr) The Long Island Rail Road serves some 280,000 commuters each day, with services from Penn Station to points in Brooklyn and Queens, and on Long Island. Prices are broken down by zones. A peak-hour ride from Penn Station to Jamaica Station (en route to JFK via AirTrain) costs $8.25 if you buy it online (or a whopping $15 onboard!).

New Jersey Transit (p287) Also operates trains from Penn Station, with services to the suburbs and the Jersey Shore.

New Jersey PATH (☎ 800-234-7284; www.panynj.gov/path) Another option for getting into NJ's northern points, such as Hoboken and Newark. Trains ($1.75) run from Penn Station along the length of Sixth Ave, with stops at 33rd, 23rd, 14th, 9th and Christopher Sts, as well as at the reopened World Trade Center site.

Bus

A growing number of budget bus lines operate from locations just outside **Penn Station** (☎ 212-582-6875,

800-872-7245; W 33rd St btwn Seventh & Eighth Aves):

BoltBus (☎ 877-265-8287; www.boltbus.com) Notable for its free wi-fi, BoltBus travels from New York to Philadelphia, Boston, Baltimore and Washington, DC (all from $8). Buses to DC and Baltimore leave from the northeast corner of 33rd and Seventh Ave; buses to Philadelphia and Boston leave from 34th St and Eighth Ave, northwest corner.

Megabus (☎ 1877-462-6342; http://us.megabus.com) Also offering free wi-fi, Megabus travels between New York and Boston (from $1), Washington, DC (from $1) and Toronto ($39), among other destinations.

Vamoose (☎ 212-695-6766, 877-393-2828; www.vamoosebus.com) Sends buses to Arlington, Virginia (one way $30), near Washington, DC. Buses leave from 255 W 31st St.

Grand Central Station

The last line departing from Grand Central Terminal, the **Metro-North Railroad** (☎ 212-532-4900; www.mta.info/mnr) serves Connecticut, Westchester County and the Hudson Valley.

Getting Around New York City

Once you've arrived in NYC, getting around is fairly easy. The 660-mile subway system is cheap and (reasonably)

efficient and can whisk you to nearly every hidden corner of the city. There are also buses, ferries, trains, pedicabs and those ubiquitous yellow taxis (though don't expect to see many available when it's raining) for zipping around and out of town when the subway simply doesn't cut it.

The sidewalks of New York, however, are the real stars in the transportation scheme - this city is made for walking. Increasingly, it's also made for bicycles, with the addition of hundreds of miles of new bike lanes and greenways over the last few years.

S Subway & Buses

The New York subway's 660-mile system, run by the **Metropolitan Transportation Authority** (MTA; ☎ 718-330-1234; www.mta.info), is iconic, cheap ($2.50 for a SingleRide, $2.25 if using MetroPass), round-the-clock and easily the fastest and most reliable way to get around the city.

It's a good idea to grab a free map, available from any attendant. When in doubt, ask someone who looks like they know what they're doing. They may not, but subway confusion (and consternation) is the great unifier in this diverse city.

Metrocards for Travelers

New York's classic subway tokens now belong to the ages: today all buses and subways use the yellow-and-blue **MetroCard** (☎ 718-330-1234; www.mta.info/metrocard), which you can purchase or add value to at one of several easy-to-use automated machines at any

Subway Cheat Sheet

A few tips for understanding the madness of the New York underground follows:

NUMBERS, LETTERS, COLORS

Color-coded subway lines are named by a letter or number, and most carry a collection of two to four trains on their tracks. For example, the red-colored line in Manhattan is the 1, 2, 3 line; these three separate trains follow roughly the same path in Manhattan, then branch out in the Bronx and Brooklyn.

EXPRESS & LOCAL LINES

A common mistake is accidentally boarding an 'express train' and passing by a local stop you want. Know that each color-coded line is shared by local trains and express trains; the latter make only select stops in Manhattan (indicated by a white circle on subway maps).

GETTING IN THE RIGHT STATION

Some stations – such as SoHo's Spring St station on the 6 line – have separate entrances for downtown or uptown lines (read the sign carefully). Also look for the green and red lamps above the stairs at each station entrance; green means that it's always open, while red means that particular entrance will be closed at certain hours, usually late at night.

LOST WEEKEND

All the rules switch on weekends, when some lines combine with others, some get suspended, some stations get passed, others get reached. Check the www.mta.info website for weekend schedules.

station. You can use cash or an ATM or credit card.

There are two types of MetroCard. The 'pay-per-ride' is $2.25 per ride, though the MTA tacks on an extra 7% bonus on MetroCards over $10. (If you buy a $20 card, you'll receive $21.70 worth of credit). If you plan to use the subway quite a bit, you can also buy an 'unlimited ride' card ($29 for a seven-day pass).

Note that the MetroCard works for buses as well as subways (and offers free transfers between them).

🚕 Taxi

Hailing and riding in a cab are rites of passage in New York – especially when you get a driver who's a neurotic speed demon, which is often. (A word of advice: don't forget to buckle your seatbelt.)

The **Taxi Limousine & Commission** (TLC; ☏ 311), the taxis' governing body, has set fares for rides (which can be paid with credit or debit card). It's $2.50 for the initial charge (first one-fifth of a mile), 40¢ each additional one-fifth mile as well as per 60 seconds of being stopped in traffic, $1 peak surcharge (weekdays 4pm to 8pm), and a 50¢ night surcharge (8pm to 6am), plus a new NY State surcharge of 50¢ per ride. Tips are expected to be 10% to 15%, but give less if you feel in any way mistreated – and be sure to ask for a receipt and use it to note the driver's license number.

The TLC keeps a Passenger's Bill of Rights, which gives you the right to tell the driver which route you'd like to take, or ask your driver to stop smoking or turn off an annoying radio station. Also, the driver does not have the right to refuse you a ride based on where you are going.

To hail a cab, look for one with a lit (center) light on its roof. It's particularly difficult to score a taxi in the rain, at rush hour and around 4pm, when many drivers end their shifts.

Private car services are a common taxi alternative in the outer boroughs. Fares differ depending on the neighborhood and length of ride, and must be determined beforehand, as they have no meters. Though these 'black cars' are quite common in Brooklyn and Queens, never get into one if a driver simply stops to offer you a ride – no matter what borough you're in. A couple of car services in Brooklyn include **Northside** (☎ 718-387-2222; 207 Bedford Ave) in Williamsburg and **Arecibo** (☎ 718-783-6465; 170 Fifth Ave at Degraw St) in Park Slope.

Walking

New York, down deep, can't be seen until you've taken the time to hit the sidewalks: the whole thing, like Nancy Sinatra's boots, is made for pedestrian transport. Broadway runs the length of Manhattan, about 13.5 miles. Crossing the East River on the pedestrian planks of the Brooklyn Bridge is a New York classic. Central Park trails can get you to wooded pockets where you can't even see or hear the city.

⛴ Ferry

New York Water Taxi (☎ 212-742-1969; www.nywatertaxi.com; hop-on, hop-off service 1-day $26) has a fleet of zippy yellow boats that provide an interesting, alternative way of getting around. Boats run along several different routes, including a hop-on, hop-off weekend service around Manhattan and Brooklyn. NY Water Taxi also runs year-round commuter service connecting a variety of locations in Manhattan, Queens and Brooklyn.

Another bigger, brighter ferry (this one's orange) is the commuter-oriented Staten Island Ferry (p71), which makes constant free journeys across New York Harbor.

Tours

There are dozens upon dozens of organized tours around the city. The following are a few favorites.

⛴ Boat

Circle Line Boat Tours (Map p188; ☎ 212-563-3200; www.circleline42.com; 42nd St at Twelfth Ave; tours $20-29.50; [S] A/C/E to 42nd-Port Authority) The classic Circle Line – whose local 1970s TV-commercial song is now the stuff of kitschy nostalgia – guides you through all the big sights from the safe distance of a boat that circumnavigates the five boroughs.

🚌 Bus

Gray Line (☎ 212-397-2620; www.newyorksightseeing.com; tours $50-75) The most ubiquitous guided tour in the city, Gray Line is responsible for bombarding New York streets with the red double-decker buses that locals love to hate. Really, though, for a comprehensive tour of the big sights, it's a great way to go.

🚲 Cycling

Bike the Big Apple (☎ 877-865-0078; www.bikethebigapple.com; tours incl bike & helmet $70-80) Bike the Big Apple, recommended by NYC & Company (the official tourism authority of New York City and operators of www.nycgo.com), offers five set tours.

Walking

Municipal Art Society (Map p188; ☎ 212-935-3960; www.mas.org; 111 W 57th St; tours adult $15) Various scheduled tours focusing on architecture and history.

Specialist

Foods of New York (☎ 212-239-1124; www.foodsofny.com; tours $40-75) The official foodie tour of NYC & Company offers various three-hour tours that help you eat your way through gourmet shops in either Chelsea or the West Village.

On Location Tours (☎ 212-209-3370; www.screentours.com; tours $15-45) This company offers four tours – covering *Sex and the City*, *The Sopranos*, general TV and movie locations, and movie locations in Central Park – that let you live out your entertainment-obsessed fantasies.

Wildman Steve Brill (☎ 914-835-2153; www.wildmanstevebrill.com; sliding scale up to $15) New York's best-known naturalist – betcha didn't know there were any! – has been leading folks on foraging expeditions through city parks for more than 20 years.

A-Z

Directory

Business Hours

Nonstandard hours are listed in specific reviews throughout this guide. Standard business hours are as follows:

Banks 9am-6pm Mon-Fri, some also 9am-noon Sat

Businesses 9am-5pm Mon-Fri

Restaurants Breakfast is served from 6am to noon, lunch from 11am to 3pm, and dinner from 5pm to 11pm. Sunday brunch (often served on Saturdays too) lasts from 11am until 4pm.

Bars & Clubs 5pm-2am

Entertainment 6pm-midnight

Shops 10am to 7pm weekdays, 11am to 8pm Saturdays. Sundays can be variable.

Discount Cards

The following discount cards offer a variety of perks to some of the city's must-sees.

Downtown Culture Pass www.downtownculturepass.org

New York CityPASS www.citypass.com

Explorer Pass www.nyexplorerpass.com

The New York Pass www.newyorkpass.com

Electricity

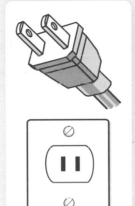

120V/60Hz

120V/60Hz

Emergency

Police, Fire, Ambulance (911)

Poison Control (800-222-1222)

Internet Access

It is rare to find accommodation in New York City that does not offer a way for guests to connect to the internet – a log in fee is often required.

New York Public Library (www.nypl.org/branch/local) offers free internet access for laptop toters and half-hour internet access via public terminals at almost all of its locations around the city. Visit the website for more information.

NYC Wireless (www.nycwireless.net) is a local free-wi-fi activist group that has an online map of free access points, which requires sign-in; the group has advocated for free hotspots in public parks including Bryant Park, Battery Park, Tompkins Square Park and Union Square Park.

Other public areas with free wi-fi include Columbia University (p246), **South Street Seaport** (Map p246; 212-732-7678; www.southstreetseaport.com; Pier 17 btwn Fulton & South Sts; 10am-9pm Mon-Sat, 11am-8pm Sun; 2/3, 4/5, J/M/Z to Fulton St) and **Apple stores** (www.apple.com).

Internet kiosks can also be found at the scatter of **Staples** (www.staples.com) and **FedEx Kinko** (www.

Practicalities

o **Newspapers** The **New York Post** (www.nypost.com) is known for screaming headlines, conservative political views and its popular Page Six gossip column. The **New York Times** (www.nytimes.com) – the gray lady – has become hip in recent years, adding sections on technology, arts and dining out. The legendary **Village Voice** (www.villagevoice.com), owned by national alternative-newspaper chain New Times, has less bite but still plenty of bark. It's home to everyone's favorite gossip columnist, Michael Musto. The intellectual daily **Wall Street Journal** (www.wallstreetjournal.com) focuses on finance, though its new owner, media mogul Rupert Murdoch, has ratcheted up the general coverage to rival that of the *Times*.

o **Magazines** Those that give a good sense of the local flavor include: **New York Magazine** (www.nymag.com), a weekly magazine with feature stories and great listings about anything and everything in NYC, with an indispensable website; **New Yorker** (www.newyorker.com), the highbrow weekly that covers politics and culture through its famously lengthy works of reportage, and also publishes fiction and poetry; and, **Time Out New York** (http://newyork.timeout.com), a weekly magazine, whose focus is on mass coverage, plus articles and interviews on arts and entertainment.

o **Radio** An excellent programming guide can be found in the *New York Times* entertainment section on Sunday. Our top pick is **WNYC93.9FM and 820AM** (820-AM & 93.9-FM; www.wnyc.org). NYC's public radio station is the local NPR affiliate, offering a blend of national and local talk and interview shows, with a switch to classical music in the day on the FM station.

o **Smoking** Smoking is strictly forbidden in any location that's considered a public place; this includes subway stations, restaurants, bars, taxis and parks.

currency based on the current exchange rate.

Public Holidays

New Year's Day January 1

Martin Luther King Day Third Monday in January

Presidents' Day Third Monday in February

Easter March/April

Memorial Day Late May

Gay Pride Last Sunday in June

Independence Day July 4

Labor Day Early September

Rosh Hashanah and Yom Kippur Mid-September to mid-October

Halloween October 31

Thanksgiving Fourth Thursday in November

Christmas Day December 25

New Year's Eve December 31

fedexkinkos.com) locations around the city.

Money

US dollars are the only accepted currency in NYC. While debit and credit cards are widely accepted, it's wise to have a combination of cash and cards.

ATMs

Automatic teller machines are on practically every corner.

You can either use your card at banks – usually in a 24-hour-access lobby, filled with up to a dozen monitors at major branches – or you can opt for the lone wolves, which sit in delis, restaurants, bars and grocery stores, charging fierce service fees that go as high as $5.

Changing Money

Banks and moneychangers, found all over New York City (including all three major airports), will give you US

Safe Travel

Crime rates in NYC are still at their lowest in years. There are few neighborhoods remaining where you might feel apprehensive, no matter what time of night it is (and they're mainly in the outer boroughs). Subway stations are generally safe, too, though some in low-income neighborhoods, especially in the outer boroughs, can be dicey. There's no reason to be paranoid, but it's better to be safe than sorry, so use common sense: don't walk around alone at night in unfamiliar, sparsely populated areas, especially if you're a woman. Carry your daily walking-around money somewhere inside your clothing or in a front pocket rather than in a handbag or a back pocket, and be aware of pickpockets particularly in mobbed areas, like Times Sq or Penn Station at rush hour.

Taxes

Restaurants and retailers never include the sales tax – 8.875% – in their prices, so beware of ordering the $4.99 lunch special when you only have $5 to your name. Several categories of so-called 'luxury items,' including rental cars and dry-cleaning, carry an additional city surcharge of 5%, so you wind up paying an extra 13.875% in total for these services. Clothing and footwear purchases under $110 are tax-free; anything over that amount has a state sales tax of 4.375%. Hotel rooms in New York City are subject to a 14.75% tax, plus a flat $3.50 occupancy tax per night. Since the US has no nationwide value-added tax (VAT), there is no opportunity for foreign visitors to make 'tax-free' purchases.

Telephone

Phone numbers within the USA consist of a three-digit area code followed by a seven-digit local number. If you're calling long distance, dial 1 +

the three-digit area code + the seven-digit number. To make an international call from NYC, call 011+ country code + area code + number. When calling Canada, there is no need to use the 011.

Area Codes in NYC

No matter where you're calling within New York City, even if it's just across the street in the same area code, you must always dial 1 + the area code first.

Manhattan ☎212, 646
....
Outer boroughs ☎347, 718, 929
....
All boroughs (usually cell phones) ☎917

Operator Services

Local directory ☎411
....
Municipal offices & information ☎311
....
National directory information ☎1-212-555-1212
....
Operator ☎0
....
Toll-free number information ☎800-555-1212

Time

New York City is in the Eastern Standard Time (EST) zone – five hours behind Greenwich Mean Time, two hours ahead of Mountain Standard Time (including Denver, Colorado) and three hours ahead of Pacific Standard Time (San Francisco and Los Angeles, California). Almost all of the USA observes daylight-saving

time: clocks go forward one hour from the second Sunday in March to the first Sunday in November, when the clocks are turned back one hour.

Tourist Information

In person, try one of the five official bureaus (the Midtown office is the shining star) of **NYC & Company** (☎212-484-1200; www.nycgo.com):
....
Midtown (☎212-484-1222; 810 Seventh Ave btwn 52nd & 53rd Sts; ◷8:30am-6pm Mon-Fri, 9am-5pm Sat & Sun; ⓈB/D, E to 7th Ave)
Times Square (☎212-484-1222; Seventh Ave btwn 46th & 47th Sts, Times Square; ◷9am-7pm; Ⓢ1/2/3, 7, N/Q/R to Times Sq)
....
Lower Manhattan (☎212-484-1222; City Hall Park at Broadway; ◷9am-6pm Mon-Fri, 10am-5pm Sat & Sun; ⓈR/W to City Hall)
....
Harlem (☎212 222 1014; 163 W 125th at Adam Clayton Powell Jr Blvd; ◷noon-6pm Mon-Fri, 10am-6pm Sat & Sun; Ⓢ1 to 125th St)
....
Chinatown (☎212-484-1222; cnr Canal, Walker & Baxter Sts; ◷10am-6pm; ⓈJ/M/Z, N/Q/R/W, 6 to Canal St)

Borough Tourism Portals

Each borough has a special tourism website:
....
Bronx ilovethebronx.com
....
Brooklyn visitbrooklyn.org

Manhattan mbpo.org

Queens discoverqueens.info

Staten Island
statenislandusa.com

Neighborhood Tourism Portals

In addition to each borough, many of the city's most popular neighborhoods have their own websites (either official or 'unofficial') dedicated to exploring the area.

Lower East Side www.lowereastsideny.com

Chinatown www.explorechinatown.com

Upper East Side www.uppereast.com

Soho www.sohonyc.com

Williamsburg www.freewilliamsburg.com

●●●
Travelers with Disabilities

Federal laws guarantee that all government offices and facilities are accessible to the disabled. For information on specific places, you can contact the mayor's **Office for People with Disabilities** (☏ 212-788-2830; ◷ 9am-5pm Mon-Fri), which will send you a free copy of its *Access New York* guide if you call and request it.

Another excellent resource is the **Society for Accessible Travel & Hospitality** (SATH; ☏ 212-447-7284; www.sath.org; 347 Fifth Ave at 34th St; ◷ 9am-5pm; Ⓢ 6 to 33rd St, 🚌 M34 to 5th Ave, M1 to 34th St), which gives advice on how to travel with a wheelchair, kidney disease, sight impairment or deafness.

For detailed information on subway and bus wheelchair accessibility, call the **Accessible Line**

(☏ 718-596-8585) or visit www.mta.info/mta/ada for a list of subway stations with elevators or escalators. Also visit NYC & Company (p293); search for 'accessibility.'

Visas

The USA Visa Waiver Program (VWP) allows nationals from 36 countries to enter the US without a visa, provided they are carrying a machine-readable passport. For the updated list of countries included in the program and current requirements, see the **US Department of State** (http://travel.state.gov/visa) website.

Citizens of VWP countries need to register with the **US Department of Homeland Security** (http://esta.cbp.dhs.gov) three days before their visit. There is a $14 fee for registration application; when approved, the registration is valid for two years.

Behind the Scenes

Author Thanks
Michael Grosberg

Many thanks to Helen Koh, Michael Hurwitz and Steve Brill for sharing their knowledge of the city with me. To Carly Neidort for her support and Sasha and Noah Grosberg for their conversations during work breaks.

Acknowledgments

Illustrations p228-9 by Javier Zarracina.
Cover photographs
Front: New York, Xavi Arnau/Getty
Back: Central Park and surrounding high rises on Manhattan, Jean-Pierre Lescourret/LPI
Many of the images in this guide are available for licensing from Lonely Planet Images: www.lonelyplanetimages.com.

This Book

This 2nd edition of Lonely Planet's *Discover New York City* guidebook was written by Michael Grosberg, Cristian Bonetto, Carolina Miranda and Brandon Presser. The previous edition was also written by Michael Grosberg. This guidebook was commissioned in Lonely Planet's Oakland office, and produced by the following:

Commissioning Editor Jennye Garibaldi
Coordinating Editor Briohny Hooper
Coordinating Cartographer Peter Shields
Coordinating Layout Designer Wendy Wright
Managing Editor Angela Tinson
Managing Cartographers Corey Hutchison, Alison Lyall
Managing Layout Designer Jane Hart
Assisting Editor Helen Yeates
Assisting Layout Designer Virginia Moreno
Cover Research Naomi Parker
Internal Image Research Nicholas Colicchia
Thanks to Dan Austin, Aurélie Baechelen, Imogen Bannister, Daniel Corbett, Laura Crawford, Janine Eberle, Ryan Evans, Larissa Frost, Mark Griffiths, Liz Heynes, Asha Ioculari, Laura Jane, Jouve India, Kellie Langdon, Wayne Murphy, Trent Paton, Raphael Richards, Averil Robertson, Mik Ruff, Amanda Sierp, Fiona Siseman, Laura Stansfeld, Gerard Walker, Clifton Wilkinson, Amanda Williamson, Juan Winata

SEND US YOUR FEEDBACK

We love to hear from travelers – your comments keep us on our toes and help make our books better. Our well-traveled team reads every word on what you loved or loathed about this book. Although we cannot reply individually to postal submissions, we always guarantee that your feedback goes straight to the appropriate authors, in time for the next edition. Each person who sends us information is thanked in the next edition, the most useful submissions are rewarded with a selection of digital PDF chapters.

Visit **lonelyplanet.com/contact** to submit your updates and suggestions or to ask for help. Our award-winning website also features inspirational travel stories, news and discussions.

Note: We may edit, reproduce and incorporate your comments in Lonely Planet products such as guidebooks, websites and digital products, so let us know if you don't want your comments reproduced or your name acknowledged. For a copy of our privacy policy visit lonelyplanet.com/privacy.

INTERNATIONAL CENTRE OF PHOTOGRAPHY
1133 AVE OF THE AMERICAS AT 43rd STREET
NY 10038   SAT + SUN 10-6
          - TUE - THU 10-6 , FRI 10-8 $14
SEPT 19 → SABASTIO SALGADO (Usi cent. FRI 5- 8pm)

B+H
420 9th Avenue @ 34th St.
NY 10001
Sun 10- 6pm

Sanctuary Hotel.
132 West 47th St.